A SHIFT IN TIME

A SHIFT IN TIME

How Historical Documents Reveal the Surprising Truth about Jesus

LENA EINHORN

YUCCA

Yucca Publishing books may be purchased in bulk at special discounts for sales promotion, corporate gifts, fund-raising, or educational purposes. Special editions can also be created to specifications. For details, contact the Special Sales Department, Yucca Publishing, 307 West 36th Street, 11th Floor, New York, NY 10018 or yucca@skyhorsepublishing.com.

Yucca Publishing® is an imprint of Skyhorse Publishing, Inc.®, a Delaware corporation.

Visit our website at www.yuccapub.com.

10 9 8 7 6 5 4 3 2 1

Library of Congress Cataloging-in-Publication Data is available on file.

Cover design by Zubothan Mahaathev of Dreamz23
Cover photo credit: Steve Collender

Print ISBN: 978-1-63158-099-4
Ebook ISBN: 978-1-63158-100-7

Printed in the United States of America

CONTENTS

PROLOGUE

In 2005, in the process of writing a book exploring an entirely different hypothesis on the historical Jesus, I read through large amounts of Christian and non-Christian historical texts from the first few centuries CE. Many have done so before me, often with the express purpose of finding non-biblical evidence for the life and work of Jesus—indeed for his existence as a historical person. It is a fairly futile exercise, in that very few of the episodes described in the New Testament find echoes in other first century historical sources. And Jesus himself—barring a disputed paragraph called the *Testimonium Flavianum*—is absent in these non-biblical early sources. This has led to the common conclusion among scholars that Jesus must have been a fairly unknown person in his own time, or, as a minority view holds, that he did not exist at all.

In the process of going through these early texts, however, and especially when reading the chronicles of Flavius Josephus (the accepted major source of information on the Jewish realm in Roman times), every now and then I found myself reacting to an event or a person described, noting that they were decidedly similar to someone, or something, I had read about in the four Gospels of the New Testament. Since, however, the episodes described by Josephus invariably took place in a different era than when Jesus was said to have been active, I tended to ignore them, or more or less subconsciously put them aside. Interestingly, I did so despite the fact that the interval between the episode in the New Testament and that described by Josephus always was the same: about twenty years. It is interesting how the human brain works when it encounters new information that does not fit with one's previous knowledge or notions. But the fact that a time gap of twenty years meant that the names of the people involved in the episodes often were different in the two sources certainly lessened my inclination to view the events as true parallels. For the longest time, they simply remained curious coincidences.

This all changed late one night, when I happened to come upon the Greek original of the Gospel of John, chapter 18. Suddenly, the parallels were absolutely impossible to ignore. It was a shocking experience, one that actually stopped me in my tracks for quite some time, before I resumed the project and published the book.[1] Postulating that Jesus was, in fact, active in the 50s CE, and not the 30s—as the Gospels claim—and that much of what is described in the New Testament actually can be found also in other contemporary historical sources would, if the hypothesis were true, open up vast new possibilities, but also create some unsettling difficulties. On the one hand, Jesus would really turn out to be a historical person—one described also by other contemporaries than those who wrote the New Testament texts—and in addition, just like the Gospels say, he would have been very prominent in his own time. On the other hand, it would be hard to ascribe a consistent twenty year time shift merely to a mistake on the part of the Gospel writers (or, for that matter, Josephus). In other words, if the time shift is real, and the parallels true, it is reasonable to assume that this editorial shift—from the 50s to the 30s—is deliberate. Additionally, an assumed time shift would produce an alternate picture of Jesus and his disciples which is not always congruent with that shown in the New Testament (although, as I will argue in this book, the New Testament provides substantial subtext on this matter).

This last predicament—that a contrasting picture of Jesus would emerge—could, one may hypothesize, actually be a reason for an applied time shift. Better an absent Jesus in the non-biblical sources, than a partially conflicting tale.

Or rather: better a veiled alternate story than an apparent one.

In the years since I first formulated the time shift hypothesis, I have at times come back to it in writing, and I have presented it in academic fora. For obvious reasons, a radical hypothesis such as this encounters resistance, also in scholarly circles. At the same time, papers I have written on the hypothesis have in the last few years been accepted for presentation at a number of sessions at the Society of Biblical Literature Annual and International Meetings—the major international conferences for biblical scholars—and each time it has stirred up much debate.[2]

Because much has happened since I first stumbled upon the time shift hypothesis, because a considerable amount of additional evidence has accumulated, and because a detailed presentation of the hypothesis still awaits publication, I write this book. All the same, I retain the ambition to present enough background material to make the book accessible to a non-scholarly audience.

It is not unproblematic for me to stay with this project. Although historical Jesus studies has been an active field in academia for well over two centuries, it is hard to fully separate the historical person Jesus from the faith associated with him. Most scholars will say that they hold the two entirely separate, but I doubt it is always possible. Especially when fundamental issues are brought to the fore. I struggle with this, and in the end always arrive at the conclusion that it is very hard to abstain from trying to answer fundamental questions.

What I present, however, will never be anything but a hypothesis. It is up to each and every individual to find their own truths.

A SHIFT
IN TIME

PREMISE ONE

ONE OF THE PROBLEMS FACING ALL HISTORICAL JESUS STUDIES HAS been, and continuous to be, that there is only one source of contemporary, first century, testimony in which Jesus is unequivocally described: the New Testament texts. This is peculiar, since that period in other respects is well documented by Roman and Jewish historians of the time.

Among scholars today, the most common explanation for this paradox has been that Jesus in reality must have been fairly unknown in his own era.

This interpretation, however, fails to account for the fact that the New Testament describes Jesus as someone with a large following, and one whose trial involved both high priests in Jerusalem (Annas and Caiaphas), as well as the Jewish ruler of Jesus's home province Galilee (Herod Antipas), and the Roman ruler of *Iudaea* (Pontius Pilate).

It also fails to account for the fact that when non-biblical accounts of Jesus do materialize, in the next century, we also find texts that speak out against him. As a rule, these neither deny his existence nor do they try to belittle his importance. In fact, also these polemic texts tend to describe Jesus as a person with a large following.

PREMISE TWO

AFTER THEY HAD FINISHED THE LAST SUPPER, JESUS AND HIS DISCIPLES went to the Mount of Olives to quietly await his arrest, which would occur at the hands of people sent out by the high priests. This is how all three Synoptic Gospels—Matthew, Mark, and Luke—present this event.

One Gospel account, however, differs slightly: in John chapter 18 we read that the people sent out by the high priests on this occasion were accompanied by "the soldiers" and "their officer" (or, in other translations, "the band" and "the captain").

But it is when we go to the Greek original of John's Gospel that we find that this account stands out more than just slightly: the original word for "the soldiers" is *speira*, and the original word for "their officer" is *chiliarchos*. A *speira* is a Roman cohort of six hundred to one thousand soldiers, and *chiliarchos* means "commander of one thousand." Thus, in the Gospel of John, there is a definite suggestion of a battle on the Mount of Olives preceding Jesus's arrest. This interpretation is reinforced by Luke 22:36, which states that Jesus prior to leaving for the Mount of Olives tells his disciples that "the one who has no sword must sell his cloak and buy one."

Curiously, the main chronicler of the times, Flavius Josephus, describes just such a battle on the Mount of Olives—indeed a battle between the followers of a Jewish messianic leader and a Roman cohort. Like Jesus, this messianic leader had previously dwelled in the wilderness. Like Jesus, he acquired a large following, and raised the fear and ire of the authorities. And like Jesus, he told his followers that he would show them from hence how, at his command, "the walls of Jerusalem would fall down."

The only problem is: according to Josephus, this event on the Mount of Olives did not occur under Pontius Pilate. It occurred twenty years later.

ON TRYING TO FIND JESUS IN THE HISTORICAL SOURCES

EVER SINCE GERMAN BIBLICAL SCHOLAR HERMANN SAMUEL REIMARUS began his quest for the historical Jesus, more than two and a half centuries ago, scholars have examined, and attempted to determine, the historical facts behind the narratives of the New Testament.[1] Did Jesus of Nazareth really exist as a historical person, and, if so, who was he? If his movement really did emerge in the late 20s or early 30s CE, as the Gospels tell us, what kind of movement was it known as among contemporaries? Can the four Gospel accounts (which are usually assumed to have been penned between 68 and 110 CE) be corroborated by non-biblical first century sources?

And the problem these scholars invariably have come up against is this: outside of the New Testament texts, first century historical sources, with one dubious exception, have nothing to tell us about the messianic leader Jesus from the Galilean town of Nazareth, crucified in the early to mid-30s CE. Nor of his movement. Contemporary historians are essentially silent.

At first glance, this may not seem so peculiar. We are, after all, talking about events that occurred two thousand years ago, perhaps long enough to have been sifted out in the ever-diluting stream of historical narrative. And yet, as we know, certain eras—even ancient eras—have been so tumultuous and historically decisive that contemporary narrators found it essential to preserve them, and others made sure that these narratives were passed down through the ages. The particular period which we are talking about, the period when Jesus is said to have lived and worked, is indeed one of those well-documented eras. Because it was the era when the Jewish nation in Judea and Galilee was destroyed.

Let us begin by taking a closer look at this pivotal period in Jewish history. Not just to paint a backdrop, but also, as we shall later see, because the tumultuous politics of the time may have had a stronger impact on the work and actions of Jesus than a superficial look at the New Testament texts might lead us to believe.

**

When Jesus, according to New Testament chronology, is born, Judea and Galilee—the centers of Jewish settlement—are in the midst of upheaval. About six decades earlier, in 63 BCE, the Jewish nation had lost its short-lived independence, after power struggles between two Hasmonean princes had led both of them to more or less invite the Roman army to intervene. Since then, Rome has ruled. But it has ruled through instinct—at times granting the Jews something akin to autonomy (or at least allowing Jewish client kings to run the affairs of the country), and at other, often more tumultuous, times taking direct control, to the point of appointing and deposing even the Jewish high priests in Jerusalem. But to the chagrin of the Roman authorities, the population often has not responded to this kindly. Each movement away from autonomy, or each perceived affront to their laws or traditions, invariably has put the Jews—who never accepted their loss of independence—on edge, and occasionally on the verge of rebellion.

When Jesus is born, King Herod the Great is either at the end of his reign (according to the Gospel of Matthew), or has been dead for ten years (according to the Gospel of Luke). And whether one looks upon this Jewish client king, Herod, as a paranoid madman or not, it is undoubtedly so that the Romans during Herod's long reign more or less had left the Jewish realm alone. Herod, after all, had been powerful, and he had put much effort into pleasing the Romans as well as the Jews (something at which he was somewhat less successful). After Herod's death, in 4 BCE, Roman Emperor Augustus at first aspires to keep things as they are, and the nation is divided between Herod's sons (they will all have the name "Herod" attached to their names, although this is not always indicated). Herod Antipas gets Galilee and Perea, in the north and east, Archelaus gets the central parts—Judea, Samaria and

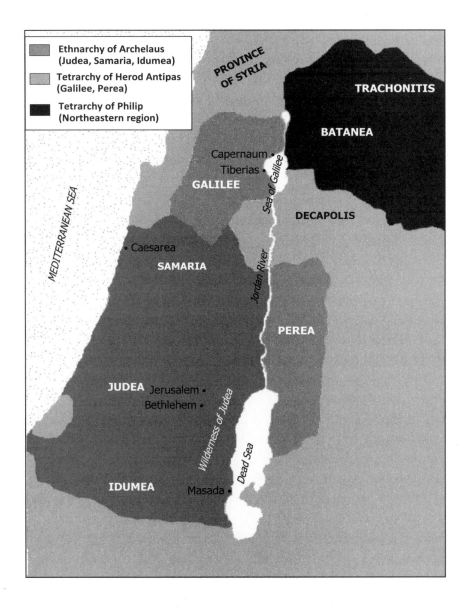

Idumea—and Philip gets the areas north-east of Lake Galilee. Herod Antipas and Philip are given the title *tetrarch* ("Ruler of a quarter"), and Archelaus is entitled *ethnarch* ("Ruler of a nation").

But the ruler of the heartland, Archelaus, in particular, had already proven to be a poor leader. Incapable of controlling the escalating tumults, he had resorted to extreme cruelty and violence. And while he is away in Rome to negotiate with Emperor Augustus about the succession, tumults erupt all over the province. This insurrection is finally crushed only after the Roman Governor of Syria, Varus, has two thousand Jews crucified. Archelaus returns, but fails to gain the trust of the people of Judea, the central and most important part of the Jewish realm (not least because Jerusalem lies here), and this Jewish king is eventually, in the year 6 CE, summoned to Rome, where he is deprived of his crown and banished to Gaul. Yet, the Roman emperor does little to please the belligerent Jews; Archelaus is not succeeded by another Jewish king. This time Rome takes direct control. And it does so by sending a new Roman governor, Quirinius, to Syria, and then putting him in charge of Judea as well. The governor immediately proceeds to start registering the Jews and leveling taxes on them, something which of course raises the ire of the population even further.

Interestingly, aspects of this crucial event appear also in the New Testament, in the Gospel of Luke:

> In those days a decree went out from Emperor Augustus that all the world should be registered. This was the first registration and was taken while Quirinius was governor of Syria. All went to their own towns to be registered. Joseph also went from the town of Nazareth in Galilee to Judea, to the city of David called Bethlehem, because he was descended from the house and family of David. He went to be registered with Mary, to whom he was engaged and who was expecting a child. While they were there, the time came for her to deliver her child.[2]

The phrase "this was the first registration and was taken while Quirinius was governor of Syria" is in fact the crucial piece of information which allows us to pinpoint the time of Jesus's birth, at least according to the Gospel of Luke. We know that Quirinius became governor in Syria shortly after Archelaus was deposed, in 6 CE. And we also know that the registration, or census, which was done in order to level the tax, was performed soon thereafter, thus in 6 or 7 CE.[3] Consequently, we can deduce that Luke puts the time of Jesus's birth at 6 or 7 CE. But curiously, the most important aspect of this census is not mentioned in the Gospel: the census, and ensuing taxation, became the starting shot for a major anti-Roman revolt. A revolt which came to define Jewish anti-Roman resistance in the following seven decades of Jewish life in this area. Roman-Jewish historian Flavius Josephus, our main source of information about the first century Jewish realm, writes, in fact, that the rebel movement was founded with the census revolt (which is, as we shall see, perhaps a matter of interpretation).[4] This seminal revolt was led by a man called Judas the Galilean.

> Judas . . . taking with him Sadduc, a Pharisee, became zealous to draw them to a revolt, who both said that this taxation was no better than an introduction to slavery, and exhorted the nation to assert their liberty.[5]

Although the revolt—as described by Josephus—was sparked by a taxation of Judea, it is no mere coincidence that Judas was a Galilean.[6] The Galileans were known as particularly averse to foreign domination—and particularly prone to act. As Josephus put it, they "have been always able to make a strong resistance on all occasions of war; for the Galileans are inured to war from their infancy, and have been always very numerous; nor hath the country been ever destitute of men of courage, or wanted a numerous set of them."[7]

The census revolt was violently crushed by the Roman authorities, and for some decades thereafter the Jewish rebel movement remained dormant. But the rebels would eventually regroup and reemerge. The religiously inspired and violent movement founded by Judas the Galilean—later often loosely referred to as the Zealot movement—would ultimately, six decades later, be at the helm of the Jewish War against Rome, the war bringing about the fall of Jerusalem, and the end of the Jewish nation as a geographical and political entity.

It is no doubt interesting that the Gospel of Luke not only places the birth of Jesus at this pivotal moment of Jewish-Roman history, the census revolt, but also defines the time of birth by specifically mentioning the census, and yet without here mentioning the historically more important revolt and de facto birth of the anti-Roman rebel movement in its organized form.[8] Headed by a Galilean, no less.

What makes Luke's narrative even more curious is the fact that the only other Gospel mentioning Jesus's birth, namely Matthew, places it in a completely different era, before the death of Herod the Great (4 BCE), thus at least ten years prior to the census.[9] To further complicate matters, Luke indicates that John the Baptist—Jesus's forerunner—who (according to the same Gospel) was the same age as Jesus, was conceived "in the days of King Herod of Judea."[10] Not at the time of the census, thus. One must ask: why this considerable discrepancy between the two Gospels—as well as within Luke itself? Is it merely due to a mistake on the part of either Matthew or Luke? Or could it be that the designated time of Jesus's birth in at least one of the cases is symbolic rather than real?

The Jewish revolt against Roman taxation is thus quickly quashed, and while Galilee continues to be ruled by a Jewish provincial ruler, Herod Antipas, the Roman province of *Iudaea*—consisting of Judea, Samaria and Idumea—now becomes home to a string of Roman procurators, or prefects, as the early ones are called.[11] One of these prefects is named Pontius Pilate—according to the New Testament, the Roman ruler at the time of the crucifixion of Jesus. Pilate rules *Iudaea* from about 26 to 36 CE.

The prefect, or procurator, resides in the coastal city of Caesarea, where he has his pretorium, formerly the palace of Herod. Only on very special occasions, usually the major Jewish festivals, does he venture to Jerusalem, a city which always had been, and would continue to be, a seat of fomenting upheaval, particularly around the festivals, when massive numbers of Jews from all over the Jewish realm gather there.

But, as mentioned, this period—from the crushing of the census revolt until almost four decades later—is still one of relative calm. On a few occasions, these decades will see major protests from the Jews—

ROMAN PREFECTS AND PROCURATORS IN JUDEA UNTIL THE JEWISH WAR	
6–9 CE	Coponius
9–12 CE	Marcus Ambibulus
12–15 CE	Annius Rufus
15–26(27) CE	Valerius Gratus
26(27)–36(37) CE	Pontius Pilate
36(37)–37 CE	Marcellus
37–41 CE	Marullus
44–46 CE	Cuspius Fadus
46–48 CE	Tiberius Julius Alexander
48–52 CE	Ventidius Cumanus
52–59(60) CE	Antonius Felix
59(60)–62 CE	Porcius Festus
62–64 CE	Albinus
64–66 CE	Gessius Florus

usually in response to a perceived desecration of Jewish law or institutions—but no armed resistance, much less any rebellion. As Roman historian Tacitus writes in his *Histories*: "Under Tiberius all was quiet."[12] Tiberius was Roman emperor between 14 and 37 CE.

It is only in the year 44 CE that the followers—in fact heirs—of Judas the Galilean are moved to act once again. And what stirs them seems to be the death of a king, one by the name of Agrippa I. After living under Roman procuratorship for many years, the Jews of Judea had in 41 CE, along with the people of the rest of the Jewish realm, been finally united under a Jewish ruler—and a popular one at that. Herod Agrippa I, nephew of Herod Antipas and grandson of Herod the Great, had developed from a spoiled child growing up in Caesar's court in Rome to a not only shrewd, but also very diplomatic—indeed empathetic—ruler of the recalcitrant Jews. His people cherished him, with a love bordering on devotion, after suffering for so many years under cruel Roman procurators. But it all ended, most abruptly, at a festival in Caesarea. As Flavius Josephus tells us, the king had put on a garment wholly of silver, and when he sat in the theater in front of the multitude, the people thought him so magnificent that they cried out that he must be a god. "Upon this the king did neither rebuke them, nor reject their impious flattery," Josephus writes, "but as he presently afterward looked

Jewish Client Kings under Roman Rule
(from Herod the Great until the Jewish War)

Judea, Samaria, and Idumea	Galilee and Perea	Northeastern region
Herod the Great 37–4 BCE		
Archelaus 4 BCE–6 CE	Herod Antipas 4 BCE–39 CE	Philip 4 BCE–34 CE
Roman Prefects 6–41		Added to the Province of Syria 34–37
Agrippa I 41–44	Agrippa I 39–44	Agrippa I 37–44
Roman Procurators 44–	Roman Procurators 44–55	Roman Procurators 44–53
	Roman Procurators 55– / Agrippa II 55–	Agrippa II 53–
Jewish War Against Rome 66–70		

up, he saw an owl sitting on a certain rope over his head, and immediately understood that this bird was the messenger of ill tidings, as it
had once been the messenger of good tidings to him; and fell into the
deepest sorrow. A severe pain also arose in his belly, and began in a most
violent manner." As the stomach pains become ever more ferocious,
Agrippa is carried off the stage. He dies five days later.[13]

Interestingly—and perhaps not without significance—this episode, or one very similar to it, is told also by those who authored the

New Testament. In the Acts of the Apostles, the fifth book of the New Testament, we find the following mysterious text (as mentioned, the name "Herod" could be attached to the name of any ruler of the Herodian dynasty):

> On an appointed day Herod put on his royal robes, took his seat on the platform, and delivered a public address to them. The people kept shouting, "The voice of a god, and not of a mortal!" 23And immediately, because he had not given the glory to God, an angel of the Lord struck him down, and he was eaten by worms and died.
>
> *Acts of the Apostles 12:21–23*

The death of Agrippa I (which may or may not have been murder at the hands of Rome) was another pivotal event in the development of the anti-Roman resistance movement. For Agrippa's death immediately brought back the hated Roman procurators, and this time not only to Judea, but also to Galilee, and virtually all of the rest of the country as well.[14] All semblances of autonomy are now lost, and the people respond accordingly.

When Cuspius Fadus, the first Roman procurator appointed after the death of Agrippa I, arrives, he finds "quarrelsome doings between the Jews that dwelt in Perea, and the people of Philadelphia." Angry at not having been consulted, Fadus has the principal men among the Jews slain or banished.[15] And soon, it appears, the tumults begin anew. Within a couple of years, the sons of Judas the Galilean—Jacob and Simon—appear on the stage, stirring what seems to be the beginnings of a revolt against Rome. Fadus' successor, Procurator Tiberius Alexander, has them crucified.[16]

But, as it turns out, rebellion is not the only recurrent response to the loss of political, social, or religious autonomy among the Jews. Something else appears to happen at these times of unrest: the emergence of messianism.

The word *Mashiach*, meaning "anointed one" (and *Khristos* is a direct translation of this into Greek), occurs about forty times in the

Hebrew Bible. From the beginning, it referred to a wise, righteous, and strong king, priest, or prophet. But with time—and especially since the Babylonian exile of the sixth century BCE—this Messiah figure came to be looked upon as someone appointed by God to lead his people against its enemies, someone who would rebuild the Jewish nation, and restore the kingdom of David. The Messiah was seen as a redeemer, sometimes even an otherworldly redeemer. The period of Roman occupation especially becomes one of eschatological thinking, thoughts about the ends of time, and of redemption found in other worlds. And so this occupation brings out not only the rebellious instincts in the Jews, but also deep thoughts of impending doom, and messianism. Not surprisingly, the spiritual and the military aspects of the appointed rebel leaders often blended into one, the leader of the rebellion often claiming, or being afforded, messianic qualities. Indeed, Judas the Galilean had by many been perceived as a messianic figure.

In line with the pattern of messianism going hand in hand with revolt, it is not long after the death of Agrippa I that we hear of a certain "magician" coming to the fore, a man by the name of Theudas. This self-appointed prophet gathers people by the river Jordan, telling them he will divide the river for them. Procurator Fadus immediately senses the danger, well aware of the link between spiritual awakening and upheaval. He sends a troop of horsemen out against the people on the Jordan, killing a great many of them. Theudas himself is decapitated, and his head carried to Jerusalem.[17]

No, it is not yet a full-fledged rebellion, but it will soon become one. The stirrings which will eventually, in 66 CE, develop into all-out war between the Jews and their Roman occupiers start slowly and hesitatingly with the death of Agrippa I, in 44 CE, and really never cease after that. The Jews of Judea and Galilee are on a descending slope toward catastrophe. And in the year 70 CE, Jerusalem will be destroyed, along with its Temple and the majority of its people. The surviving Jews will be scattered around the then-known world.

The century before the destruction of Jerusalem is thus a tumultuous time indeed. It is the era which, in retrospect, heralds not only the destruction of Jerusalem and its Temple, but the near-destruction of the Jewish people. And it all occurs at the hands of Rome, then the central power of the civilized world. Consequently, it is no surprise that it is an era which has gone down in history, in more versions than one.

The Roman empire of the first century boasts a number of exceptional historians: Tacitus, Suetonius, Velleius Paterculus, to name only a few. Several of them found reason to write about Judea and Galilee, and the events that unfolded there. But one historian in particular stands out, in that he made the history of the Jews, and especially the Jewish War against Rome (including its preamble), the focus of his entire life's work. His name is Flavius Josephus. And he is the main reason why we know so much about the era in which Jesus lived and worked. Indeed, his chronicles are the main source of comparison for any scholar interested in the historical aspects of the New Testament.

So who was this man, Flavius Josephus?

Yosef ben Matitiahu (or Joseph son of Matthias), as Josephus was originally named, was born in Jerusalem in the year 37 or 38 CE. His family was one of great prominence, with both priestly and aristocratic ancestry. As Josephus himself writes in his autobiography, *Vita*: "By my mother I am of the Royal blood."[18] Being thus part of the Jewish establishment, Josephus had more of an intellectual, and sometimes opportunistic approach, rather than an activist one, to the politics of the day. He tells us that when he was sixteen he devoted himself to the study of the three Jewish main factions—the Sadducees, the Pharisees, and the Essenes. But toward the zealously religious rebels, the "fourth philosophic sect," as he calls them, he only feels disdain.[19] This is a disdain, not to say hatred, that will stay with him for the rest of his life (which is something to take into account when judging Josephus's texts on the Zealots, and their messianic leaders).

As a nineteen-year-old, Josephus becomes a Pharisee, the most popular Jewish faction at that time.[20] Or so he says. Whether this is true or not is a matter of opinion; Josephus was an opportunistic man, and he may have wished to ingratiate himself with the Jewish mainstream at the time *Vita* was written, around 99 CE. Defending himself, as it turns out, was of prime concern to Josephus. Because by this time, the Jews regarded him as a traitor.

For Joseph son of Matthias, the beginning of adulthood coincided with the final phase of escalation of tensions between the Jews and their Roman masters. It is the religiously fanatic rebels, above all, who have intensified their activity against Rome. And they have not only provoked the anger of the occupiers, they have also caused considerable internal strife among the Jews, many of whom wished, above all, to stay quiet and non-provocative. But the rebels will not be passive this time. As Josephus writes: "They [. . .] do not value dying any kinds of death, nor indeed do they heed the deaths of their relations and friends, nor can any such fear make them call any man lord."[21] And these rebels are beginning to influence the rest of the population.

About 63 CE, Josephus travels to Rome, in order to intervene on behalf of some Jewish priests who had been imprisoned. Being of aristocratic origins, and having well-developed social skills, Josephus will spend the next couple of years in the court of the emperor, Nero, having acquainted himself with Nero's wife Poppaea. The priests are finally released, much thanks to Josephus, and he subsequently returns to Jerusalem, in the year 66—a year which will see the beginning of what would soon be perceived as the final apocalypse, the Jewish War.

Like other persons from the elite, Josephus was in the beginning not sympathetic to the revolt. But, inevitably, the more conservative and privileged Jews would be pulled along with the masses—especially after the rebels had begun to meet with success. What had started out as a fringe rebellion thus eventually became a war, involving everyone—Jew against Roman. Josephus, having demonstrated leadership skills as well as those of a diplomat, was appointed, probably by the Jewish Council in Jerusalem, the Sanhedrin, to lead the fight against the Romans in Galilee.

Josephus is, however, not an uncontested leader. There is a rival northern militia led by a man named John of Gischala. The competition and enmity between John and Josephus will have disastrous results, leading to a failure to secure the old capital of Galilee, Sepphoris.

It is in the summer of 67 CE that this turn of events will have decisive consequences for Josephus personally. Roman commander Vespasian leads a massive attack against the rebel stronghold in the town of

Jotapata, which controls the road to Sepphoris, and Josephus's forces are surrounded. After six weeks they are finally defeated, and most are killed. Josephus himself, however, is hiding in a hole, with forty other "persons of eminence."[22] On the third day, they are discovered by the Romans, and told to surrender. Josephus is on the verge of doing so, but then his compatriots demand that he take his life rather than give himself up to the enemy. This leads Josephus to present an alternative idea to them: they should all die, he suggests, determining the order through lots; the one drawing the first lot would be killed by the man who drew the second, who, in turn, would be killed by the third, and so on. The others finally agree. And when all lots have been drawn, it turns out that Josephus got the last one . . . When it comes time for him to kill, Josephus asks the only other man left alive to surrender with him, "as he was very desirous neither to be condemned by the lot, nor, if he had been left to the last, to imbrue his right hand in the blood of his countryman" (Josephus writes about himself in the third person). No one is left to stop them, and they emerge unharmed from the hole to surrender themselves to the Romans.[23]

This episode, perhaps, is the main reason why Josephus would forever be considered a betrayer among his fellow Jews; and also why the chronicles of his people, that he would ultimately bequeath to history, would be preserved not by those whose lives he had documented, but rather by their victors, the Romans, and then by their descendants in Roman lands, the Christians.

Upon being arrested, Josephus is taken to Vespasian himself. And there, he presents the commander with a sweet prophecy: Vespasian will soon, his captive says, be emperor![24] Vespasian is immediately taken with the young man. And so is his son, Titus. This does not stop them from arresting Josephus, however, and keep him as a prisoner. But one year later Emperor Nero commits suicide, and in yet another year, Vespasian is, as Josephus prophesied, proclaimed emperor. Josephus is now let free, and given his patron's name, Flavius.[25]

The war is at its peak, and Josephus is in Jerusalem, with Titus, witnessing how the city, and its Temple, are destroyed utterly. He had tried to persuade his fellow Jews to surrender, but was not heeded. In the year 70 CE, the Jewish nation is crushed (although a small pocket of rebels hold out on the desert rock Masada for another three years). Josephus now travels to Rome, in the company of his triumphant friend Titus. This former Jewish revolutionary, and later turncoat, is richly rewarded for his changed loyalties: he becomes a privileged Roman citizen, with an annual salary. And as a latter-day colonialist he is given some land in his former home, Judea. But Josephus will not forget where he came from. And it is this man who—if not single-handedly, then certainly superiorly—has brought us the story of the long and painful final struggle of the unrelenting freedom-hungering Jews.

Josephus in Rome writes four major works: *War of the Jews* (ca. 75–79 CE), describing the war and its preludes, a work of seven books; *Antiquities of the Jews* (ca. 93 CE), a work of Jewish history from ancient times to the revolt against the Romans, encompassing twenty books; *Against Apion* (ca. 97 CE), a work in defence of the Jews; and the autobiographical *Life of Flavius Josephus* (or *Vita;* ca. 94–99 CE). Thus, interestingly, Josephus appears to write almost simultaneously with the Gospel authors.

Josephus's books were deposited in the Public Library of Rome.[26] But the oldest substantial manuscripts in the original Greek that we still have today were written in the ninth, tenth, or eleventh centuries.[27] Parts of his works were, however, cited or referred to by other authors, principally Christian, much earlier. We shall soon come back to this.

Of Josephus's works, the multi-volumed *War of the Jews* and *Antiquities of the Jews* are the ones that have proven to be such rich sources of knowledge about Roman *Iudaea* and neighboring territories in the times of Jesus and later. Josephus writes in great detail, not only about the war, but about all the important events in the decades and centuries preceding it. And not only once; he describes the century before the fall of Jerusalem in both *War* and *Antiquities*, often providing different (and occasionally contradictory) details in the two sources. It is a rich trove indeed, telling us about procurators and revolutionaries, about high priests and messianic claimants.

But does it tell us anything about Jesus of Nazareth?

Now there was about this time Jesus, a wise man, if it be lawful to call him a man; for he was a doer of wonderful works, a teacher of such men as receive the truth with pleasure. He drew over to him both many of the Jews and many of the Gentiles. He was [the] Christ. And when Pilate, at the suggestion of the principal men amongst us, had condemned him to the cross, those that loved him at the first did not forsake him; for he appeared to them alive again the third day; as the divine prophets had foretold these and ten thousand other wonderful things concerning him. And the tribe of Christians, so named from him, are not extinct at this day.[28]

This paragraph, often referred to as the *Testimonium Flavianum,* is found in the eighteenth book of *Antiquities of the Jews.* And with the exception of a sentence in Book Twenty ("[High priest Ananus] assembled the Sanhedrin of judges, and brought before them the brother of Jesus, who was called Christ, whose name was James, and some others" [29]), the *Testimonium Flavianum* is the only reference to either Jesus or Christianity in Josephus's entire works.

It could be considered sufficient—sufficient, at least, to determine that Jesus was a historical person. But there is a problem with this paragraph: it was probably not written by Josephus. At least it was not written by Josephus as it stands. Although many scholars still believe that aspects of the *Testimonium* may be original, few are prepared to state that this segment of Josephus's book has not been tampered with.[30] And there are many reasons for this.

First, the text of the *Testimonium Flavianum* is decidedly confessional. It states that Jesus may not have been "a man"; it calls him "Christ," i.e. Messiah; it says that he rose from the dead; and it is clearly written by a person believing in Jesus as the Messiah, and worshipping him. This is not only unlike Josephus—in all other cases so spiteful, not to say hateful, of messianic claimants among the Jews—it also finds no reverberation in the rest of his writings. Outside of these two excerpts, Flavius Josephus simply does not seem to know about the Christians. They are otherwise not present in his chronicles—and completely absent in *War of the Jews.* And yet he wrote *War* in the 70s, and

Antiquities in the 90s, some four and six decades, respectively, after the Gospels tell us that Jesus was crucified.

Secondly, as a number of scholars have pointed out, the text seems to be squeezed in between two other paragraphs that deal with the revolutionary sentiments among the Jews, and which would flow much better if the *Testimonium Flavianum* was not in the middle.[31] This, indeed, is an argument also against the claim that perhaps Josephus did write a less confessional version of the text, which was later augmented.[32] As Charles Guignebert, an early twentieth century scholar of the history of Christianity, once put it: "the short digression, even with the proposed corrections, interrupts the thread of the discourse into which it is introduced."[33]

Thirdly, and perhaps most importantly, the early church fathers, although in some cases having read Josephus, do not mention the *Testimonium*. Since Josephus was not accepted by his fellow Jews, nor were his works preserved among them for posterity, the oldest preserved substantial manuscripts of *Antiquities of the Jews* date from around the tenth century. The work had been quoted considerably earlier than that, but the earliest known to have done so were not Jewish or Roman historians, they were Christian church fathers. And yet, in the beginning these Christian leaders failed to mention the *Testimonium Flavianum*.

Church Father Origen (ca. 185–254) was an early Christian scholar, pupil of Clement of Alexandria, and today regarded as one the most distinguished of the early church fathers, and the foremost Christian textual critic of his time. Around 246–248 CE, Origen wrote two works, in which he mentions *Antiquities of the Jews* by Josephus, with particular reference to its views on Jesus.[34] Significantly, Origen mentions a text similar to, but different than, the one we now see in Book 20 verse 200 of *Antiquities*, mentioning "the brother of Jesus, who was called Christ, whose name was James." But more importantly, although Origen talks also about the eighteenth book of *Antiquities*, and in fact cites five passages from it, he entirely omits to mention the *Testimonium Flavianum*.[35] Not only that: Origen in one of his books writes that Josephus "did not accept Jesus as Christ," and in another that Josephus was "not believing in Jesus as the Christ."[36]

Some decades later, Church Father Eusebius, bishop of Caesarea, also feels moved to bring up Flavius Josephus, historian of Roman Judea and Galilee, in relation to Jesus. And in not one, but three of his books, Eusebius quotes the *Testimonium Flavianum* almost word for word as it is known today.[37] Suddenly, thus, this passage is known. But since when? Origen, obviously, had not known about it. And he was not the only one. In his book *Josephus, Judaism, and Christianity*, prominent Josephus scholar Louis Feldman writes: "I have counted no fewer than eleven church fathers prior to or contemporary with Eusebius who cite various passages from Josephus (including the *Antiquities*) but who do not mention the *Testimonium*." He continues: "Moreover, during the century after Eusebius there are five church fathers, including Augustine, who certainly had many occasions to find it useful and who cite passages from Josephus but not this one."[38] Although others have countered that the earlier writers appear to have mostly read Josephus's other works, or other books of *Antiquities*, the fact remains: Origen states clearly that he read Book 18 of *Antiquities,* and although doing so with an eye to evidence about Jesus, he fails entirely to mention the *Testimonium Flavianum*.[39]

The first time we hear of this absolutely fundamental passage in the quest for the historical Jesus is in the fourth century. And we hear about it from a Christian bishop. It is not an uncommon suggestion, thus, that Eusebius may have written the *Testimonium* himself.[40]

But why, then, is this passage of such "monumental importance," as Jesus scholar John P. Meier puts it?[41] Why is there so much focus on the *Testimonium*? Quite simply because Josephus ought to have written about Jesus. He wrote about everything else that befell the Jews during this century. And he wrote about it at length. To put it bluntly: if Jesus of Nazareth had been a person of importance during the time of the Roman presence in Judea and Galilee, then Josephus most certainly would have recorded this.

So were there other local chroniclers, beside Josephus, covering this significant era of Jewish history? Yes, there were—at least two.

Like Josephus, Justus of Tiberias was a Jewish military leader during the war against Rome. And like Josephus, he was active primarily in the Galilee. In fact, the two men, although fighting for the same cause, became enemies (for a time Justus and his father Pistus apparently attached themselves to John of Gischala).[42] They became enemies to the extent that each of them dedicated a book to demolishing the reputation of the other. Josephus's autobiography, *Vita*, was written in defense against Justus's *History of the Jewish War*, in which the latter apparently accused Josephus of not writing truthfully in *War of the Jews*, and of instigating the sedition in Galilee. As the revolt, at the time these accounts were written, had long been crushed, both authors were probably motivated by a desire to put themselves in a more favorable light toward the Romans.

Justus of Tiberias seems to have written at least two works of history—one concerning itself with the Jewish War, mentioned above, and the other, a book he called *A Chronicle of the Kings of the Jews in the Form of a Genealogy*, documenting the history of the Jews from the time of Moses until the death of Agrippa II. Thus, Justus did much the same thing as Josephus did. The difference is, unlike in the case of Josephus, the works of Justus have not been preserved for posterity. Fragments or commentaries have, however, been related by others.[43] And in one significant case, Photius, patriarch of Constantinople in the ninth century, read through the entire *Chronicle of the Kings of the Jews*, looking for descriptions of Jesus. And this is what he found:

> Read the Chronicle of Justus of Tiberias, entitled "A Chronicle of the Kings of the Jews in the Form of a Genealogy, by Justus of Tiberias." He came from Tiberias in Galilee, from which he took his name. He begins his history with Moses and carries it down to the death of the seventh Agrippa of the family of Herod, and the last of the kings of the Jews. His kingdom, which was bestowed upon him by Claudius, was extended by Nero, and still more by Vespasian. He died in the third year of the reign of Trajan, when the history ends. Justus's style is very concise, and he omits a great deal that is of the utmost importance. Suffering from the common fault of the Jews, to which race he belonged, he does not even mention the coming of Christ, the events of His life, or the miracles performed by Him.[44]

So Justus also does not provide any evidence of Justus's existence. Nor do we find Jesus in the works of Philo (ca. 20 BCE–after 40 CE), a Jewish philosopher who would be much read by early Christians, as his ideas seemed to touch on ideas of theirs. Although Philo describes both Pontius Pilate and the Essenes (a faction among the Jews that many historians have later associated with Jesus or John the Baptist), he nevertheless fails to mention Jesus.

It is not until we enter the second century CE that we begin to find what seem to be incontestable (although, it should be stated, sometimes still contested) non-biblical accounts about Jesus, or his movement.[45]

In his 1909 book, *The Christ: A Critical Review and Analysis of the Evidence of His Existence*, American historian and freethinker John E. Remsburg published a table listing forty-two authors active at the time of Jesus, or within the first century after him. "Enough of the writings of the authors named in the foregoing list remains to form a library," writes Remsburg. "Yet in this mass of Jewish and Pagan literature, aside from two forged passages in the works of a Jewish author, and two disputed passages in the works of Roman writers, there is to be found no mention of Jesus Christ."[46] The "two disputed passages," it should be mentioned, were written in the second century. And although more than two-thirds of the authors listed by Remsburg were active in the first century, only the chronicles by Josephus contain any texts referring to Jesus—texts which most likely have been tampered with.

How can we explain this meager result? We are, after all, talking about a period otherwise well documented. And if, as the Gospels state, Jesus of Nazareth was a messianic leader with a large following, a leader who was tried and crucified, a leader whose trial involved two high priests, the tetrarch of Galilee, and the prefect of *Iudaea*, the discrepancy between the Gospel narratives and other contemporary sources is major. What could the reason be?

The predominant explanation among Jesus scholars has been, and continues to be, that although Jesus of Nazareth most likely existed, he was probably less significant in his own time than the Gospel accounts suggest. As Jesus scholar E. P. Sanders puts it: "When he was executed, Jesus was no more important to the outside world than the two brigands or insurgents executed with him—whose names we do not know."[47] A view represented by fewer scholars is that the lack of historical evidence can be explained by the likely fact that Jesus was an entirely mythological character.[48]

There may, however, be a third explanation for our failure to detect Jesus in the contemporary historical sources outside of the New Testament, an explanation which is rarely put forth: perhaps Jesus of Nazareth lived and acted in a slightly different era than we think. Perhaps our chronology is off by some years. Perhaps we can find a prominent and influential Jesus of Nazareth in those other contemporary historical sources, if we only look a little bit earlier—or later.

THE TIMING OF EVENTS DEPICTED
IN THE GOSPELS

How do we know when Jesus lived, preached, and was crucified? We know because the New Testament tells us. But it doesn't tell us by providing us with dates—and our present calendar (based on the birth of Jesus) naturally did not exist then. It tells us in a different way: by providing names.

The New Testament is actually very generous with names of people in authority when Jesus was active—Roman emperors, governors and procurators, Jewish client kings and high priests—and because we have such rich parallel sources of information concerning many of these authority figures, we know when they were in power, and conversions to our present Gregorian calendar are generally uncomplicated. From this, we can easily deduce when Jesus preached and was crucified.

Do we then have any reason to suspect that the New Testament authors could have been badly informed with regard to who ruled when? Well, no obvious reason. The New Testament, as we now know it, was more or less set by the end of the fourth century. But the various texts were written long before that. The most important segments—the four Gospels—were all likely written in the first century, or the beginning of the second. Although dating of the Gospels is difficult, and a matter of argument, Mark is often estimated to have been written 68–73 CE, Matthew 70–90, Luke 80–100, and John 90–110.[1] Thus, they were probably written only a few decades after Jesus is said to have been active. And we have reason to assume that the authors knew which dignitaries were in power then.

Furthermore, when it comes to chronological information, the Gospel authors as a rule are consistent, at least each individual author is; i.e. if one dignitary associated with a particular event is mentioned in a Gospel, then other dignitaries mentioned in connection with the same event will be of the same era. In other words, kings and emperors and procurators and high priests mentioned will tend to be of the same era.

This, at least, indicates that the Gospel authors were familiar with the political structures of the time they describe.

Who, then, were these Gospel authors?

The simple answer is: we don't know. At least three of the Gospels—Mark being the possible exception—are considered to be written after the fall of Jerusalem (mostly because of the authors' seeming knowledge of its destruction), and so it is thought that they were composed in exile. All four Gospels, except possibly Matthew, are assumed to have been written in Greek, despite the fact that Jesus and his disciples spoke Aramaic. Although Greek at that time was *lingua franca* in the eastern part of the Roman Empire, this would strengthen the assumption that they were written outside of the Jewish realm.

Although considered separate testimonies on the life of Jesus, the Gospels nevertheless are regarded as interdependent. Three of them—the three that are believed to be the earliest ones, Mark, Matthew and Luke—have so much in common that they are thought to be partially based on each other, or on common sources. They are therefore called the *synoptic*, comparable, Gospels ("taking a common view"). It is possible to line up long segments of text from these three Gospels, and put them side by side. Often they agree word for word. The Gospel that sticks out is John. This Gospel, although not often in disagreement, differs considerably in content and style from the other three.

All the same, the Gospels seem to be partially directed at different audiences:

Mark, likely the earliest Gospel, is regarded as a Hellenistic Gospel, written for the Greek-speaking people in the Roman Empire. The information is sparse, and the style of writing non-literary.

Matthew appears more to be directed towards the Jews, or towards Judaeo-Christians, who themselves would have some prior knowledge of Judaism, and perhaps connection to the land. It continually refers to the Old Testament, and even emphasizes that the message of Jesus is directed specifically towards Jews. The argument it has is against the mainstream faction of Judaism after the fall of Jerusalem: the Pharisees.

Perhaps the most interesting Gospel from the point of view of chronology is, as we shall soon see, Luke, the third Gospel. The author of Luke is regarded as the historian among the Gospel writers. He is possibly also a person we can identify, since the Apostle Paul had a disciple, and fellow traveler, called Luke. The author of the Gospel has an obvious patron when he writes, as he starts with the words:

> Since many have undertaken to set down an orderly account of the events that have been fulfilled among us, just as they were handed on to us by those who from the beginning were eyewitnesses and servants of the word, I too decided, after investigating everything carefully from the very first, to write an orderly account for you, most excellent Theophilus, so that you may know the truth concerning the things about which you have been instructed.[2]

Who this patron "Theophilus" (meaning "lover of God") is, we are not told. But Luke states clearly that he himself has not been an eye-witness to the events he describes. He has gathered information from others. Most agree that Luke is also the probable author of the Acts of the Apostles, the New Testament book which describes what happened after the crucifixion of Jesus (and which starts with the words: "In the first book, Theophilus, I wrote about all that Jesus did and taught from the beginning").[3]

Which sources, then, has Luke made use of? Apart from using information from the other Synoptic Gospels—Mark, and either

Matthew or sources used by Matthew—it is a fairly common, although not uncontested, opinion that Luke would have read another historical source central to us: the chronicles of Flavius Josephus, and in particular his *Antiquities of the Jews* (which, if true, would push the writing of Luke and Acts into the 90s, at least).[4] For one, there are a couple of episodes described by both Luke-Acts and Josephus, where the accounts are decidedly similar (see, for instance, the description of the death of Agrippa I, mentioned above), but more important are the similarities in themes, vocabulary, and literary style, and the sense that the author of Luke-Acts knows the highlights and viewpoints of Josephus's work. As Josephus scholar Steve Mason puts it in his book *Josephus and the New Testament*:

> Luke-Acts is unique among the NT writings in the extent of its affinities with Josephus's narratives [. . .] I cannot prove beyond doubt that Luke knew the writings of Josephus. If he did not, however, we have a nearly incredible series of coincidences, which require that Luke knew something that closely approximated Josephus's narrative in several distinct ways.[5]

It is worthwhile to bear this in mind: the Gospel writers were probably not unaware of what other contemporary historians wrote about the Jewish realm during Roman occupation. Including what those historians wrote about the times when Jesus was said to have lived and preached.

The Gospel of John, finally, is, as mentioned, quite different from the other three Gospels, both in its content and in its tone. John lingers on certain episodes, and the writing is more meditative or philosophical in its tone. Most scholars consider the Gospel of John to be the least reliable in a historical sense (perhaps because it differs from the other three). But sometimes John provides unique material, and this material can not automatically be dismissed.[6]

In these four testimonies, the Gospels, written mostly by unknown scribes, we find descriptions of the life and work of Jesus, from his birth to his crucifixion and resurrection. The narratives are nevertheless focused on particular periods of his life—mostly on his final year, and above all on the last week of his life, when he was arrested on the Mount of Olives, put to trial, crucified, buried, and resurrected. As mentioned, two of the Gospels, Matthew and Luke (but interestingly not the oldest Gospel, Mark) also provide descriptions of Jesus's birth, and events surrounding it.

The Gospels thus tell us about the preaching and life of Jesus Christ. But they are also careful to place Jesus in a historical context. It is a fact that all four Gospels—and Luke in particular—are at pains to provide chronological parameters that should allow us to pinpoint the time of Jesus's life and mission.

So let us now look at some of the chronological information provided by the four Gospels, information that will tell us when Jesus is said to have lived and worked.

The Gospel of Luke tells us that Jesus was born when Augustus was Roman emperor. We know that Augustus ruled from 27 BCE until 14 CE. The same Gospel specifies the time of birth further, by providing the information that Jesus was born during the tax census under Quirinius, which we know happened just after Quirinius arrived as governor of Syria, in 6 or 7 CE. Interestingly, as mentioned, the Gospel of Matthew provides a differing time for Jesus birth—prior to the death of Herod the Great, which occurred in 4 BCE. We shall come back to this discrepancy between Luke and Matthew later.

After the description of Jesus's birth, the Gospels basically tell us nothing about his childhood and youth, except a description in Luke of when Jesus at age twelve goes to Jerusalem with his parents, and unbeknownst to them stays behind in the Temple ("Why were you searching for me? Did you not know that I must be in my Father's house?").[7] But no names of dignitaries are provided in these verses.

The next time we meet Jesus is when he comes down to the Jordan River, to be baptized by John the Baptist. But prior to this, we are given some significant chronological information. The Gospel of Luke, in fact, provides us with a whole slew of chronological references concerning the timepoint of the emergence of John the Baptist as a preacher. Luke 3:1–2 says: "In the fifteenth year of the reign of Emperor Tiberius, when

Pontius Pilate was governor of Judea, and Herod was ruler of Galilee, and his brother Philip ruler of the region of Ituraea and Trachonitis, and Lysanias ruler of Abilene, during the high priesthood of Annas and Caiaphas, the word of God came to John son of Zechariah in the wilderness."[8] All of the named dignitaries except one—Lysanias ruler of Abilene—are known, as are their periods in office (which all overlap to some extent). But the most specific date is provided by the line "in the fifteenth year of the reign of Emperor Tiberius." Tiberius ruled the Roman empire alone from 14 to 37 CE. Thus (assuming that Luke's dating does not include the co-regency with Augustus, which started about two years earlier), the fifteenth year of Tiberius's rule was in 28 or 29 CE, which should be the year when John the Baptist, according to Luke, started his missionary work.[9] Since Jesus was baptized by John, and only subsequent to this started his own missionary activity (which lasted anywhere from less than one to almost four years), the missionary work, and the crucifixion, of Jesus must have happened after 28 CE. Since, however, the Gospels do not tell us how long the period was between John the Baptist's emergence as a preacher and the baptism of Jesus, it is from this information hard to arrive at an actual timepoint when Jesus himself started preaching (or of a last possible date for the crucifixion). Luke does say that "Jesus was about thirty years old when he began his work," but this is confusing information.[10] If he was born when Matthew says, before the death of Herod the Great (4 BCE), this would mean he started his missionary work around, or before, 24 CE, which of course is too early, if John the Baptist started his in 28 CE. If, on the other hand, we go by Luke's own information, that Jesus was born at the time of the tax census, in 6 or 7 CE, he would have started preaching around 36 or 37 CE, which, as we shall see, is possible, but bordering on too late.

After being baptized, Jesus goes out into the wilderness, where he spends forty days, resisting temptation by the devil. After this, and seemingly before Jesus starts his own missionary work (at least according to Mark and Matthew), John the Baptist is arrested. And although John the Baptist is based "in the wilderness of Judea," the person who has him arrested, curiously enough, is the tetrarch of Galilee, Herod Antipas.[11] We know that Herod Antipas was in power between 4 BCE and 39 CE.[12] This means that John the Baptist must have been arrested (and then killed) before 39 CE. And since Herod Antipas is present during the trial of Jesus, Jesus must have begun his work before 39 CE, as well. This fits with the chronological data mentioned so far.

After John is arrested, Jesus goes to the Galilee, to his hometown Nazareth, and to the Sea of Galilee, where he first meets with his closest disciples. Now starts Jesus's missionary work which, as mentioned, lasts for anywhere between less than one to perhaps as many as four years, depending on which Gospel we read, and how we interpret it. And then follows the major, and most significant, part of the Gospel narratives: the final visit to Jerusalem, with the tumults at the Temple, the Last Supper, the arrest on the Mount of Olives, the trial, and the crucifixion.

It is here, during Jesus's arrest, trial and crucifixion, that the Gospels provide us with the most important names to establish a chronology. Because we are told that the following four people were present as judges at his trial: Roman prefect Pontius Pilate, Jewish high priests Caiaphas and Annas, and the ruler of Galilee—Herod Antipas, here only called "Herod."[13] So if we know their times in office, we can also determine the outer limits of when Jesus could have been crucified. And we do have that information:

- Pilate held his position as prefect over *Iudaea* from 26 (or 27) to 36 (or early 37) CE.[14]
- Herod Antipas ruled Galilee from 4 BCE to 39 CE.[15]
- Caiaphas was high priest in Jerusalem from ca. 18 to 36 (or early 37) CE.[16] The information on Annas we shall come back to later.

Thus, if we take into account that John the Baptist started preaching in 28 or 29 CE, we may conclude that the entire period of Jesus's missionary activity, and his crucifixion, must have occurred sometime between 28 and 37 CE. That seems like clear and succinct dating, and we ought to feel fairly certain that this chronology is correct.

The only problem is this: some of the accounts presented in the New Testament simply do not fit within that timeframe. That is the basis for the hypothesis presented in this book.

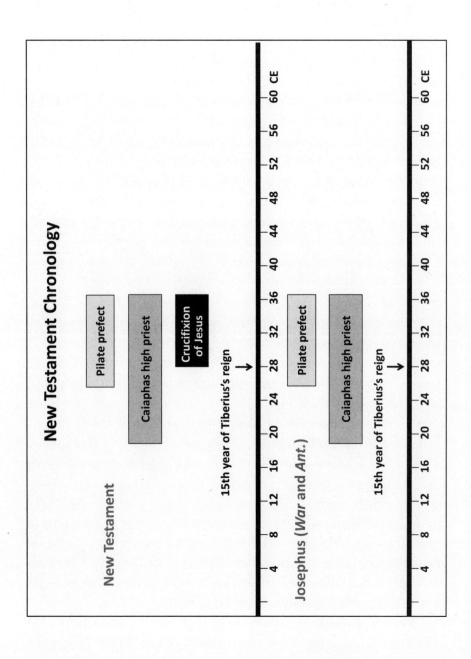

CHRONOLOGICAL ENIGMA ONE: ON THEUDAS, AND OTHER MESSIANIC LEADERS

LET US BEGIN WITH A WIDELY ACKNOWLEDGED CHRONOLOGICAL ODD-ity in the New Testament narrative. It concerns one of the Jewish mes-sianic leaders under Roman rule.

In his chronicles, Flavius Josephus mentions a number of Jewish messianic claimants during the dramatic fourteen decades of Roman occupation. And he also provides a few with names. As previously alluded to, the pattern of their emergence largely follows that of ris-ing and abating rebellion. Thus, with the exception of the naming of Jesus in the *Testimonium Flavianum*, the appearance of messianic leaders among the Jews, at least named ones, is restricted to the peri-ods of outright revolt. On the following page is a list of those Jew-ish messianic leaders uniformly recognized as having been named in Josephus's chronicles, from after the death of Herod the Great until the fall of Jerusalem.

Interestingly, at least three of these messianic leaders are named also in the New Testament—all three of them in the Acts of the Apostles.

The Acts of the Apostles (which, as mentioned, was probably writ-ten by the same author who wrote the Gospel of Luke) is the fifth book of the New Testament, and it relates what happened after the

---

Jewish messianic leaders named by Josephus 4 BCE–70 CE

Simon of Peraea: 4 BCE
During the revolt after the death of Herod the Great

Athronges: 4–2? BCE
During the revolt after the death of Herod the Great

Judas the Galilean: 6 CE
Leads the revolt against the Tax Census, under Quirinius

Theudas: 44–46 CE
Messianic leader by the Jordan River, under Fadus

The Egyptian: 52–59 CE
Tries to conquer Jerusalem, under Felix

Menahem: 66 CE
Sicarii leader at the beginning of the Jewish War

Simon bar Giora: 66–70 CE
Rebel leader during and at the end of the Jewish War

---

crucifixion of Jesus. Acts essentially alternates between describing the actions of the apostles—the closest disciples of Jesus—who remained in Jerusalem after the crucifixion, and the actions of Saint Paul. Paul, who is not part of the Gospel narratives, first appears in Acts when outside Jerusalem he is an observer of the stoning of Stephen, proto-martyr of Christianity. After this, Paul himself becomes a persecutor of Christians, but is converted to the faith during a journey to Damascus. Paul subsequently, and essentially singlehandedly, becomes responsible for spreading Christianity around the Mediterranean. At one point he is arrested in Jerusalem—apparently after being recognized by Jews in the Temple, who want to kill him. He is subsequently imprisoned by the Roman authorities, but after two years he is allowed to travel to Rome, where his missionary work continues. The Acts of the Apostles (together with the Letters of Paul) documents this. But, as mentioned, Acts in parallel relates events occurring among the apostles remaining in Judea and Galilee.

But what is really interesting in this context is that Acts also name-drops; Acts suddenly mentions the names of individuals who appear to fly in and out of the narrative, seemingly without explanation.

Judas the Galilean, Theudas, and "the Egyptian"—they are three of the major messianic leaders in the century leading up to the Jewish War. And all three of them are mentioned in Acts.[1] Why Acts, in particular, would be the book naming these three messianic leaders (otherwise absent in the New Testament narrative) is hard to say. And the circumstances under which they are mentioned are mystifying as well, because the names are just thrown into the New Testament narrative, only once for each person and almost without context, at least without a context which is explained. The New Testament tells us virtually nothing about who these three men are. We would have to go to Josephus to get that information.

But let us start by looking at the situations in which they are mentioned in the New Testament:

"The Egyptian," a messianic rebel leader active during the procuratorship of Felix, appears in Acts in a sentence uttered by the commander who arrests Paul in Jerusalem, after Paul has been discovered and beaten by the multitude in the Temple: "Do you know Greek?" the commander says to Paul. "Then you are not the Egyptian who recently stirred up a revolt and led the four thousand *Sicarii* out into the wilderness?"[2] No further explanation of this question is given—we are not told who "the Egyptian" is, nor who the *Sicarii* are. And the name "the Egyptian" never appears again in the New Testament.

Judas the Galilean and Theudas, in turn, are both mentioned in the fifth chapter of Acts, in a situation involving the apostles of the Jerusalem community. After the crucifixion, Acts tells us, the apostles continued preaching and teaching about Jesus in and around the Temple. The Jewish authorities in Jerusalem were not, however, pleased with these agitators in their midst, and had them arrested and imprisoned.[3] "But during the night," Acts tells us, "an angel of the Lord opened the prison doors, brought them out, and said, 'Go, stand in the temple and tell the people the whole message about this life.' When they heard this, they entered the temple at daybreak and went on with their teaching."[4] The determination of these apostles to continue Jesus's work is thus strong. But so is the opposition. The temple police once again have the apostles arrested, this time bringing them to the high priest and the Jewish Council, the Sanhedrin. But also in front of the Jewish authorities, these disciples of Jesus continue preaching about him. And now Acts tells us the following:

> When they [the rabbis] heard this, they were enraged and want-ed to kill them. But a Pharisee in the council named Gamaliel, a teacher of the law, respected by all the people, stood up and ordered the men to be put outside for a short time. Then he said to them, "Fellow Israelites, consider carefully what you propose to do to these men. For some time ago *Theudas* rose up, claim-ing to be somebody, and a number of men, about four hundred, joined him; but he was killed, and all who followed him were dispersed and disappeared. After him *Judas the Galilean* rose up at the time of the census and got people to follow him; he also perished, and all who followed him were scattered. So in the present case, I tell you, keep away from these men and let them alone."[5]

The three major messianic leaders of the decades preceding the Jewish War are thus all mentioned in the New Testament—once for each name, and each time without any explaining context. But there is an additional oddity with this last paragraph, the one nam-ing Theudas and Judas the Galilean: the timing is off. The event itself, i.e. the interrogation of the apostles at the Sanhedrin, must have happened in the 30s, at the latest. For one, as it is described, it appears to follow closely on the crucifixion of Jesus. But more importantly, the interrogation precedes the narrative of the conver-sion of the Apostle Paul, on the road to Damascus. In one of the Letters of Paul, we are told that he arrived in Damascus when Aretas was king of the Nabateans.[6] Aretas died in 40 CE, at the latest.[7] Thus, the conversion of Paul—and the events preceding it—must have happened in the 30s.

But the thing is: this interrogation of the apostles could not have happened in the 30s. And the reason is one word: "Theudas." Because this is what Josephus writes about the messianic leader Theudas:

> Now it came to pass, while Fadus was procurator of Judea, that a certain magician, whose name was Theudas, persuaded a great part of the people to take their effects with them, and follow him to the river Jordan; for he told them he was a prophet, and that he would, by his own command, divide the river, and afford them an easy passage over it; and many were deluded by his words. However, Fadus did not permit them to make any advantage of his wild attempt, but sent a troop of horsemen out against them; who, falling upon them unexpectedly, slew many of them, and took many of them alive. They also took Theudas alive, and cut off his head, and carried it to Jerusalem.[8]

Fadus was Roman procurator of Judea from 44 to 46 CE—appointed by Emperor Claudius immediately following the death of King Agrippa I.[9] And Theudas was a spiritual leader who was active and killed during Fadus' procuratorship. So says Josephus. Yet Acts tells us that Theudas is already dead in the 30s! How is this possible? How can Josephus say that Theudas is killed 44 to 46 CE, and the New Testament that he is already dead in the 30s? This is a discrepancy between the New Testament narrative and that of Josephus which is generally acknowledged.[10]

The most common assumption has been that the author of Luke-Acts confused the order of the messianic leaders, especially since the paragraph subsequently relates Rabbi Gamaliel's statement that Judas the Galilean came *after* Theudas.[11] As we know, Judas the Galilean was the leader of the census revolt, under Quirinius, which took place already in 6 or 7 CE, several decades *before* Theudas appeared on the scene.[12] The author of Acts thus seems to make not only one, but two chronological mistakes.

An alternative attempt at explanation has been that there were perhaps two major Jewish messianic leaders named Theudas—a valid suggestion, if it were not for the fact that only one is mentioned by Josephus.[13]

Another, and quite interesting, explanation has been that Luke perhaps refers to Judas the Galilean by mistake, and really means the *sons of Judas*, who, according to Josephus's *Antiquities*, were killed soon after Theudas.[14] As mentioned, a number of scholars have come to the conclusion that the author of Luke and Acts had probably read *Antiquities of the Jews*. Thus, if this was the case, Luke might, according to this interpretation, have mistaken "the sons of Judas" for Judas the Galilean himself, and as a consequence mistakenly placed him after Theudas. This possible mistake would not, however, explain how Theudas could already be dead when the apostles are brought to the Sanhedrin in the 30s. It would only explain the reversed order between Theudas and Judas.

In conclusion, Josephus places the death of Theudas in the mid-40s, at least a decade later than Acts does. This is by most scholars attributed to a mistake by the author of Luke-Acts.

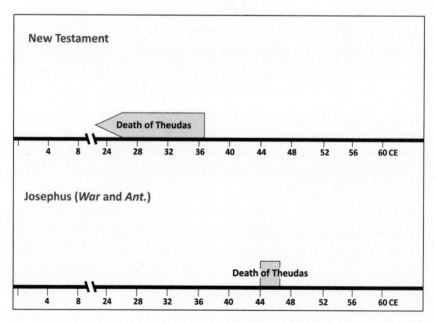

There are, however, other chronological inconsistencies in the New Testament texts, most of them rarely addressed.

CHRONOLOGICAL ENIGMA TWO: OF ROBBERS AND REBELS

OUR NEXT CHRONOLOGICAL ENIGMA IN THE NEW TESTAMENT concerns a group of people mentioned on a number of occasions in the narrative: the so called "robbers" ("bandits" or "thieves" in some translations).

The Gospels tell us that Jesus was crucified between two "robbers." It also tells us that the person who was released in his stead, Barabbas, was a "robber."[1] And when he is arrested on the Mount of Olives, Jesus meets his adversaries with the words: "Have you come out with swords and clubs to arrest me as though I were a robber?"[2]

"Robbers" were obviously prevalent in the time of Jesus.

Who, then, were these "robbers"?

One sentence in the Gospel of Mark seems to give us a hint. It says: "Now a man called Barabbas was in prison with the rebels who had committed murder during the insurrection."[3] If John tells us that Barabbas was a "robber," and Mark tells us that Barabbas was in prison with "the rebels," it does not seem too far-fetched to assume that "robbers" were Jewish rebels.

Were they?

In descriptions of the rebel activity occurring in the Jewish realm in the century leading up to the Jewish War, we see more than one term being applied to these religiously motivated fighters. The designation most often used today is "Zealot." The word, *zelotes* in Greek, means "one most eagerly desirous of a thing," "one burning with zeal." This has become something of an umbrella term for the Jewish insurgents against Rome. But in fact, if we go by Josephus, he only starts applying this term during the Jewish War, and perhaps only in reference to a subgroup of insurgents.[4] The first time he describes the rebels at length he in fact only calls them "the fourth sect of Jewish philosophy":

> But of the fourth sect of Jewish philosophy, Judas the Galilean was the author. These men agree in all other things with the Pharisaic notions; but they have an inviolable attachment to liberty, and say that God is to be their only Ruler and Lord. They also do not value dying any kinds of death, nor indeed do they heed the deaths of their relations and friends, nor can any such fear make them call any man lord.[5]

If we look in the Talmud (the Jewish Oral Law, which was put down in writing only after the Jewish War against Rome) the terms usually used to designate the rebels are *kanaim*—Hebrew for Zealots—and *biryonim* or *barione* (Aramaic, singular *bariona*)—"the boorish ones," or "wild ones."[6] But if we look through Josephus's works, next to "Zealots" the terms primarily used by him when describing these spiritually driven, and often very fanatical, freedom fighters are: *lestai* (singular: *lestes*), and *Sicarii* (singular: *Sicarius*). The designation most frequent of all is *lestai*. And *lestai* is Greek for "robbers." Josephus thus confirms what is only hinted at in the Gospels: a "robber"—a *lestes*—is a Jewish rebel.[7]

Why, then, would the rebels be called "robbers"? Well, the term would seem to convey not only how these fighters were regarded—not least by Josephus—but partly also which methods they used. The rebels were not always particular with regard to the means they applied to accomplish their political goals, nor of the consequences these had for their fellow countrymen. Robbery would on occasion be part of their arsenal, as would violence targeted also against other

Jews, primarily those associated with the leading Jewish factions (perceived by the rebels to be collaborators with the Roman occupier). It is for this reason, perhaps, that Josephus describes the "robbers" with such disdain:

> This seems to me to have been the reason why God, out of his hatred of these men's wickedness, rejected our city; and as for the temple, he no longer esteemed it sufficiently pure for him to inhabit therein, but brought the Romans upon us, and threw a fire upon the city to purge it; and brought upon us, our wives, and children, slavery, as desirous to make us wiser by our calamities.[8]

Let us now briefly look at the third term used by Josephus: *Sicarii*. Because also this is a term that we recognize from the New Testament. Remember the following sentence in Acts: "Then you are not the Egyptian who recently stirred up a revolt and led the four thousand *Sicarii* out into the wilderness?"[9]

Who, then, were the *Sicarii*?

Sicarii is a Latin term best translated as "daggermen." The use of curved daggers—*sicae* in latin—usually hidden inside voluminous garments, became their telltale sign. And the Sicarii are often described as the most persistent and fanatical of the anti-Roman resistance groups.

The origins of the Sicarii are, however, a little unclear. Josephus introduces them as a new faction on two different occasions fifty years apart: in the second book of *War*, and in *Antiquities*, Josephus tells us that it was under Felix, Roman procurator from 52 to 59/60 CE, that the Sicarii first appeared on the stage:

> . . . there sprang up another sort of robbers in Jerusalem, which were called Sicarii, who slew men in the day time, and in the midst of the city; this they did chiefly at the festivals, when they mingled themselves among the multitude, and concealed daggers under their garments, with which they stabbed those that were their enemies [. . .] The first man who was slain by them was Jonathan the high priest[10]

In the last book of *War*, however, Josephus writes that the Sicarii had been present already in the times of Judas the Galilean, in 6 or 7 CE— that they *were*, in fact, the followers of Judas. And this interpretation is strengthened by the fact that several later Sicarii leaders were blood relatives of Judas. [11]

So what distinguished the Sicarii from the "robbers," the "robbers" from the Zealots, and the Zealots from the *barione*? Perhaps nothing, or at least nothing consistent. At times in Josephus's writings, or the writings of the Talmud, it seems that we are dealing with different anti-Roman resistance factions, at other times they seem to blend into each other. Occasionally, Josephus will distinguish between the Sicarii and other "robbers," and on other occasions he will not.

Now, as we know, the "robbers," according to the New Testament, are very much present during Jesus's crucifixion.

So does this fit with what other sources tell us about them?

Well, let us look more closely at the pattern of their appearance. To start with, when did they first arrive on the stage?

Josephus writes that "of the fourth sect of Jewish philosophy, Judas the Galilean was the author," thus implying that the Jewish rebel movement started with Judas. [12] But this seems to be a matter of definition. As an organized political movement, anti-Roman resistance may have originated in Judas's times. But Josephus himself tells us about an event as early as during the reign of Herod the Great—thus well before the tax revolt—when daggermen, of sorts, appeared on the stage. Herod was a powerful king of the Jews, but one whose dependence on Rome made him obsequious to his faraway patrons, something which would provoke the anger of his subjects. Josephus writes about the games Herod arranged every five years in honor of Caesar:

> And truly foreigners were greatly surprised and delighted at the
> vastness of the expenses here exhibited, and at the great dangers
> that were here seen; but to natural Jews, this was no better than
> a dissolution of those customs for which they had so great a ven-
> eration. It appeared also no better than an instance of barefaced

impiety, to throw men to wild beasts, for the affording delight to the spectators; and it appeared an instance of no less impiety, to change their own laws for such foreign exercises: but, above all the rest, the trophies gave most distaste to the Jews; for as they imagined them to be images, included within the armor that hung round about them, they were sorely displeased at them, because it was not the custom of their country to pay honors to such images.

Graven images are forbidden in Judaism. Despite the fact that Herod tried to appease the protesting Jews by stripping the trophies of their ornaments, there were still those who would not be mollified. Josephus writes of ten men who conspire to kill Herod during an appointment, by hiding daggers under their garments. They are found out, and arrested:

> When they were seized, they showed their daggers, and professed that the conspiracy they had sworn to was a holy and a pious action; that what they intended to do was not for gain, or out of any indulgence to their passions, but principally for those common customs of their country, which all the Jews were obliged to observe, or to die for them.[13]

So violent actions in defense of Jewish customs and traditions were obviously carried out well before Judas the Galilean came on the stage. As was the use of hidden daggers.

And with regard to the term "robbers" (*lestai*), Josephus actually mentions that the man who was likely the father of Judas, Hezekiah, was the leader of a band of "robbers" more than four decades before the tax census revolt.[14] One could even say that elements of what would be considered zealotry were present as early as during the Maccabean revolt against the Seleucid Empire, starting in 167 BCE, the uprising which had given the Jews their short-lived independence ("Let every one who is zealous for the law and supports the covenant come out with me!" as Mattathias, leader of the revolt, called out to his fellow Jews[15]). And even as far back as in the fourth book of Moses, Numbers, we find the person considered to be the "Model Zealot," the man to be emulated for all rebels to come: Numbers relates how the priest, and later high priest, Phinehas, grandson of Aaron, takes the law in his own hands, and kills an Israelite leader and his Midianite mistress, when these were participating in what Phinehas regarded as idolatrous and licentious actions.[16] The priest, who had used the head of his spear as a dagger, inspired God to declare that "Phinehas . . . has turned back my wrath from the Israelites by manifesting such zeal among them on my behalf that in my jealousy I did not consume the Israelites."[17]

So the seeds of zealotry appear to have been there for a long time. All the same, it was Roman occupation which would bring it out in its organized political form.

Now, of course, the New Testament covers a certain period of this Roman occupation. And indeed, we do seem to see signs of Jewish rebellion in the Gospels and in Acts. In fact, one of Jesus's disciples is called Simon the Zealot. And in Acts we read of "the Egyptian" with his four thousand Sicarii.[18] The most prevalent term, however—in the New Testament, as in the works of Josephus—is "robbers," *lestai*.[19] And the "robbers" appear not only in name in the Gospels; they are clearly active. They are, after all, crucified with Jesus.

So the New Testament does provide us with seemingly strong evidence that rebels are operating at that time. Indeed, Mark 15:7 directly states: "Now a man called Barabbas was in prison with the rebels who had committed murder during the insurrection." And Luke concurs: "[Barabbas] was a man who had been put in prison for an insurrection that had taken place in the city."[20]

But something doesn't add up here.

If Jesus is active in the late 20s or early 30s, how could there have been an insurrection? Remember that Roman historian Tacitus writes that "under Tiberius all was quiet" in Judea and Galilee.[21] Tiberius was Roman emperor from 14 to 37 CE, for almost all of Jesus's life, and certainly for all of his missionary period. So could the "robbers" still have been operating in that period? Would that not seem like a contradiction?

Let us return to Josephus, who wrote so many books about the Jewish rebels. Do his chronicles provide any evidence of their presence in the times of Jesus?

Fortunately, we have a very good way of assessing this: by simply counting. The words "robbers," Zealots, and Sicarii appear in *Antiquities*, *War*, and *Vita* on hundreds of occasions. The Sicarii are introduced only in the 50s—even if Josephus in the last book of *War* writes that they were the heirs of Judas the Galilean. And the Zealots are mentioned only during the Jewish War. But the word "robbers" is found all through Josephus's writings—seemingly as his umbrella term for anti-Roman insurgents. In fact, from the moment the Romans appear in the Jewish land, so do the "robbers." And they will hold out after everyone else has fled or died. So are they there the entire time, from 63 BCE until 73 CE, from the beginning of Roman occupation until the war is over, and Masada has fallen? No, they are not, not judging by Josephus. There is one period during this Roman occupation, one single sustained period, when the "robbers" seem to be completely absent, or at least quiet: during the years when Jesus was active! Just like Tacitus states that "under Tiberius all was quiet," so does a scanning of the word *lestai* in Josephus's writings provide us with a matching finding: From 6 CE—after the census revolt was crushed—until 44 CE—when Agrippa I dies—Josephus *never once* talks about robber activity, in any of his works. In contrast, after 44 CE we find some form of the word "robber" on sixty-two occasions in *War*, twenty-one times in *Antiquities*, and ten times in *Vita*. An actual tabulation of Josephus's mentioning of "robbers" in different eras (up until the beginning of the Jewish War) is seen in the diagram on the next page.

The only hint about activity during Jesus's time is a sentence in *War*, saying that "Eleazar the arch-robber," active in the 50s, together with his associates "had ravaged the country for twenty years together."[22] In *Antiquities*, however, it only says that Eleazar "had many years made his abode in the mountains."[23]

Now this does not mean that the Jews were not, on occasion, unhappy with their situation also in the interim period. Josephus does describe two occasions of Jewish mass protests under Pilate. But on the part of the Jews there were on these occasions never any expressions of violence—much less any rebellion. As Josephus states (and Philo supports), "the people were unarmed."[24] And there are no signs of any "robbers."

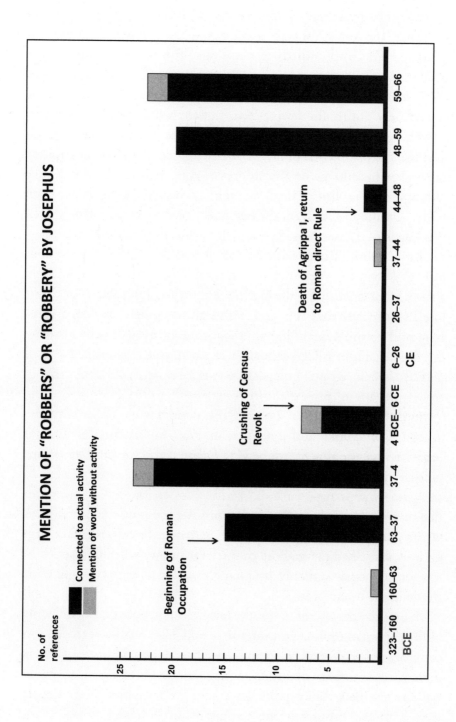

MENTION OF "ROBBERS" OR "ROBBERY" BY JOSEPHUS

Under Roman emperor Caligula (37–41 CE), the tension and protests increased, especially when the emperor wanted to erect a statue of himself in the Temple. The danger was averted, however, by the death of Caligula.[25] And then came Agrippa I, and unified the nation. For an all too brief period of time. It is after this that they reappear: the "robbers."

The time of the re-emergence of the "robbers" in the writings of Josephus is thus not random. When, after the death of Agrippa I, the areas returned to provincial status, the disappointment among the Jews was immense. To quote Second Temple historian Menahem Stern: "The twenty-two years from [Agrippa's death] until the outbreak of the Great Revolt may be summed up as a period that marked the decline of that rule and the progressive deterioration of the relations between the Roman authorities and the general Jewish population."[26]

In conclusion, not only is there a reintroduction of "robbers" in Josephus's narratives after 44 CE (and then a dramatic increase from 48 CE), but this pattern fits with the actual state of relations between the Jews and the Romans in the decades leading up to the Jewish War.

It is therefore difficult to explain how Jesus could be crucified with lestai, "rebels who had committed murder during the insurrection," if this took place in the 30s.

Equally mysterious are the names of some of the disciples. We have already mentioned Simon the Zealot, a name that would seem much more appropriate in a different era. Possibly the same could be said for Judas Iscariot (Scarioth in Latin). There are several interpretations of this name, but perhaps the most common one is that it is derived from the word Sicarius (sikarios in Greek).[27] If so, and if it is true, as Josephus writes, that Judas the Galilean was a Sicarius, in fact their leader, it is curious that a disciple of Jesus would bear a name so similar to his.

Another curious disciple name is the one Simon Peter is assigned in Matthew 16:17. He is here called Simon Bariona (as one word, "Bariona," in the Alexandrian Greek original—not "bar Jonah"). As already mentioned, bariona in the Talmud is an Aramaic designation for a type of Zealot. And in one Talmud tractate it says that "Abba Sikara [was] the head of the barione in Jerusalem," which implies that barione essentially are synonymous with Sicarii (Abba Sikara simply means "head of the Sicarii" in Aramaic).[28] In light of this, it is no doubt curious that the Gospel of John names Simon Peter as the person who, when Jesus is arrested, "had a sword [*machaira*—short sword or dagger], drew it, struck the high priest's slave, and cut off his right ear."[29]

Finally, Mark 3:17 tells us that Jesus among his apostles appointed "James son of Zebedee and John the brother of James (to whom he gave the name Boanerges, that is, Sons of Thunder)." Boanerges is usually said to be derived from *benei*, meaning sons, and *regesh*, which figuratively may mean "thunder"—and in Luke 9:54 James and John ask Jesus, "do you want us to command fire to come down from heaven and consume [the Samaritans]?" But the word usually implies "commotion," "uproar," "tumult," "insurrection."[30]

Thus, not only are Jesus and his disciples surrounded by *lestai*, several of the disciples themselves have names which seem to imply a connection with the Jewish rebels.

In addition, an indication of tumults going on in the times of Jesus can be found not only in Mark, but also in the following sentence from Matthew 11:12: "From the days of John the Baptist until now the kingdom of heaven has suffered violence, and the violent take it by force."[31]

This is remarkable, since, in fact, of the more than one-hundred-thirty years of Roman occupation, the period between 6 and 44 CE— the period when John the Baptist and Jesus of Nazareth are said to have been active—by most other accounts would be the least likely to be characterized as violent.

Thus, we are left with the perplexing conclusion that the New Testament describes a tumultuous era in the final years of Jesus's life, whereas all other sources describe those years as the least tumultuous of that century—and, furthermore, as a time when no "robber" activity is documented.

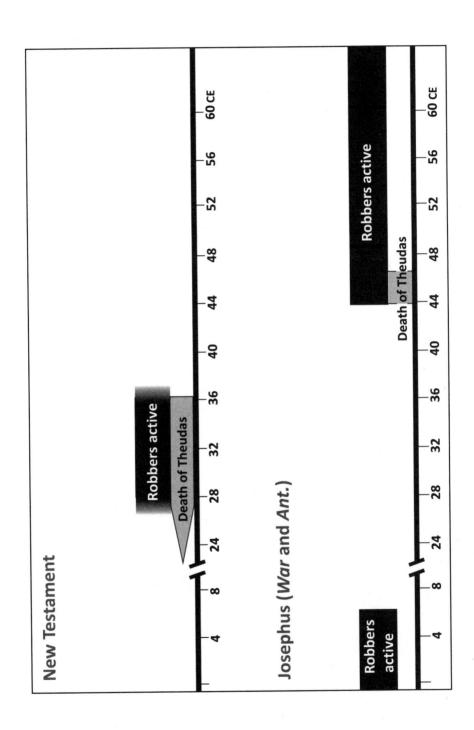

CHRONOLOGICAL ENIGMA THREE: CRUCIFIXIONS

How did the Romans punish and deter those involved in threatening actions against the occupier?

Judging both by Josephus and by the New Testament, crucifixion was the preferred mode of execution. It is a very old form of capital punishment, perhaps originating with the Assyrians and Babylonians, practiced systematically by the Persians in the sixth century BCE, but later used quite frequently also by other nations, like the Romans. It was a form of capital punishment practiced against rebels, slaves who rose up against their masters, or pirates.

Among the Romans, at least, crucifixion was considered such a cruel form of execution that it was eventually abandoned in the fourth century, during the rule of the Christianized emperor Constantine.

But was this form of execution practiced all through the period of Roman occupation of the Jewish realm? This is of course difficult to say. Josephus does not mention periods when the Roman rulers abstained from crucifying Jews in Judea or Galilee. But just like with the robbers, and the messianic claimants, he is silent on the topic during some periods, while mentioning crucifixions (sometimes mass crucifixions) during other eras. And it is interesting to note that the pattern repeats itself again: barring the *Testimonium Flavianum*, Josephus makes no note of crucifixions of Jews between 4 BCE and 46 CE. He mentions them, however, under Varus (4 BCE), Tiberius Alexander (46 to 48 CE), Cumanus (48 to 52 CE), Felix (52 to ca. 59 CE), and Florus (64 to 66 CE), as well as during the Jewish War (66 to 73 CE).

All the same, the pattern is nowhere near as clear as with robbers, since the words "crucifixion," "crucifixions," or "crucified" are mentioned much less frequently in Josephus's texts than the words "robber," "robbers," and "robbery." Suffice it to say, that it fits with the general pattern of relative calm under Tiberius, and does not contradict it.

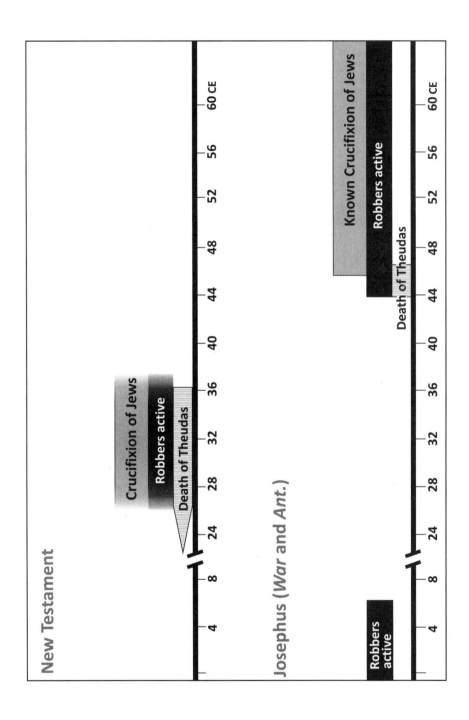

CHRONOLOGICAL ENIGMA FOUR: THE CONFLICT BETWEEN JEWS AND SAMARITANS

In looking at chronological contradictions between the New Testament and other historical sources, we have until now found ourselves repeatedly encountering the Jewish rebels. This may seem peculiar, but the fact is that the pattern persists, as we shall see from the next example.

In the chronicles of Josephus, there are certain significant events signaling the rekindling of the Jewish rebellion in the 40s, and the parallel re-emergence of the "robbers." And these triggering events seem to accumulate in the four-year reign of Roman procurator Ventidius Cumanus.

Cumanus arrived as procurator of Judea (and, according to Josephus, "the rest," except the small northern territory of Chalcis) in 48 CE.[1] Although stirrings of rebellion had been there since the death of Agrippa I, four years earlier, things took a radical turn for the worse with Cumanus's arrival. This procurator, as it turned out, would be a person who more often than not would stoke the flames, rather than smother them. Josephus writes about the first such occasion:

> Under . . . Cumanus began the troubles, and the Jews' ruin came on; for when the multitude were come together to Jerusalem, to

the feast of unleavened bread, and a Roman cohort stood over the cloisters of the temple (for they always were armed, and kept guard at the festivals, to prevent any innovation which the multitude thus gathered together might make), one of the soldiers pulled back his garment, and cowering down after an indecent manner, turned his breech to the Jews, and spake such words as you might expect upon such a posture. At this the whole multitude had indignation, and made a clamor to Cumanus, that he would punish the soldier; while the rasher part of the youth, and such as were naturally the most tumultuous, fell to fighting, and caught up stones, and threw them at the soldiers. Upon which Cumanus was afraid lest all the people should make an assault upon him, and sent to call for more armed men, who, when they came in great numbers into the cloisters, the Jews were in a very great consternation; and being beaten out of the temple, they ran into the city; and the violence with which they crowded to get out was so great, that they trod upon each other, and squeezed one another, till ten thousand of them were killed, insomuch that this feast became the cause of mourning to the whole nation, and every family lamented their own relations.[2]

Things would continue intensifying under this procurator, because right after this event came the next trigger: the attack against the Roman slave Stephen, which we shall come back to in the next chapter. And then came the third—a small, seemingly innocuous confrontation, which would soon escalate into a war.[3] A war not between Jews and Romans, but one between Jews and Samaritans, neighbors in the Roman province of *Iudaea*.

The province of *Iudaea* from 6 CE consisted of Judea, Samaria, and Idumea. Judea was the central and most important part of this province, with its spiritual and, at least in the Jewish context, political heart, the city of Jerusalem. The other important part of the Jewish realm, Galilee in the north, was then still nominally ruled by a Jewish tetrarch (Herod Antipas), and thus not formally part of *Iudaea*. Samaria, the northernmost region of *Iudaea*, lay between these two Jewish territories.

Samaria had for centuries maintained a tenuous calm with its neighbors. Although adhering to a religion closely affiliated with Judaism, the Samaritans' claim of representing original Judaism—as well as their self-identification as direct descendants of the northern Israelite tribes of Ephraim and Manasseh—were as a rule rejected by the Jews. Also, the Samaritans eventually rejected Jerusalem as their central holy place of worship, and built their own temple at the top of Mount Gerizim, near what is today Nablus. Under Roman rule, Samaritans were sometimes favored, especially under Herod the Great, who built much in their region. Josephus, however, notes that Pilate struck down on Samaritan followers of a charismatic leader.[4] Rome would at times also use the religious schism between Jews and Samaritans for their own political purposes. Despite this, the tensions between Jews and Samaritans rarely turned into violence, and Josephus mentions only one period of outright conflict between them in the first century. But this one conflict developed into war.

In both his major works, Josephus describes how this Galilean-Samaritan war begins, in 48 CE, with a seemingly banal incident:

> It was the custom of the Galileans, when they came to the holy city at the festivals, to take their journeys through the country of the Samaritans; and at this time there lay, in the road they took, a village that was called Ginea, which was situated in the limits of Samaria and the great plain, where certain persons thereto belonging fought with the Galileans, and killed a great many of them.[5]

This attack leads to Jewish *lestai*, "robbers," in turn attacking the Samaritans, and they "set the villages on fire," as Josephus writes.[6] After this, the war is in full flame, and, as Josephus puts it, "all of Judea was overrun with robberies."[7] The war between the Jews and the Samaritans only ends when Roman emperor Claudius banishes procurator Cumanus—whom the Jews had accused of being partial to the Samaritans—and in 52 CE appoints Procurator Felix in his stead.

The Galilean-Samaritan war is thus a war with a distinct beginning and end, to a significant extent involving Jewish *lestai*, "robbers." Although the question of how the relationship between Samaritans and

Jews evolved at different times is a matter of debate, tensions seem mostly to have been kept within bounds until after the first century.[8] As mentioned, the Galilean-Samaritan war of 48–52 is the only first century period of conflict between them described by Josephus.

Now in the New Testament, we also find evidence of hostilities between Jews and Samaritans, but in a different era: that of Pilate—26 to 36 CE. Famous, for instance is the story in the Gospel of John of how Jesus "had to go through Samaria," and sits down for a drink of water:

> He left Judea and started back to Galilee. But he had to go through Samaria. So he came to a Samaritan city called Sychar, near the plot of ground that Jacob had given to his son Joseph. Jacob's well was there, and Jesus, tired out by his journey, was sitting by the well. It was about noon. A Samaritan woman came to draw water, and Jesus said to her, "Give me a drink." (His disciples had gone to the city to buy food.) The Samaritan woman said to him, "How is it that you, a Jew, ask a drink of me, a woman of Samaria?" (Jews do not share things in common with Samaritans.)[9]

Other signs of enmity between Jews and Samaritans are found in the Gospels of Luke and Matthew.[10] This in itself would perhaps not be significant, if it were not for the fact that later, in Acts, such evidence of animosity is not only absent, but Samaria and Samaritans are mentioned on several occasions, without any suggestions of hostility. This is despite the fact that the time period when the Galilean-Samaritan war happened, 48 to 52 CE, is represented in Acts.[11] A pattern of abating conflict between Jews and Samaritans can thus possibly be discerned also in the New Testament, but in a different period than that described by Josephus (see diagram on the next page).

This differing time pattern of hostility could still, of course, be coincidental. Underlying tensions between Jews and Samaritans were, after all, there also at other times. There is, however, one additional element in Josephus's narrative of the Galilean-Samaritan war which warrants attention: the triggering event, as described by Josephus, bears some similarities to an episode described in the Gospel of Luke. We shall put these two narratives side by side:

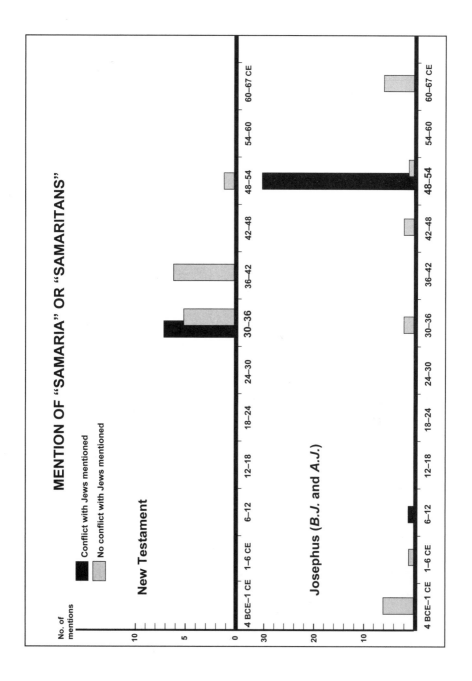

MENTION OF "SAMARIA" OR "SAMARITANS"

No. of mentions

■ Conflict with Jews mentioned

☐ No conflict with Jews mentioned

New Testament

Josephus (*B.J.* and *A.J.*)

Josephus:	New Testament:
Antiquities 20.118–121	Luke 9:51–56
"It was the custom of the Galileans, when they came to the holy city at the festivals, to take their journeys through the country of the Samaritans; and at this time there lay, in the road they took, a village that was called Ginea, which was situated in the limits of Samaria and the great plain, where certain persons thereto belonging fought with the Galileans, and killed a great many of them."	"When the days drew near for him to be taken up, he set his face to go to Jerusalem. And he sent messengers ahead of him. On their way they entered a village of the Samaritans to make ready for him; but they did not receive him, because his face was set towards Jerusalem. When his disciples James and John saw it, they said, 'Lord, do you want us to command fire to come down from heaven and consume them?' But he turned and rebuked them. Then they went on to another village."
War 2.232–235	
"[Jewish lēstai then] set the villages on fire"	

These narratives—from *Antiquities* and *War* on the one hand, and from the New Testament on the other—share several distinct elements:

- Both accounts concern Galileans traveling through Samaria on their way to Jerusalem for the festivals.
- Both accounts mention that the Galileans are not welcomed by the Samaritans, and that this leads to a conflict.
- Both accounts mention these events occurring in a particular Samaritan village.
- Both accounts mention "fire" as a means of punishment on the part of the Galileans. But in Luke, the suggestion to bring down fire meets with a pacifist reaction. We shall come back to this later.

The similarities between Josephus's account of the start of the Galilean-Samaritan War and Luke 9:51–56 have previously been noted by a number of scholars.[12] Gary Goldberg, for instance, notes that "in both passages there is a mention of Galileans setting fire to Samaritan villages (or wanting to) as revenge." Albert Hogeterp writes: "On the Galilean-Samaritan conflict about Jewish pilgrimage to Jerusalem passing through Samaritan territory, cf. Luke 9:53." And Reinhard

Pummer states: "Josephus narrative about the clashes between Galileans and Samaritans in the times of Ventidius Cumanus belongs to the same category [as Luke 9:51–56]."

Despite this, the accounts have not been viewed as depictions of the same event. One has to assume that this is due to the fact that the event described by Josephus occurs in 48 CE, about fifteen years later than that described by Luke.

This very delay, however, seems to exactly fit the pattern seen in the figure on page 59 ("Mention of Samaria or Samaritans").

And thus, we are once again faced with an event described in the New Testament narrative which finds no reverberation in depictions of the same era in non-biblical sources—where a similar event instead is described some two decades later.

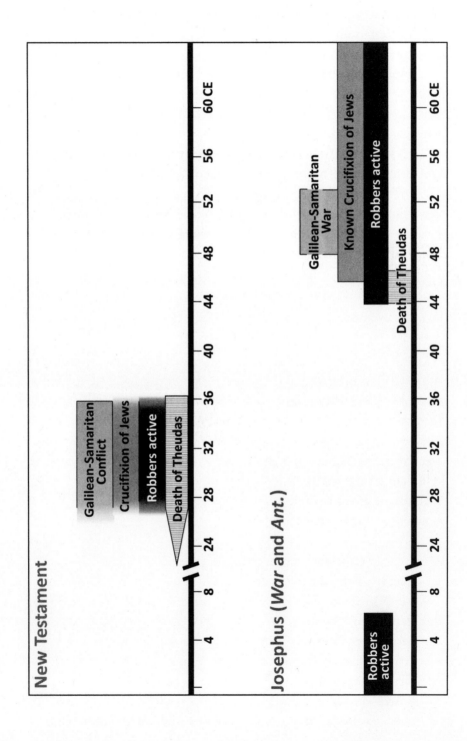

CHRONOLOGICAL ENIGMA FIVE: STEPHEN

As mentioned in the previous chapter, Cumanus, during his procuratorship, violently put down three Jewish tumults—and the last one, the Galilean-Samaritan war, led to his being removed from office. All three conflicts had, however, started with seemingly small provocations: in the first instance, a Roman soldier had let down his breeches over the cloisters of the Temple; in the third one, Galileans traveling to Jerusalem for the festivals had been stopped in a Samaritan village. We shall now come to the intermediate tumult. It starts with a robbery. A robbery of a man named Stephen:

> Some of those that raised the foregoing tumult, when they were traveling along the public road, about a hundred furlongs from the city, robbed Stephen, a servant of Caesar, as he was journeying, and plundered him of all that he had with him; which things when Cumanus heard of, he sent soldiers immediately, and ordered them to plunder the neighboring villages, and to bring the most eminent persons among them in bonds to him. Now as this devastation was making, one of the soldiers seized the laws of Moses that lay in one of those villages, and brought them out

before the eyes of all present, and tore them to pieces; and this was done with reproachful language, and much scurrility; which things when the Jews heard of, they ran together, and that in great numbers, and came down to Caesarea, where Cumanus then was, and besought him that he would avenge, not themselves, but God himself, whose laws had been affronted; for that they could not bear to live any longer, if the laws of their forefathers must be affronted after this manner. Accordingly Cumanus, out of fear lest the multitude should go into a sedition, and by the advice of his friends also, took care that the soldier who had offered the affront to the laws should be beheaded, and thereby put a stop to the sedition which was ready to be kindled a second time.

This attack on Stephen, and its aftermath, is so pivotal in the violent re-emergence of the "robbers," that Josephus describes it at length in both his major works.[1]

On the surface, it would seem that there are no echoes of this event in the New Testament. Except for one thing: the name, Stephen. This name is familiar to any reader of the Christian Bible. Stephen was the proto-martyr of Christianity (his fate is described in Acts 6:5–8:2).

Interestingly, Stephen was an uncommon name in Judea and Galilee, at least at the time. In fact, Josephus only mentions one single Stephen in his entire works. It is therefore remarkable that a man by the name of Stephen is described also in the New Testament. And incidentally, also in this case, he is the only person by that name mentioned in the entire Bible—Old or New Testament.

Thus, there is one Stephen in each source, which seems curious. At first glance, however, the two Stephens appear to have nothing in common. For one thing, they appear ten to twenty years apart. And in addition, they seem to be entirely different people. The Stephen of Acts is no servant of Caesar, he is a deacon of the early Church in Jerusalem.

The tale of Stephen in the New Testament is pivotal, because it introduces Paul into the narrative. Stephen is presented as an early Christian preacher in Jerusalem, one who is often confronted by traditional Jews of the city. But on one occasion this leads to an outright clash. Some members of the synagogue of freedmen (freed slaves within the Roman empire) claim they have "heard him speak blasphemous words against Moses and God."[2] As a consequence, Stephen is seized and brought before the Jewish Council in Jerusalem, where his accusers say that "we have heard him say that this Jesus of Nazareth will destroy this place and will change the customs that Moses handed on to us."[3] Stephen himself now proceeds to give a long account of the history of the Jews, ending with the accusation: "You are the ones that received the law as ordained by angels, and yet you have not kept it." When he also accuses those present of having betrayed and murdered the Righteous One, his confronters become enraged. As it says in Acts chapter 7, "they dragged him out of the city and began to stone him; and the witnesses laid their coats at the feet of a young man named Saul." Stephen is killed, and Saul (who would later be the Apostle Paul), is inspired to become a violent persecutor of members of the Church.

Thus the tales of the two Stephens—the one in the New Testament and the one in Josephus's chronicles—are different. And yet, there are some eye-catching similarities: not only does the main character in each story have the seemingly unique name Stephen; in each case Stephen is also the target of an attack by Jews; and in each case the attack occurs on a road outside Jerusalem. One interpretation of Josephus's text (leaning on a saying in the Jewish Mishnah) furthermore claims that Stephen is identical to the Roman soldier subsequently tearing the Torah to pieces, "and this was done with reproachful language."[4] If correct, this interpretation would also make both Stephens the target of an accusation of blasphemy.

Could these be coincidences? Is it really possible that the two separate narratives describing a man by the unusual name of Stephen would both center on Stephen being attacked by a mob, in both cases on a road, in both cases a road outside Jerusalem—and this is a coincidence? What are the chances?

There is yet another similarity between the tales: both of these attacks on a man named Stephen on a road outside Jerusalem constitute significant

Stephen	**Stephen**
(*Ant.* 20.113–114; *War* 2.228–229)	(Acts 6:5–8:2)
Servant of Roman Emperor	Early Christian deacon
48 CE	**30s CE**
Attacked by a mob	**Attacked by a mob**
of Jewish lēstai	of Jews
on a road outside Jerusalem	**on a road outside Jerusalem**
The only Stephen **in the works of Josephus**	**The only Stephen** **in the Bible**
Starting point for the violent activity of the Jewish rebels	**Starting point for Saul's violent persecution of early Christians**

starting points for violence. In Josephus's narrative, it is the starting point for the violent activity of the Jewish rebels. In Acts, it is the starting point for Saul's violent persecution of the early Christian movement.

Different groups, thus. For in Josephus's Stephen narrative there are no Christians present.

This might seem like a clear distinction, if it were not for the fact that outside of the contested *Testimonium Flavianum,* Josephus *nowhere* in his works describes a Christian movement. In his chronicles we find no information about the Church, nor of the disciples, or Stephen, or Paul. It is as if Josephus does not *know* about Christianity. And yet he wrote as late as the 90s CE.

Could it be that that which the New Testament describes as the early Christian movement, originally, and in other sources, was depicted as something else? Could it be that it was described as a rebel movement? Let us briefly investigate this idea. Because it is not new.

Ever since Reimarus began his quest for the historical Jesus more than two and a half centuries ago, one recurring interpretation of the Gospel narratives of the complex, multifaceted trial of Jesus has been that Jesus, in fact, may have been a spiritual revolutionary leader not only against the Jewish establishment, but also against Rome. Very much a leader of the times, in other words. A political rebel. "It was then clearly not the intention or the object of Jesus to suffer and to die," writes Reimarus, "but to build up a worldly kingdom, and to deliver the Israelites from bondage."[5] Other proponents of variations of this idea have been, among others, Robert Eisler, Joel Carmichael, Samuel G.F. Brandon, Hyam Maccoby, and, more recently, Fernando Bermejo-Rubio.[6] Their suggestions range from Jesus and the disciples themselves being political rebels to them merely expressing sympathy with the ideals and aims of the anti-Roman resistance movement.

Eisler, for instance, quotes third century Christian author Lactantius, who in his work *The Divine Institutes* refers to a statement by a contemporary anti-Christian: "But he affirmed that Christ Himself was put to flight by the Jews, and having collected a band of nine hundred men, committed robberies."[7]

Another early polemicist placing Jesus in the context of political rebellion is second century Greek philosopher Celsus: "In the days of Jesus, others who were Jews rebelled against the Jewish state, and became His followers." This statement made Church Father Origen object that "neither Celsus nor they who think with him are able to point out any act on the part of Christians which savours of rebellion."[8]

Early polemical statements are not, however, what the later proponents of this hypothesis—that Jesus had rebel affiliations, and may himself have been a political revolutionary—primarily base their conclusions on. In fact, their main source of reference is the New Testament itself. Because yes, the New Testament is full of pronouncements of struggle and confrontation, pronouncements usually interpreted in an eschatological light, but which often as easily could be understood as insurrectionary in a political sense.

"Do not think that I have come to bring peace to the earth," says Jesus in the Gospel of Matthew, "I have not come to bring peace, but a sword."[9] And in the Gospel of Mark: "When you hear of wars and rumors of wars, do not be alarmed; this must take place, but the end is still to come. For nation will rise against nation, and kingdom against kingdom; there will be earthquakes in various places; there will be fam-ines. This is but the beginning of the birth pangs."[10]

And such pronouncements are not the only indications of a pos-sible political context for Jesus's activity. Jesus was, after all, eventually sentenced by the worldly authorities, the Romans—who as a rule did not get involved in religious quarrels among the Jews. He was executed by the means the Romans used for rebels. On the cross, he was sur-rounded, on each side, by "robbers." One of his disciples was even called Simon the Zealot (Simon the Cananaean in two of the Gospels; see the Hebrew term *kanai*[11])—and as previously described, several of his other disciples had names implying connections to the rebels. The *titulus* on the cross described Jesus as "King of the Jews." And when the apostles are brought to the Jewish Council after preaching in the Temple (Acts 5:33–38), Rabbi Gamaliel—according to the New Testament narra-tive—compares them to the followers of rebel leaders Judas the Galilean and Theudas, rather than to members of other merely religious factions.

The political aspirations of Jesus, as well as his being perceived as a threat by the Romans, are conceivably also expressed in the following passage from the Gospel of John:

> So the chief priests and the Pharisees called a meeting of the coun-cil, and said, "What are we to do? This man is performing many signs. If we let him go on like this, everyone will believe in him, and the Romans will come and destroy both our holy place and our nation." But one of them, Caiaphas, who was high priest that year, said to them, "You know nothing at all! You do not under-stand that it is better for you to have one man die for the people than to have the whole nation destroyed."[12]

And in Acts 1:6 we read:

> So when they had come together, they asked him, "Lord, is this the time when you will restore the kingdom to Israel?"

There are even more direct implications of armed resistance. Take, for instance, Jesus's admonition to his disciples that "the one who has no sword must sell his cloak and buy one." And the next sentence: "For I tell you, this scripture must be fulfilled in me, 'And he was counted among the lawless'; and indeed what is written about me is being fulfilled."[13]

Putting Jesus in the context of the times in which he lived makes tremendous sense. This, after all, was a period when messianic leaders almost invariably appeared in connection with political rebellion—and usually at the helm of it. And all it takes to perceive Jesus as more aligned with his times is a preparedness to perceive double entendres in the New Testament narrative. Ambiguities are not infrequent, and sometimes we even see contradictions. Take for instance the Gospel statements on taxes. Remember that it was taxes levied by the Romans on the Jews which had sparked the first revolt, in 6–7 CE. Paying taxes to Rome was thus a highly aggravating thing to those identifying with the rebel cause. But here Jesus is somewhat equivocal. Although in Mark 12:17 he says, "Give to the emperor the things that are the emperor's, and to God the things that are God's," Luke 23:1–2 seems to paint a different picture:

> Then the assembly rose as a body and brought Jesus before Pilate. They began to accuse him, saying, "We found this man perverting our nation, forbidding us to pay taxes to the emperor, and saying that he himself is the Messiah, a king."

Also in Matthew 17:24–27, Jesus seems to tell his disciples both that they should and that they shouldn't pay taxes:

> When they reached Capernaum, the collectors of the temple tax came to Peter and said, "Does your teacher not pay the temple tax?" He said, "Yes, he does." And when he came home, Jesus spoke of it first, asking, "What do you think, Simon? From whom do kings of the earth take toll or tribute? From their children or from others?" When Peter said, "From others," Jesus said to him, "Then the children are free. However, so that we do not give offense to them, go to the sea and cast a hook; take the first fish that comes up; and when you open its mouth, you will find a coin; take that and give it to them for you and me."

Here, Jesus seems to say that although the citizens are free not to pay the emperor, they should nevertheless catch a fish, and a coin, and pay him, "so that we do not give offense." The symbol of the caught fish is, however, also ambigious. Because what is really the meaning of "fish" here? Mark 1:16–17 says: "As Jesus passed along the Sea of Galilee, he saw Simon and his brother Andrew casting a net into the sea—for they were fishermen. And Jesus said to them, 'Follow me and I will make you fish for people.'"[14] And in Luke 5:10: "Then Jesus said to Simon [the fisherman], 'Do not be afraid; from now on you will be catching people.'" There is a close analogy to this in the Old Testament, in Jeremiah 16:16: "I am now sending for many fishermen, says the Lord, and they shall catch them."[15] "Them", in this case, is "the people of Israel," who, because they had forsaken God, will suffer severe calamities. "I will," says God, "hurl you out of this land into a land that neither you nor your ancestors have known." But ultimately, "I will bring [the people of Israel] back to their own land that I gave to their ancestors."[16]

Catching of fish, thus, has a deep eschatological meaning. And the fish seem to be people—in Jeremiah, and also in some Gospel verses.

Is the fish with the coin in its mouth also a person? Perhaps. But if so, the message is even more complex. Yes, someone is supposed to pay the tax to the emperor. But who? And how will Peter acquire the coin from this person?

Or is the fish in this case just a fish? Which in the life of a fisherman equals currency. If so, Jesus here seems to give conciliatory advice: although you have no moral obligation to pay the tax, you still should, so as not to offend the authorities.

Jesus's remarks (or remarks about him) sometimes do seem contradictory, or multifaceted. And the view of him as a possible rebel leader is certainly countered by his many pronouncements of an opposite, pacifist, nature. In fact, the prevailing thought among scholars today is that Brandon and his colleagues overinterpreted the words implying that Jesus could have been a political revolutionary. As Martin Hengel puts it:

Neither his behavior during the last dramatic days in Jerusalem nor his total activity and proclamation support such assumptions.

They rest upon details which are torn out of context and are arbitrarily interpreted.[17]

Pacifist, or revolutionary? They seem like opposites, and we shall come back to this contradictory picture later.

Even if one were to postulate, however, that the early Church could have been part of the Jewish rebel movement, and even if one were to assume that the two narratives of an attack on Stephen could be depictions of the same event, we are clearly not dealing with a straight-forward analogy when comparing Josephus's narrative with that in Acts. In Josephus's account, Stephen is not a rebel, he is a representative of Rome. It is those who *attack* him who are rebels. If there is an analogy, thus, it would be one where the roles have been reversed. We shall come back to this later as well.

At this stage, suffice it to say that one recurring word in the descriptions of Saul/Paul could add fuel to the suggestion that rebels may have been on the attacking end also in the New Testament tale of Stephen. If one reads the original Greek text of the Acts of the Apostles and Paul's Letters, Paul—who partook in the attack against Stephen—in both sources describes himself with a word that we recognize: *zelotes*— "Zealot." But in most translations, this word is presented as an adjective or an adverb. In the New Revised Standard Version of the English Bible, the sentence in Acts has Paul say: "I am a Jew, born in Tarsus in Cilicia, but brought up in this city at the feet of Gamaliel, educated strictly according to our ancestral law, being zealous for God, just as all of you are today." But a literal translation of the end of the sentence reads: "I was a Zealot for God just as all of you are today."[18]

The text in Paul's Letter to the Galatians, in the same English translation, is as follows: "I advanced in Judaism beyond many among my people of the same age, for I was far more zealous for the traditions of my ancestors." But a literal translation from the Greek is: "I advanced in Judaism beyond many among my people of the same age, for to a much higher degree, I was a Zealot for the traditions of our ancestors."[19]

One could, perhaps, argue that the use of the word "Zealot" in this context is more figurative than literal—that it connotes ardor rather than Zealotry. But the fact is: each time the words "Zealot" or "Zealots" appear in the New Testament in reference to a particular individual, that individual is only one of two people: Paul, or Simon the Zealot.[20]

That Paul could have had early connections with the Jewish rebels is an idea which has been discussed previously.[21]

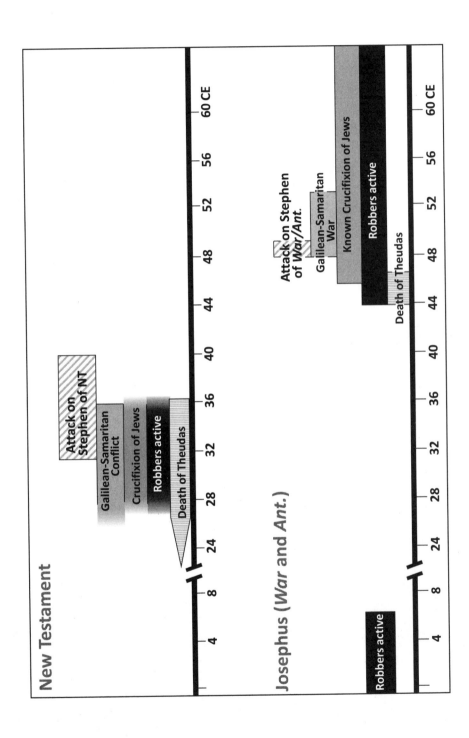

PEOPLE IN POSITIONS
OF AUTHORITY

THE CHRONOLOGICAL INCONSISTENCIES MENTIONED SO FAR HAVE ALL concerned major events in the period leading up to the Jewish War—usually involving Jewish rebels. They have concerned discrepancies in the time of death of the messianic leader Theudas; discrepancies in the presence and activity of so called "robbers"; they have concerned the use of crucifixions as a means of execution; and they have concerned two rebellion-triggering events during the procuratorship of Cumanus.

There are, however, also inconsistencies involving the very elements which provide us with the tools to create a New Testament chronology, namely people in positions of authority. The New Testament presents us with the names of various high priests, emperors, Jewish kings, Roman procurators, etc.—individuals also described in the chronicles of Josephus. The presence of their names in both these sources (and in other historical texts) is what allows us to pinpoint when Jesus was active, and when he was crucified. There is, however, a problem with these names—a general problem. And the problem does not involve their times in office. It involves their activities. Because their activities do not match. They have the same names in both sources—the New

Testament and the works of Josephus. But they do not do the same things. Almost never.

Let us begin with an example concerning the two high priests presiding at Jesus's trial.

CHRONOLOGICAL ENIGMA SIX:
THE TWO HIGH PRIESTS

THE OFFICE OF HIGH PRIEST WAS ONE OF VERY HIGH PROMINENCE among the Jews. According to scripture, the first to assume the office was Aaron, brother of Moses. And, as Josephus puts it, "no one should take the high priesthood of God but he who is of the blood of Aaron, while every one that is of another stock, though he were a king, can never obtain that high priesthood."[1] It also seems to have been an office ordinarily held for life, like that of a monarch.[2] The properties of this office did, however, change over time. Whereas the high priest originally held purely religious authority, the position would with time become political as well, especially in periods when the Jewish realm was under foreign rule. And irrespective of who had ultimate political and military power over the Jewish people, the Jews for the longest time retained power over the choice for the highest religious office. But with the arrival of Antiochus IV Epiphanes—from 175 BCE ruler of the Seleucid Empire, which then controlled Jerusalem—things changed entirely. Antiochus, in rabbinical sources called "the wicked," not only had the desire to denationalize his subjects, he also interfered greatly with their religious practices, plundered the Temple treasury, and took it upon himself to appoint and sack the Jewish high priests at his pleasure—usually after having been paid a substantial bribe from the incumbent. And although Antiochus soon lost power over the Jews (who for a hundred years thereafter were autonomous) the role of the high priest—and the manner in which he was chosen—after this was irrevocably altered, and, some would say, corrupted. After the Maccabean revolt, and the attainment of Jewish independence, high priest and ruler soon blended into one. The Hasmonean kings, descendants of Mattathias and his son Judah Maccabee, liberators of the Jewish nation, early on took on this dual dignity. In 141 BCE, at an assembly of "the priests and the people and the rulers of the nation," a resolution was taken to the effect that Simon, last surviving brother of Judah Maccabee, "should be their leader and high priest forever, until a trustworthy prophet should arise."[3] This omnipotent dual position would be inherited from ruler to ruler, and thus the "politico-messianic" and the religious aspects were combined in the Hasmonean rulers, in a manner which much later would be reflected in the approach of the Jewish rebels under Roman rule: messianic spiritual leader, warrior, and aspiring ruler, all in one.[4] As already described, the Maccabean revolt had held the seeds of Zealotry, and the descendant rulers of these warriors would continue to blend the political with the religious.

But in the case of the Hasmonean dynasty, glory held the seeds of self-destruction. Internal strife between two brothers, Hyrcanus II and Aristobolus II—a conflict partially sparked by the power struggle of two religious factions, the Pharisees and the Sadducees—led each brother to seek the assistance of the Romans, ending in a conquest which would seal the fate of the Jewish nation, in the year 63 BCE.

With the Roman occupation, the office of high priest would become one that was completely subjugated to the goodwill of the secular rulers—be they Romans or Jewish client kings of Rome. Nevertheless, the high priest was permitted to retain a certain political power, as long as he did not act in opposition to the ultimate ruler. And in those periods when the nation was ruled by procurators, the high priest was the person among the Jews who held the highest secular power. Nevertheless, Roman prefects and procurators at times tended to appoint and dismiss high priests at very short intervals, even less than one year. An antagonistic high priest would thus be a very short-lived high priest. Consequently, this was an office which gradually lost its esteem in the period of Roman rule.

High Priests (from Herod the Great to the fall of Jerusalem)

Name	Approx. time in office
Ananel	37–36 BCE
Aristobolus III	36
Ananel	36–30
Jesus, the son of Phabi	30–23
Simon, the son of Boethus	23–5
Mattathias, the son of Theophilus	5–4
Joazar, the son of Boethus	4
Eleazar, the son of Boethus	4–3
Jesus, the son of Sie	3–?
Joazar, the son of Boethus	?–6 CE
Annas, the son of Seth	6–15
Ismael, the son of Phabi	15–16
Eleazar, the son of Annas	16–17
Simon, the son of Camithus	17–18
Joseph Caiaphas	18–36
Jonathan, the son of Annas	36–37
Theophilus, the son of Annas	37–41
Simon Cantheras, the son of Boethus	41–43
Mattathias, the son of Annas	43
Elioneus, the son of Cantheras	43–44
Joseph, the son of Camydus	44–46
Ananias, the son of Nebedeus	46-?
Jonathan, the son of Annas	4?–56
Ismael, the son of Phabi	58–61
Joseph Cabi, the son of Simon	61–62
Ananus, the son of Ananus (Annas)	62
Jesus, the son of Damneus	62–63
Jesus, the son of Gamaliel	63–65
Mattathias, the son of Theophilus	65–67
Phinehas, the son of Samuel	67–70

The New Testament names a few high priests—primarily in the period when Jesus is active, and in connection with the arrest and imprisonment of Paul in Jerusalem. In a Christian context, the most important of these high priests are undoubtedly Annas and Caiaphas, who presided over parts of Jesus's trial. The fact that they were two is in itself interesting and noteworthy. According to the New Testament, Annas and Caiaphas held the office of high priest jointly, or—as might be deduced from the Gospel of John—in alternating years.[5] Both are according to John present during the trial, and Luke earlier writes: ". . . during the high priesthood of Annas and Caiaphas, the word of God came to John son of Zechariah in the wilderness."[6]

So is there any support for this joint high priesthood of Annas and Caiaphas in the chronicles of Josephus?

No, there is not (see table above).

Annas (Ananus, Hannan, Hanin), son of Seth, is by Josephus described as one of the most successful of the high priests in the Roman province. Josephus writes:

> Now the report goes that this eldest Ananus proved a most fortunate man; for he had five sons who had all performed the office of a high priest to God, and who had himself enjoyed that dignity a long time formerly, which had never happened to any other of our high priests.[7]

Annas had been appointed high priest by Quirinius, the Roman governor of Syria, in the year 6 (or 7) CE, the year of the tax revolt. "And when the taxings were come to a conclusion," writes Josephus, "he [Quirinius] deprived Joazar of the high priesthood, which dignity had been conferred on him by the multitude, and he appointed Ananus, the son of Seth, to be high priest."[8]

Josephus provides little information on what took place during Annas's time in office. He does, however, tell us how he was deposed, nine years later, in the year 15 CE:

> He [Tiberius] was now the third emperor; and he sent Valerius Gratus to be prefect of Judea, and to succeed Annius Rufus. This

man deprived Ananus of the high priesthood, and appointed Ismael, the son of Phabi, to be high priest.[9]

Annas is never reinstated again.

What now happens is that we enter a period in which high priests are appointed and dismissed in short order. Ismael, the son of Phabi, is succeeded by Eleazar, the son of Annas, who is succeeded by Simon, the son of Camithus. All within a period of three years. But then, finally, in 18 CE, Gratus appoints Joseph Caiaphas to the office. And Caiaphas is allowed to remain in his position for as long as eighteen or nineteen years. Furthermore, Caiaphas holds the office alone, at least judging by Josephus's account. When the trial of Jesus, according to New Testament chronology, takes place, some time between 28 and 37 CE, Annas has, according to Josephus, been out of office for between thirteen and twenty-two years. And Josephus has not written about him since he was deposed.

As one of the great rabbis of Jewish history, Maimonides, put it: "Two high priests should not be initiated together."[10] And in the chronicles of Josephus, the appointment of a new high priest is almost invariably presented like this: "He now deprived XX of the high priesthood, and gave it to YY."

Nevertheless, it seems that joint high priesthoods on occasion *did* exist. Josephus himself gives us what seems to be a clear example, in the middle of the first century. In fact, it concerns two high priests mentioned also in the New Testament: Jonathan son of Annas (possibly mentioned in Acts, after the crucifixion of Jesus), and Ananias son of Nebedeus (mentioned in Acts in connection with the arrest of Paul).[11]

High Priest Jonathan holds an important place in the books of Flavius Josephus, and seems to be one of the most prominent high priests of the Roman era. Jonathan son of Annas is first appointed to his position in the year 36 CE, or early 37, immediately succeeding Caiaphas. But after only one year, Jonathan is dismissed, and replaced with his brother Theophilus, only to be approached again about six years later, by Agrippa I, and asked to once again be high priest. This man, Jonathan, was held in very high esteem by the Jews, and the king considered him "more worthy of that dignity" than other candidates, or the previous high priest. But this time, Jonathan declines, with the words: "O king! I rejoice in the honor that thou hast for me, and take it kindly that thou wouldst give me such a dignity of thy own inclinations, although God hath judged that I am not at all worthy of the high priesthood. I am satisfied with having once put on the sacred garments; for I then put them on after a more holy manner than I should now receive them again." Instead, Jonathan proposes yet another brother, Mattathias (Matthias), to be appointed to the office of high priest, and King Agrippa I, "according to his brother's desire, bestowed the high priesthood upon Matthias."[12]

Nevertheless, although the time of his reinstatement is not clearly indicated by Josephus, Jonathan *does* become high priest once again, because under procurator Cumanus (48 to 52 CE), Jonathan son of Annas is repeatedly referred to as "the high priest," and clearly in an active capacity.[13] Simultaneously, however, we hear of yet another high priest, Ananias son of Nebedeus, who is appointed to the position just before the arrival of Cumanus.[14] And to make their joint holding of office evident, Josephus in *War* refers to them as "Jonathan and Ananias, the high priests."[15] Some authors have assumed that the occasional use of the title high priest in the plural in the New Testament and in Josephus's texts could be explained by the retention of the title after dethronement, but this seems unlikely in this particular case, where Jonathan so obviously is involved in the affairs of the state. For instance, at the height of the Galilean-Samaritan war, Jonathan, not Ananias son of Nebedeus, is referred to as the high priest who intervenes with the Roman authorities on behalf of his people:

> And the men of power among the Samaritans came to Tyre, to Ummidius Quadratus, the president of Syria, and desired that they that had laid waste the country might be punished: the great men also of the Jews, and Jonathan the son of Ananus, the high priest, came thither, and said that the Samaritans were the beginners of the disturbance, on account of that murder they had committed; and that Cumanus had given occasion to what had happened, by his unwillingness to punish the original authors of that murder.[16]

Many sources on high priests under the Roman era thus list Jonathan son of Annas as "reinstated" or "restored" in the late 40s or early 50s.[17] And yet, Ananias son of Nebedeus is *also* still referred to as the high priest, when later, together with high priest Jonathan, he is sent to the emperor to give an account of the the Galilean-Samaritan war.

After Cumanus is subsequently deposed, it is Jonathan who suggests to the emperor whom he should appoint as next Roman procurator: Antonius Felix. A few years later, Jonathan is killed by the Sicarii, at the instigation of Felix (a curious collusion indeed). Josephus explains the circumstances: "Felix also bore an ill will to Jonathan, the high priest, because he frequently gave him admonitions about governing the Jewish affairs better than he did, lest he should himself have complaints made of him by the multitude, since he it was who had desired Caesar to send him as procurator of Judea." When he is killed in the 50s, Jonathan is still, according to both *Antiquities* and *War*, "the high priest."[18]

Is Ananias also still high priest at this point? Interestingly, the New Testament says he is. When the Apostle Paul is arrested in Jerusalem, Acts tells us that Felix is the acting procurator and that Ananias is the high priest. Two years later, Acts further says, Felix is replaced by Festus (who, according to Josephus, became procurator in 59 or 60 CE). Thus, judging by the New Testament, Ananias was high priest at least until 57 CE.[19] And there are some indications he may even have continued after this, once again sharing the high priesthood.[20]

In conclusion, not only does Josephus refer to these two men as "Jonathan and Ananias, the high priests," additional descriptions from his chronicles, as well as the New Testament, indicate that their times in office overlapped.

Again, at least on the surface, a better fit appears to be seen when comparing the New Testament narrative with events Josephus places in the late 40s or 50s.

Were one to surmise, however, that this is a true parallel, and that the high priests of the Gospels in reality were active in the 40s and 50s, rather than the 30s, the shift would be more difficult to ascribe to a chronological mistake on the part of a Gospel writer. Because it would entail a change of names. The question, then, is this: does a pattern like this—one dignitary in the Gospels better fitting the characteristics and life circumstances of another dignitary in non-biblical sources—repeat itself?

CHRONOLOGICAL ENIGMA SEVEN: PILATE VS. FELIX

CHANGING THE NAMES OF AUTHORITY FIGURES IN THE GOSPEL TEXTS, in order to detect—or disguise—parallels in the historical sources, would at the same time be a simple and a radical intervention. As mentioned, New Testament chronology is entirely based on the presence of names of dignitaries whose period of rule is known from other sources. In fact, little else than the names can be used as chronological markers, since the actual circumstances of their rule—as described in the Gospels—very rarely find echoes in non-biblical sources. In other words, despite the presence of a plethora of well-known dignitaries in the Gospel texts, their actions and circumstances do not match the descriptions in other contemporaneous sources. In fact, in the example above (concerning the co-reigning high priests), the circumstances of the dignitaries named in the Gospels better match those of *other* dignitaries in the chronicles of Josephus. And, as we shall see, not only does this seem to be a pattern, but there is some consistency with regard to *which* dignitaries better match the descriptions in the Gospels, and when they are active.

Let us look at two of the Roman procurators/prefects, described both in the New Testament and in non-biblical sources.

Pontius Pilate ruled Judea for some ten years, from 26 (or 27) to 36 (or 37) CE. Not much about his previous life and career is known. It has been assumed that he was an equestrian of the Pontii family of Samnium—a region in what is today central Italy—and one tradition connects him to the small village of Bisenti. What is known with certainty is that he was sent by Emperor Tiberius to serve as prefect over Judea, Samaria, and Idumea (the Roman province of *Iudaea*), probably in the year 26 CE, succeeding Valerius Gratus in the position (and like his predecessor settling in the coastal town of Caesarea). The other major Jewish territory, Galilee, was in this period still ruled by a Jewish client king, Herod Antipas.

With regard to Pilate's personal traits, Philo describes him as "a man of a very inflexible disposition, and very merciless as well as very obstinate," and furthermore notes "his corruption, and his acts of insolence, and his rapine, and his habit of insulting people, and his cruelty, and his continual murders of people untried and uncondemned, and his never ending, and gratuitous, and most grievous inhumanity."[1] Pilate, thus, was a man of few sensitivities.

Despite this—and probably more as a function of the times than of his superior qualities as a leader—Pilate ruled during one of the calmest periods in the more than one hundred years of Roman occupation. First century sources describe only two occasions where Pilate's actions did inspire protests among the Jews, on both occasions non-violent demonstrations, and on both occasions because of perceived transgressions against Jewish law or traditions. One of Josephus's narratives on the first event reads as follows:

> But now Pilate, the procurator [*hegemon*=leader] of Judea, removed the army from Caesarea to Jerusalem, to take their winter quarters there, in order to abolish the Jewish laws. So he introduced Caesar's effigies, which were upon the ensigns, and brought them into the city; whereas our law forbids us the very making of images; on which account the former procurators were wont to make their entry into the city with such ensigns as had not those ornaments. Pilate was the first who brought those images to Jerusalem, and set them up there; which was done without the

knowledge of the people, because it was done in the nighttime; but as soon as they knew it, they came in multitudes to Caesarea, and interceded with Pilate many days, that he would remove the images; and when he would not grant their requests, because it would tend to the injury of Caesar, while yet they persevered in their request, on the sixth day he ordered his soldiers to have their weapons privately, while he came and sat upon his judgment seat, which seat was so prepared in the open place of the city, that it concealed the army that lay ready to oppress them; and when the Jews petitioned him again, he gave a signal to the soldiers to encompass them round, and threatened that their punishment should be no less than immediate death, unless they would leave off disturbing him, and go their ways home. But they threw themselves upon the ground, and laid their necks bare, and said they would take their death very willingly, rather than the wisdom of their laws should be transgressed; upon which Pilate was deeply affected with their firm resolution to keep their laws inviolable, and presently commanded the images to be carried back from Jerusalem to Caesarea.[2]

Although Philo's narrative is similar, it differs from that of Josephus on two counts: Philo claims that the hated ensigns were "gilt shields" with inscriptions but without images. And he claims that the leaders of the Jews pleaded with Emperor Tiberius to interfere, which he did, thus compelling Pilate to remove the shields from Jerusalem to Caesarea.[3]

On the second occasion of protest, Pilate had decided to have aqueducts built to Jerusalem, and used "sacred money," i.e. the temple tax, to finance this. "However," writes Josephus, "the Jews were not pleased with what had been done about this water; and many ten thousands of the people got together, and made a clamor against him, and insisted that he should leave off that design." In reaction to these protests, Pilate ordered his soldiers to attack the crowd, and many people were killed.[4] This is the only registered violent encounter between Pilate's soldiers and the Judeans. But the violence was completely unilateral, as "the people were unarmed."[5] Nor does the killing lead to a violent reaction

on the part of the Jews. "The multitude," writes Josephus, "was aston-
ished at the calamity of those that were slain, and held their peace."[6]

With the exception of these two incidents, things seemed to have
been politically relatively tranquil between Pilate and his Jewish subjects. Indeed, Josephus writes of no "robbers," no Jewish messianic
leaders, and no armed rebellion during this period. Nor does Philo.
And, as mentioned, Tacitus states that "under Tiberius all was quiet."[7]

This stands in stark contrast to how things turned out under some
later Roman leaders of the Jewish realm. In particular, we shall now
concern ourselves with the procurator succeeding Cumanus (under
whose reign the three rebellion-triggering events occurred), namely
Antonius Felix, who ruled from 52 to ca. 59 CE.

Antonius Felix was from a family of freedmen, former Roman slaves,
to the royal family. His brother, Marcus Antonius Pallas, after being
freed, rose to prominence as a favorite of Emperor Claudius and as
imperial minister of finance. He later became one of the richest men
of the empire. Most likely due to the influence of Pallas, his brother
Felix also acquired prominence. In 52 CE, he was by Claudius appointed
procurator of Judea, Galilee, Samaria, and Perea, on account of the
emperor's dissatisfaction with how his predecessor Cumanus had handled
the Galilean-Samaritan war.[8] Later—after the death of Claudius—Felix
retained the procuratorship, but parts of eastern Galilee were given to
Jewish client king Agrippa II.[9] Claudius's choice of procurator seems
to have been inspired by advice from high priest Jonathan, who later
came to regret this deeply.[10] Although Felix appears to have had a
calming effect on the Galilean-Samaritan tensions, he nevertheless soon
started alienating not only his new subjects, but, in fact, the entire local
leadership. And one of the reasons was personal: Felix fell in love with
King Agrippa's married sister, princess Drusilla. As Josephus writes:

> While Felix was procurator of Judea, he saw this Drusilla, and fell
> in love with her; for she did indeed exceed all other women in
> beauty; and he sent to her a person whose name was Simon, one
> of his friends; a Jew he was, and by birth a Cypriot, and one who
> pretended to be a magician, and endeavored to persuade her to

forsake her present husband, and marry him; and promised, that if she would not refuse him, he would make her a happy woman. Accordingly she acted ill, and because she was desirous to avoid her sister Bernice's envy, for she was very ill treated by her on account of her beauty, was prevailed upon to transgress the laws of her forefathers, and to marry Felix.[11]

The words "prevailed upon to transgress the laws of her forefathers" are key. Because Agrippa II had demanded from Drusilla's first husband, King Azizus of Emesa, that he convert to Judaism and get circumcised, which he had done. An earlier intended groom had in fact been rejected on the grounds that he had refused this conversion.[12] Thus, the transgression against "the laws of her forefathers" obviously refers not to the divorce from King Azizus (which is permitted in Judaism), but to the marriage to a non-Jew, Felix. This was done against the wishes of the king.

But Felix did more than that to provoke his subjects. As Roman historian Tacitus writes: "Antonius Felix, indulging in every kind of barbarity and lust, exercised the power of a king in the spirit of a slave."[13] Tacitus, in fact, puts much of the blame for the now emerging rebellion on the two procurators Cumanus and Felix.[14] As can be seen from the figure on page 46, it is in the year 48, the year when Cumanus comes to power, that the "robbers" become really prevalent in Josephus's texts— after the three ill-handled provocations. But Felix was to exceed his predecessor in ruthlessness when dealing with these "robbers," as well as the concomitant aspiring messianic leaders ("impostors," as Josephus calls them). Josephus writes in *Antiquities*:

> Now as for the affairs of the Jews, they grew worse and worse continually, for the country was again filled with robbers and impostors, who deluded the multitude. Yet did Felix catch and put to death many of those impostors every day, together with the robbers.[15]

And in *War*, Josephus has the following to say about Felix's interaction with the insurgents:

> But as to the number of the robbers whom he caused to be crucified,
> and of those who were caught among them, and whom he brought
> to punishment, they were a multitude not to be enumerated.[16]

Despite his obvious inability to quell these insurgencies, Felix was allowed to remain in his position for something like seven or eight years—the time of his departure is not certain, but is usually set at 59 or 60 CE.

The intriguing thing is that procurator Felix, as he is depicted in Josephus's texts, in several ways appears to bear stronger similarities to the Pilate described in the Gospels, than Pilate himself. As we have already seen, Josephus describes no robbers during Pilate's rule, nor any mass crucifixions of Jews, nor any co-reigning high priests, and no conflict between Galileans and Samaritans—all elements of the Gospel narratives. But under Felix, and also under his predecessor Cumanus, he does. But Felix, in particular, stands out. Because when it comes to this procurator, there are more statements in the Gospels better fitting him than Pilate. Take, for instance, the Gospel of Luke, chapter 13, where we read the following verses:

> At that very time there were some present who told him [Jesus]
> about the Galileans whose blood Pilate had mingled with their
> sacrifices. He asked them, "Do you think that because these Gali-
> leans suffered in this way they were worse sinners than all other
> Galileans? No, I tell you; but unless you repent, you will all perish
> as they did."[17]

There is one sentence in the paragraph above, which sticks out: "At that very time there were some present who told him about the Galileans whose blood Pilate had mingled with their sacrifices." The mystifying thing with this statement is that Pilate was not the ruler of Galilee, Herod Antipas was. And there is no indication that he ever interfered in the business of Galilee.

Besides, the only registered violent encounter between Pilate's soldiers and the Jews occurred in Judea, when non-violent protests against the aqueduct prompted Pilate to instruct his men "with their staves to beat those that made the clamor."[18]

This stands in stark contrast to what occurred under Felix. Felix, unlike Pilate, was the ruler not only of Judea, but also of "Galilee, and Samaria, and Perea" (parts of Galilee after 55 CE).[19] At this point, "the country was again filled with robbers and impostors," a disproportionate amount of whom were Galileans, and Felix was exceptionally cruel in dealing with these insurgents, crucifying them en masse.[20]

There are other examples of statements in the Gospels which seem to better fit Felix. For instance, the Gospels attribute great influence to Pilate's wife. In Matthew 27:19 it says: "While he [Pilate] was sitting on the judgment seat, his wife sent word to him, 'Have nothing to do with that innocent man, for today I have suffered a great deal because of a dream about him.'"

Since we know nothing about Pilate's wife, we cannot, of course, say that she was not influential. What we can say, is that it fits very well with Felix's wife, a Jewish princess no less.

The Gospels furthermore mention a feud between Pilate and the Jewish king. As we read in Luke 23:12: "That same day Herod and Pilate became friends with each other; before this they had been enemies."

No animosity between Pilate and Herod Antipas is mentioned by Josephus, although Philo mentions one possible occasion of disagreement—when "the four sons of the king" [Herod] are asked by the people to implore Pilate to remove the guilt shields, or ensigns, from Jerusalem.[21] Josephus, on the other hand, does describe a significant, and personal, cause of antagonism between Felix and Agrippa II: Felix marries Agrippa's sister, princess Drusilla, against the will of the king.[22]

Hence, a prominent wife, and enmity with a Jewish ruler, more seem like aspects of Felix's life than of Pilate's.

Another example comes from the trial of Jesus, when Jesus is brought to Pilate by the high priests and other members of the Jewish Council. The Council members try to persuade a reluctant Pilate of Jesus's guilt.

And the text in Luke 23:6–7 then reads: "When Pilate heard this, he asked whether the man was a Galilean. And when he learned that he was under Herod's jurisdiction, he sent him off to Herod . . ." If this sentence pertains to Pilate and Herod Antipas, it contains a curious tautology. Since Pilate ruled Judea, and Herod Antipas ruled Galilee, the words "under Herod's jurisdiction" seem entirely superfluous. A more logical sentence would have read: "When Pilate heard this, he asked whether the man was a Galilean. And when he learned that he was, he sent him off to Herod . . ."

With Felix and Agrippa II, however, the sentence makes perfect sense. From around 55 CE, jurisdiction over Galilee was divided between them—with Felix ruling over western Galilee, and Agrippa II ruling over some eastern parts.[23] Consequently, the information that Jesus is a Galilean would not automatically have put him under Herod's jurisdiction.

Thus, there are in the Gospels a number of characteristics and events ascribed to Pilate or his times which, judging by Josephus, fit better with later procurators, principally Felix, procurator in the 50s (see table on next page).

Rulers associated with various events (1-66 CE)

Event	According to New Testament	According to Josephus
"Robbers" active	Pilate	Archelaus, Fadus, Tiberius Alexander, Cumanus, Felix, Festus, Albinus, Florus
Known crucifixions of Jews	Pilate	Tiberius Alexander, Cumanus, Felix, Florus
Two named co-reigning High Priests	Pilate	Cumanus, Felix
Prefect/Procurator slaughtering Galileans	Pilate	Cumanus, Felix (Festus, Albinus, Florus)
Conflict between Prefect/Procurator and Jewish King	Pilate and Herod Antipas	Felix and Agrippa II (Pilate and Herod Antipas)
Prefect/Procurator known to have an influential wife	Pilate	Felix, Florus
Conflict between Galileans and Samaritans	Pilate	Cumanus, Felix
Messianic Jewish leaders mentioned	Pilate (Archelaus, Fadus, Felix)	Archelaus, Fadus, Felix, Festus
Attack on a man named Stephen outside Jerusalem	Pilate, Marcellus or Marullus	Cumanus
Theudas killed	Pilate, or earlier	Fadus
Census	Quirinius	Quirinius

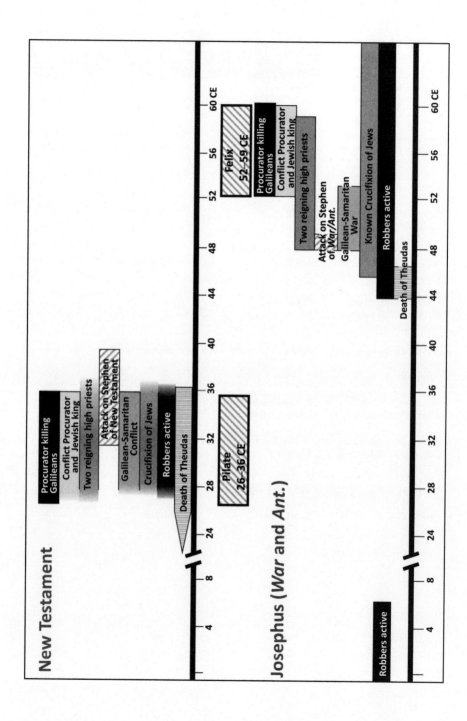

CHRONOLOGICAL ENIGMA EIGHT: THE RETURN FROM EGYPT

PERHAPS THE MOST WIDELY NOTED CHRONOLOGICAL INCONSISTENCY in the New Testament concerns the birth narratives. Only two of the four Gospels relate Jesus's birth—Matthew and Luke. But, as already mentioned, their stories are profoundly different. In the Gospel of Matthew we are told that Jesus was brought by his parents to Egypt as an infant, and returned "when Herod died." Since many of the Jewish kings are called "Herod," we can not from this statement deduce that the king in question is Herod the Great, who died in the year 4 BCE. Just a couple of sentences later, however, it says: "But when he heard that Archelaus was ruling over Judea in place of his father Herod, he was afraid to go there."[1] And we know for certain that Archelaus was the son and successor of Herod the Great. Thus, according to Matthew, Jesus must have been born in the year 4 BCE at the latest.

In the Gospel of Luke, however, we are told that Jesus is born while Mary and Joseph are in Bethlehem "to be registered" (the Greek word for the carrying out of this registration, or census, is *apographo*, which in this context means "to enter in public records the names of men, their property and income"). This registration is key. Because Luke also says: "This was the first registration and was taken while Quirinius was governor of Syria."[2] Since we know from Josephus that Quirinius became governor of Syria—to which Judea now was added—in 6 or 7 CE, after the banishment of Archelaus, and that he immediately proceeded "to take an account of their substance," we have a fairly exact time point when Luke says Jesus was born: in 6 or 7 CE.[3] Luke thus puts the time of Jesus's birth at least ten years later than does Matthew.

This discrepancy is generally noted—and further complicated by the fact that Luke himself writes that John the Baptist (who according to the same Gospel was about six months older than Jesus), was conceived "in the days of King Herod of Judea"![4] If one assumes that "King Herod" also in this case refers to Herod the Great, this is an internal contradiction in Luke which is not explained. As stated earlier, Luke's placement of Jesus's birth at the time of the tax census, around 6 CE, may be symbolic, and we shall come back to this later.

Interestingly, however, also Matthew's narrative has a significant internal contradiction, and this contradiction is rarely addressed. Right after we are told of Jesus's and his parents' return from Egypt, Matthew says: "Now in those days John the Baptist came, preaching in the wilderness of Judea."[5] There is no indication of time passing between the two events. In fact, the words "in those days" (*en de tais hēmerais ekeinais*) tie them together, and places the beginning of John the Baptist's ministry in the same period as Jesus's return from Egypt. But how is this possible, if Jesus and John are the same age? Jesus had, according to Matthew, returned from Egypt as a child! This, in fact, is clearly stated:

> When Herod died, an angel of the Lord suddenly appeared in a dream to Joseph in Egypt and said, "Get up, take the child and his mother, and go to the land of Israel, for those who were seeking the child's life are dead." Then Joseph got up, took the child and his mother, and went to the land of Israel.[6]

The problem with this information is not only that John the Baptist is about six months older than Jesus, and hardly could have started preaching when he himself was a child.[7] In addition, Luke 3:1 places the beginning of John the Baptist's ministry "in the fifteenth year of the reign of Emperor Tiberius," thus in 28 or 29 CE, or thirty-two to thirty-three years after the death of Herod the Great! So how can Matthew state that John the Baptist starts preaching at the same time as the child Jesus returns from Egypt, just after Herod the Great died? Even accounting for the fact that the return from Egypt may not have occurred immediately after Herod's death, Matthew 2:22 definitely places it in the reign of Archelaus, i.e. in 6 CE at the latest. Thus, there seems to be a paradoxical gap of at least twenty-two years between Matthew 2:23 and 3:1, a gap which is contradicted by the words "in those days" at the beginning of 3:1. A gap which nevertheless *has* to be there if Jesus returned from Egypt as a child.

But did he?

Remarkably, there are two early non-Christian sources which state that Jesus spent years as an adult in Egypt. The later, and less unequivocal, of the two is the Talmud, the Jewish Oral Law, which consists not only of interpretations of the Torah, the Five Books of Moses, but also of illustrative and instructive tales. The Talmud was put down in writing after the fall of Jerusalem, to preserve laws and traditions for a dispersing Jewry. And as the work was developing with time, it was done in stages: the so called *Mishnah* was codified around the year 200 CE, the *Jerusalem Gemara* around 400 CE, and the *Babylonian Gemara* in 500 to 600 CE. But much of what was preserved were earlier traditions.

Yeshu, Yeshu ben Pantera, ben Stada, Balaam, Peloni. These are some of the names in the Talmud that historically—but not without debate—have been associated with Jesus. The names occur in negative, or warning, contexts, and the assumption that they referred to Jesus led to much conflict between the Church and Jewish authorities in the Middle Ages, and to the ultimate censoring of the passages with these names. Thus, the passages are mostly recreated from earlier versions. One of the more direct excerpts is the following one:

> It was taught: on the eve of the Passover Yeshu was hanged. For forty days before the execution took place, a herald went forth and cried, 'He is going to be stoned because he has practised sorcery

and enticed Israel to apostasy. Any one who can say anything in his favor, let him come forward and plead on his behalf.' But since nothing was brought forward in his favor he was hanged on the eve of the Passover![8]

Perhaps the most relevant names in this context, however, are *Yeshu Ben Pantera* (*Pandira, Pandera*), or simply *ben Pantera* which means "son of Pantera," and *ben Stada* (son of Stada). We shall in a bit come back to the issue of why these names are considered the most likely to refer to Jesus.[9] But to start with, the Talmud in several places states that ben Pantera and ben Stada are the same person (and that Pantera was his biological father, whereas Stada was the husband of his mother):

> And this they did to ben Stada in Lydda, and they hung him on the eve of Passover. Ben Stada was ben Pandira.
> Rabbi Hisda said: "The husband was Stada, the paramour Pandira."[10]

And in another Talmud tractate:

> Rabbi Eliezer said to the Sages: "But did not ben Stada bring forth witchcraft from Egypt by means of scratches [in the form of charms] upon his flesh?" Was he then the son of Stada: surely he was the son of Pandira?" Said Rabbi Hisda: "The husband was Stada, the paramour was Pandira." "He was a fool," answered they, "and proof cannot be adduced from fools."[11]

The above lines from the *Babylonian Gemara* represent just one of several examples in the Talmud where it is stated that ben Stada/ben Pantera had been in Egypt. It is also one of several examples where it says that he brought spells with him when he came back. Yet another example:

> He who scratches on the skin in the fashion of writing is guilty, but he who makes marks on the skin in the fashion of writing is exempt from punishment. Rabbi Eliezer said to them: "But has

not ben Stada brought (magic) spells out of Egypt just in this way?" They answered him: "On account of one fool we do not ruin a multitude of reasonable men."[12]

What is more specifically dealt with in these last two passages is the question of whether one may under certain conditions write on the Sabbath, for example by writing words on one's skin—and ben Stada/ben Pantera is said to have brought "witchcraft from Egypt by means of scratches upon his flesh." In reading this, and as an aside, it is interesting to note that the last book in the New Testament, the Book of Revelation, describes one of the four riders of the apocalypse, the one mostly interpreted as Jesus Christ, in the following way:

> His eyes are like a flame of fire, and on his head are many diadems; and he has a name inscribed that no one knows but himself [. . .] On his robe and on his thigh he has a name inscribed, "King of kings and Lord of lords."[13]

There is yet another story from the Babylonian Talmud which may be relevant, in that it deals with Egypt, and the person concerned is called Yeshu (in one manuscript he is even called Yeshu the Nazarene). In this story, Yeshu is fleeing to Egypt to escape an evil king who kills rabbis. He flees together with a well-known rabbi by the name of Yehoshua ben Perachyah, but is later rejected by him "with both hands," on account of his behavior. The story ends with the words: "Yeshu practiced magic and led Israel astray."[14]

This account, however, is, despite the use of the name "Yeshu," less often associated with Jesus, since the rabbi, and the king (Alexander Yannai), lived about one hundred years before the birth of Jesus.[15] All the same, the tale finds a certain echo in the Gospels, since, according to the Gospel of Matthew, Jesus flees to Egypt to escape an evil king ("Herod"). Something in this Talmud story is also reminiscent of the parable of the prodigal son, in the Gospel of Luke.[16]

In conclusion, there are a number of tales in the Talmud which deal with a person who is often assumed to be Jesus, who lived in Egypt, and who came to the Jewish land bringing knowledge of magic.

But the tales are written down four or five hundred years after Jesus was active. And one cannot, based solely on the information provided by the Talmud, be certain that the names ben Pantera and ben Stada refer to Jesus. Thus, we would be left with not much more than conjecture and assumptions, if it were not for the fact that there is one other source in which these issues are discussed. And it was written considerably earlier.

We do not know a lot about Celsus. What we know, is that he was a Greek or Roman philosopher, and that he was a fierce opponent of Christianity. Celsus wrote his only known work *Alethes logos* ("The True Word") between 175 and 180 CE, a work which has not survived in its original form. We still can read parts of it, however, for the following reason: about sixty years after it was written, a man called Ambrosius sent *Alethes logos* to Church Father Origen, asking him to make a refutation. The narrative, he claimed, should not go unchallenged by the Church. Celsus had written a fierce polemic against Christianity, and certain segments also dealt with the personal history of Jesus (segments in which Celsus lets a fictive Jew challenge Jesus).

In the end, and after much deliberation, Origen did write a work, entirely concerned with disproving Celsus. It was called *Contra Celsum* ("Against Celsus"). But the interesting thing is that in his narrative, Origen did not only attempt to refute Celsus's claims, in the process he quoted massive amounts of Celsus's text, verbatim. Thus, it is in *Contra Celsum* that Celsus's words have been preserved. And these are remarkable words indeed (Celsus's words are in quotes):

> But let us now return to where the Jew is introduced, speaking of the mother of Jesus, and saying that "when she was pregnant she was turned out of doors by the carpenter to whom she had been betrothed, as having been guilty of adultery, and that she bore a child to a certain soldier named Panthera."[17]

These, thus, are the words of Celsus, quoted by Origen. And here the person "Pantera" turns up again, this time clearly assigned the role as the biological father of Jesus, whose mother, nevertheless, was betrothed to someone else.

This does not mean that we are here served the truth—the information in *Alethes logos* and in the Talmud (which are both wholly or partially antagonistic to Christianity) could come from a common source. What it does provide, however, is support for the assumption that the name ben Pantera in the Talmud most likely refers to Jesus.

The name Pantera, in fact, was so well known in the early Church that Church Father Epiphanius (ca. 310–403) weaved it into the family tree of Jesus—he wrote that Joseph's father was named Jacob Panther.[18] And in the eighth century, Church Father John of Damascus in another account of Jesus's genealogy, writes: "Panther begot Barpanther, so called. This Barpanther begot Joachim: Joachim begot the holy Mother of God."[19]

Whether they had obtained knowledge of the name Pantera from Celsus or from other, now lost, sources is impossible to say. But at any rate, the name obviously had to be dealt with by the church fathers. It should in this context be mentioned that in the satirical Jewish Gospel called *Sepher Toldoth Yeshu*, which in various versions circulated mainly in the Middle Ages—but according to some scholars may have originated as early as the fourth, or even third or second, century—Jesus's biological father is usually given the name "Joseph Panthera."[20]

Celsus provides us with more text on the history of Jesus, text which once again echoes what is later put down in the Talmud. Here, again, is Origen quoting Celsus (who lets the fictive Jew argue with Jesus):

> He [the fictive Jew] accuses Him [Jesus] of having "invented his birth from a virgin" and upbraids Him with being "born in a certain Jewish village, of a poor woman of the country, who gained her subsistence by spinning, and who was turned out of doors by her husband, a carpenter by trade, because she was convicted of adultery; that after being driven away by her husband, and wandering about for a time, she disgracefully gave birth to Jesus, an illegitimate child, who having hired himself out as a servant in Egypt on account of his poverty, and having there acquired some

miraculous powers, on which the Egyptians greatly pride themselves, returned to his own country, highly elated on account of them, and by means of these proclaimed himself a God."[21]

Thus, in Origen's citations of Celsus, the adult sojourn to Egypt turns up once again, this time four hundred years before the codification of the Babylonian Talmud. Interestingly, Church Father Origen closes the quote with the following words of his own: "Now, as I cannot allow anything said by unbelievers to remain unexamined, but must investigate everything from the beginning, I give it as my opinion that all these things worthily harmonize with the predictions that Jesus is the Son of God." Church Father Origen, in other words, does not deny Celsus's assertion that Jesus had labored in Egypt, something Origen even stresses in the next chapter: "And now, our Jesus, who is reproached with being born in a village . . . and being despised as the son of a poor laboring woman, and as having on account of his poverty left his native country and hired himself out in Egypt . . . has yet been able to shake the whole inhabited world."[22]

And a few decades later, Arnobius of Sicca, a North African convert to Christianity, writes the following in his book *Adversus Gentes*:

> My opponent will perhaps meet me with many other slanderous and childish charges which are commonly urged. Jesus was a Magician; he effected all these things by secret arts. From the shrines of the Egyptians he stole the names of angels of might, and the religious system of a remote country.[23]

Do we, then, find any reverberation of such an adult long-term absence from home in the New Testament? Well, perhaps we do, at least indirectly.

It is a fact that also in the Gospels, Jesus reappears when he is "about thirty years old."[24] Nothing is said about where he had been previously. In fact, as we have already seen, the Gospel of Matthew goes straight from Jesus's childhood return from Egypt to John the Baptist's appearance as a preacher, and then directly from there to an adult Jesus meeting and being baptized by John.

In Luke, we go from Jesus's birth to an episode when he is twelve years old and visits Jerusalem. From there we go directly to John the Baptist, and Jesus being baptized by him. And then it says: "Jesus was about thirty years old when he began his work."

In Mark, the first time we hear of Jesus he is an adult, and meets John the Baptist. And the situation is the same in the Gospel of John.

It is as if Jesus has not been visible before age thirty—at least not between twelve and thirty. He turns up, as if from nowhere, to see John the Baptist in the Judean desert.

Interestingly, this sudden appearance at age thirty is not the only indication in the Gospels of a long absence. In fact, all three Synoptic Gospels—Mark, Matthew, and Luke—describe how Jesus comes to his hometown, Nazareth. And at first, he does not seem to be recognized:

> He came to his hometown and began to teach the people in their synagogue, so that they were astounded and said, "Where did this man get this wisdom and these deeds of power? Is not this the carpenter's son? Is not his mother called Mary? And are not his brothers James and Joseph and Simon and Judas? And are not all his sisters with us?"
>
> *Matt. 13:54–56*

> When he came to Nazareth, where he had been brought up, he went to the synagogue on the sabbath day, as was his custom. He stood up to read, and the scroll of the prophet Isaiah was given to him. [. . .] All spoke well of him and were amazed at the gracious words that came from his mouth. They said, "Is not this Joseph's son?" He said to them, "Doubtless you will quote to me this proverb, 'Doctor, cure yourself!' And you will say, 'Do here also in your hometown the things that we have heard you did at Capernaum.'"
>
> *Luke 4:16–23*

> He left that place and came to his hometown, and his disciples followed him. On the sabbath he began to teach in the synagogue,

and many who heard him were astounded. They said, "Where did this man get all this? What is this wisdom that has been given to him? What deeds of power are being done by his hands! Is not this the carpenter, the son of Mary and brother of James and Joses and Judas and Simon, and are not his sisters here with us?" And they took offense at him.

Mark 6:1–3

When the people in the synagogue finally recognize Jesus, they do so in relation to his parents and siblings, thus presumably as a child or youth. If Jesus had simply left Nazareth to go down to the Judean desert to be baptized by John, and then returned home, there is no reason why the people would not have immediately known who he was, in his own right. And yet, the fact that they do eventually recognize him means that he is somehow known to them. From some time, seemingly long ago.

In conclusion, there are at least four pieces of information which indicate that Jesus spent time in Egypt as an adult:

- The Talmud excerpts mentioning ben Pantera as someone who had come as an adult out of Egypt.
- Celsus's statement that Jesus returned from Egypt as an adult (and his identification of ben Pantera as Jesus).
- Early Christian writers who refer to a claim that Jesus had spent time in Egypt as an adult.
- The absence of information about Jesus's adulthood before age thirty, and the Gospel descriptions of Jesus's return to his hometown Nazareth, seemingly after a long absence.

In addition, there is one piece of information from the Gospels indicating that this adult return from Egypt is identical to that described in Matthew 2:21–23, namely the simultaneous appearance of John the Baptist as a preacher.

Is there a way, then, to reconcile the information from Matthew with that from the Talmud and from Celsus? And is there a way to bridge the anomalous multi-year gap between Matthew 2:23 and

Matthew 3:1? Possibly, but it would require changing the name of the person in authority, with a resulting shift in time of fifteen to twenty years.

If the ruler whose death preceded the return of Jesus from Egypt was Herod Antipas (king of Galilee, 4 BCE–39 CE), or more likely Herod Agrippa I (39–44 CE), and not Herod the Great (42–4 BCE), there would be no inconsistency in the statements that Jesus returned both "when Herod died" and when "John the Baptist appeared in the wilderness of Judea" (assuming that the fifteen to twenty year time shift applies also to John the Baptist).[25] In that case, Jesus would not have been a child when he returned from Egypt, but an adult, just like Celsus and the Talmud state.

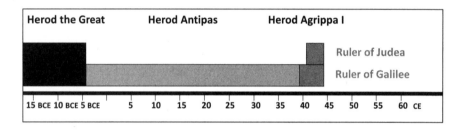

Whether, and if so why, a deliberate shift of events from one era to another was brought about will be discussed below. But if, at some point in the writing or editing of the Gospel texts, there was an impetus to create such a shift, the easiest way to accomplish this would have been to change the names of authority figures. If, however, a number of other adjustments were not made, this might create internal inconsistencies in the text. In the example above, describing Herod the Great as the king whose death preceded Jesus return from Egypt creates such a significant problem with chronology that the text fails to be fully logical—Jesus simply could not have been a child when returning from Egypt, if John the Baptist simultaneously started preaching. Thus, if a change of names was performed, this modification (at least in Matthew) most likely would have occurred after the initial text was written, and would have been fairly minimal.

Alternatively, the discrepancies could be interpreted as deliberate traces of another story. This is something which will be further discussed later.

CHRONOLOGICAL ENIGMA NINE: JESUS VS. "THE EGYPTIAN"

As we have seen in the previous chapters, there seems to be a pattern in which a number of episodes described in the New Testament display significant similarities to events described by Josephus, but with a fairly consistent delay of fifteen to twenty years. Activities depicted in the Gospels more often than not resemble events other historians place not in the times of Pilate, but later, mainly in the times of Felix (see table on page 93).

And from our point of view, we now come to perhaps the most significant aspect of Felix's procuratorship: if the 30s—judging by Josephus—are devoid of strong Jewish messianic leaders, the times of Felix, the 50s, are not.[1] And the most important of these messianic leaders is one that Josephus describes at length, in both his major works:

> There came out of Egypt about this time to Jerusalem one that said he was a prophet, and advised the multitude of the common people to go along with him to the Mount of Olives, as it was called, which lay over against the city, and at the distance of five furlongs. He said further, that he would show them from hence how, at his command, the walls of Jerusalem would fall down; and

he promised them that he would procure them an entrance into the city through those walls, when they were fallen down. Now when Felix was informed of these things, he ordered his soldiers to take their weapons, and came against them with a great number of horsemen and footmen from Jerusalem, and attacked the Egyptian and the people that were with him. He also slew four hundred of them, and took two hundred alive. But the Egyptian himself escaped out of the fight, but did not appear any more.

Antiquities of the Jews 20.169–172

"One of his disciples said to him: 'Look, Teacher, what large stones and what large buildings!' Then Jesus asked him, 'Do you see these great buildings? Not one stone will be left here upon another; all will be thrown down.' When he was sitting on the Mount of Olives opposite the temple, Peter, James, John, and Andrew asked him privately, 'Tell us, when will this be, and what will be the sign that all these things are about to be accomplished?' Then Jesus began to say to them, 'Beware that no one leads you astray. Many will come in my name and say, "I am he!" and they will lead many astray. When you hear of wars and rumors of wars, do not be alarmed; this must take place, but the end is still to come.'"(Mark 13:1–7)[2]

No, the stories are not identical, but if "the Egyptian" had been active in the 30s instead of in the 50s, historians would undoubtedly have compared him with Jesus of Nazareth.

Josephus's description of this event in his other major work, *War of the Jews*, differs on some accounts from that in *Antiquities*—and it is decidedly more negative, in line with Josephus's general loathing of messianic leaders and their followers—but it nevertheless adds fuel to a comparison:

But there was an Egyptian false prophet that did the Jews more mischief than the former; for he was a sorcerer[*goes*], and pretended to be a prophet also, and got together thirty thousand men that were deluded by him; these he led round about from the wilderness to the mount which was called the Mount of Olives, and was ready to break into Jerusalem by force from that place; and if he could but once conquer the Roman garrison and the people, he intended to domineer over them by the assistance of those guards of his that were to break into the city with him. But Felix prevented his attempt, and met him with his Roman soldiers, while all the people assisted him in his attack upon them, insomuch that when it came to a battle, the Egyptian ran away, with a few others, while the greatest part of those that were with him were either destroyed or taken alive; but the rest of the multitude were dispersed every one to their own homes, and there concealed themselves.

War of the Jews 2.261–263

Yes, there are obvious differences, but the parallels between Josephus's two accounts of "the Egyptian" and the Gospel accounts of Jesus are numerous:

- Like Jesus, "the Egyptian" had previously lingered in "the wilderness" or "desert" (*eremia*, in Greek).
- Like Jesus, "the Egyptian" had lived in Egypt.
- Like Jesus, "the Egyptian" spoke of tearing down the walls of Jerusalem.
- Like Jesus, "the Egyptian" is described as a messianic leader with a great following.
- Like Jesus, "the Egyptian" is perceived as a major threat by the authorities.
- Like Jesus, "the Egyptian" seems to have been betrayed—at least the authorities were informed beforehand about his plans.
- And last, but not least, "the Egyptian" is defeated on the Mount of Olives, which is where Jesus was arrested. It is also from there that both men have declared their prophecies.

Aside from chronology, the one thing which most clearly distinguishes Jesus and "the Egyptian" are the circumstances surrounding their defeat: Jesus is arrested in the presence of his disciples on the Mount of Olives, crucified, resurrected, and then vanishes. "The Egyptian" is defeated in battle on the Mount of Olives, and then vanishes. There are thus two major differences: the battle, and the crucifixion.

But let us look more closely at the events surrounding Jesus's arrest, as they are described in the Gospels.

THE EVENTS ON
THE MOUNT OF OLIVES

In its description of the trial against Jesus, the Gospel of Mark states that "a man called Barabbas was in prison with the rebels who had committed murder during the insurrection."[1] And Luke similarly says that Barabbas "was a man who had been put in prison for an insurrection that had taken place in the city."[2]

The fact is, however, that neither Mark nor Luke has described any insurrection, nor have the other two Gospel authors. The only reported disturbances in the Gospels are the ones occurring when Jesus is arrested on the Mount of Olives (meeting his adversaries with the words: "Have you come out with swords and clubs to arrest me as though I were a robber?").[3] Prior to this, Jesus had only been resting with his disciples. The reason for his arrest, furthermore, is predominately religious, as it is the Sanhedrin, the Jewish Council, which sends out people to arrest him. This is what Mark, Matthew, and Luke all write.[4]

One Gospel, however, differs in its account of this event. In the Gospel of John 18:12, we read that when arriving at the Mount of Olives, "the Jewish police" are accompanied by "the soldiers" and "their officer." This sounds innocuous enough, and is rarely considered a decisive difference from the other three accounts. So the Sanhedrin brought along some Roman soldiers, just in case. It is only when we go to the Greek original of John that we suddenly get the full picture, and it most certainly stands out: the original word for "soldiers" is *speira*. The word for the "officer" is *chiliarchos*. A *speira* is a Roman cohort numbering six hundred to one thousand soldiers. And the exact translation of *chiliarchos* is: "commander of one thousand" (*chilioi*: 'thousand'; *archos*: 'commander').

If John's account is correct, then what occurred on the Mount of Olives must have been some sort of battle, a battle involving the Roman army. It is difficult to imagine that the Romans would send out hundreds of soldiers to arrest one resting man. Indeed, from this account it seems that we might really be dealing with an insurrection in Jerusalem, like Mark and Luke state.

So do we find any additional corroborating evidence for such a battle or insurrection in the Gospels? In fact we do—evidence interspersed with accounts of the resting Jesus and his disciples, and therefore usually disregarded. Remember that prior to the departure for the Mount of Olives, Jesus admonishes his disciples that "the one who has no sword must sell his cloak and buy one." And he continues: "For I tell you, this scripture must be fulfilled in me, 'And he was counted among the lawless.'"[5]

Furthermore, all four Gospels mention the use of swords in the ensuing encounter on the Mount of Olives. And although Jesus had previously told his disciples to bring along these swords to the Mount of Olives, he now tells them to put them away.[6] We shall come back to these contradictory statements later.

Suffice it to say: in all four Gospels, a narrative describing a man quietly resting with his disciples, awaiting his arrest, is interspersed with numerous allusions to a very calamitous event indeed.

Thus, were we to judge by the account in John—and to some extent Luke—the events preceding the arrest of Jesus bear distinct similarities to the events surrounding the defeat of "the Egyptian." And the location is the same: the Mount of Olives.

So what about the crucifixion? Is there in Josephus's chronicles any mention of "the Egyptian" being crucified? No, there is not. And if we assume that Josephus did not simply fail to mention this, or was unaware of it, this could be a decisive difference between the fates of these two men. In fact the one remaining non-chronological difference. But before we leave the issue of the crucifixion, it might be worth bringing up another event described in the Gospels: the release of Barabbas.

Barabbas is a curious character in the New Testament narrative. He appears in all four Gospels, where he is variously described as a "robber," "a notorious prisoner," and someone who "was in prison with the rebels who had committed murder during the insurrection."[7] Barabbas had been sentenced to be executed simultaneously with Jesus. He was, however, let go, whereas Jesus was crucified (between two other "robbers," that were presumably associated with Barabbas). What makes Barabbas curious, however, is not only that he leads an "insurrection" at the same time as Jesus provokes the authorities—added to this is his intriguing name. Barabbas means "Son of the Father," a name seemingly more appropriate to Jesus (who often referred to God as *Abba,* "Father"). But actually, Barabbas is not the man's full name. In Matthew 27:16–17 we are told that his name is "Jesus Barabbas," which means "Jesus, Son of the Father"!

Could Jesus of Nazareth and Jesus "Son of the Father" really be two different people? And why would one of them be crucified between the followers of the other?

That Jesus of Nazareth and Jesus Barabbas is one and the same person is a proposition that has been made before, by scholars as well as in fictional accounts.[8] The peculiar resemblance of the names, as well as a failure to find either a biblical or a non-biblical precedent for the described custom of releasing a prisoner at the feast, are generally cited as reasons for the hypothesis.[9] The various proponents of this theory, that Jesus and Barabbas are the same man, suggest different explanations for why a Galilean rebel leader would later be remembered as two separate individuals, ranging from a simple mistake to a deliberate play on words—almost like a parable. Perhaps the purpose would be to create a choice for the reader: do you want to choose violence or will you turn the other cheek? H.A. Rigg, in his 1945 article, suggests that the division was necessary: "It was Jesus, the Christ of the great Passion story, that was vividly remembered and on whom the Gentiles built the Christianity of history. To them Barabbas became simply one of those taken in a riot and Christ the crucified Lord and Saviour."[10]

Adding Barabbas to our mix may confuse matters. But it is difficult to entirely neglect the intriguing Gospel account of a rebel leader caught at the same time as Jesus, bearing the same name as Jesus—possibly being identical to Jesus—but escaping crucifixion.

A man the Gospel of Mark, and the Gospel of Luke, in fact, state was involved with "the insurrection."

His fate may deserve to be taken into account when one looks at the one distinct non-chronological difference between Jesus and "the Egyptian."

As it is, "the Egyptian" has been virtually completely neglected by scholars attempting to find evidence for Jesus's presence in the historical narratives. R. Travers Herford, in his 1903 work *Christianity in Talmud and Midrash,* does touch upon "the Egyptian," in an attempt to separate ben Stada from ben Pantera, the two names most often associated with Jesus in the Talmud. Herford suggests that perhaps only ben Pantera is Jesus, and that ben Stada is someone else. Then he adds: "I venture to suggest, as worth consideration, the hypothesis that ben Stada originally denoted 'that Egyptian' . . . who gave himself out as a prophet, led a crowd of followers to the Mount of Olives, and was routed there by the Procurator Felix. This man is called a sorcerer . . . Now Rabbi Eliezer said of Ben Stada that he brought magical spells from Egypt; and the Rabbis, to whom he made this remark, replied that 'Ben Stada was a fool.' This verdict is more appropriate to the Jewish-Egyptian impostor than to the much more dangerous Jeshu ha-Notzri."[11] In other words, Herford does note the similarities between "the Egyptian" and ben Stada (thought to be Jesus), but he does so in an attempt to find an alternative identity for ben Stada, other than Jesus. Despite their clear similarities, Herford never considers Jesus and "the Egyptian" to be the same man. One may assume that the reason is that "the Egyptian" appeared twenty years later than Jesus.

Postulating that Jesus could be identical to "the Egyptian" would require us to also assume the radical idea that the events as they occurred have been shifted in the Gospels back in time, from the 50s to the 30s. It would, however, offer us a plausible explanation for the paradoxical fact that a person, Jesus, who according to the New Testament arouses such attention in his time, and is perceived as such a threat by the authorities, nevertheless appears to be invisible in other contemporary sources. The additional fact that a better general concordance between the Gospel texts and those of Flavius Josephus would be achieved by such a shift is cause enough to consider this possibility.[12]

Interestingly, this identification between Jesus and "the Egyptian" may actually have traveled through history, at least oral history. Although the source of his information is unclear,[13] Amulo, Archbishop of Lyons, in the ninth century (ca. 847) writes a book called *Letter, or Book, Against the Jews to King Charles,* where he states that the following is the name that the Jews give to Jesus:

> In their own language they call him *Ussum Hamizri,* which is to say in Latin *Dissipator Ægyptius* [the Egyptian Destroyer/Disperser].[14]

And in the Huldreich version of the *Sepher Toldoth Yeshu,* from 1705, the name of Jesus's father is said to be "*Mezaria* [or *Mizria,* meaning "Egyptian"], because he did the work of the Egyptians."[15]

Also found in a version of the *Sepher Toldoth Yeshu* is the assertion that upon entering Jerusalem, Jesus "hath with him two thousand men." After Judas betrays him, the text goes, the citizens of Jerusalem conquer Jesus and his crowd, "killing many of them, while the rest fled to the mountains."[16]

And then there is the very strange, and long, rendering of the *Testimonium Flavianum* found not in *Antiquities of the Jews,* but in the so called Slavonic version of Josephus's *War of the Jews*—a later, and in many respects different, and often discredited, adaptation of Josephus's work, which contains several passages on Jesus. In the Slavonic *Testimonium,* we find the following lines about him:

And many of the people followed and listened to his [Jesus's] teachings. And many souls were aroused, thinking that by him the Jewish tribes would free themselves from the hands of the Romans.

But it was his habit rather to remain in front of the city on the Mount of Olives; and there he also [freely] gave cures to people. And there 150 servants and a multitude of people joined him, seeing his power [and] how by word he did everything he wished.

They bade him enter the city, kill the Roman troops and Pilate, and reign over these.

But he did not care [to do so].

Later, when news of this came to the Jewish leaders, they assembled to the chief priests and said, "We are powerless and [too] weak to oppose the Romans, like a slackened bow. Let us go and inform Pilate what we have heard; and we shall be free of anxiety; if at some time he shall hear [of this] from others, we shall be deprived of [our] property, ourselves slaughtered, and [our] children exiled."

And they went and informed Pilate. And he sent and killed many of the people and brought in that wonder-worker. After inquiring about him, Pilate understood that he was a doer of good, not of evil, [and] not a rebel nor one desirous of kingship, and he released him.[17]

Although, according to this version of the *Testimonium,* Jesus is later crucified (after people conspire to have him caught), this does not happen after the slaughtering of the multitude on the Mount of Olives. After this tumultuous event, he is set free.

A mystifying pronouncement on the same theme can be found in the following second century statement by Celsus (who quotes a fictitious Jew on Jesus):

After we had convicted him, and condemned him as deserving of punishment, [he] was found attempting to conceal himself, and endeavouring to escape in a most disgraceful manner, and [he] was betrayed by those whom he called disciples . . .[18]

Celsus was a fierce opponent of Christianity, something which comes through in this quote. But he is also one of the absolutely earliest non-biblical sources we have on Jesus—having written as early as 175 CE. Filtering out the polemical aspects of this paragraph, we are still left with the perplexing question: from where did Celsus get the information that Jesus was first captured, then managed to escape, and then was betrayed? A sequence of events almost identical to that of the pro-Christian Slavonic *Testimonium,*[19] but absent in the traditional *Testimonium Flavianum,* or in the Gospels.

Unless it is this event that the Gospel of John 10:39–40 hints at: "Then they tried to arrest him again, but he escaped from their hands. He went away again across the Jordan to the place where John had been baptizing earlier, and he remained there."[20]

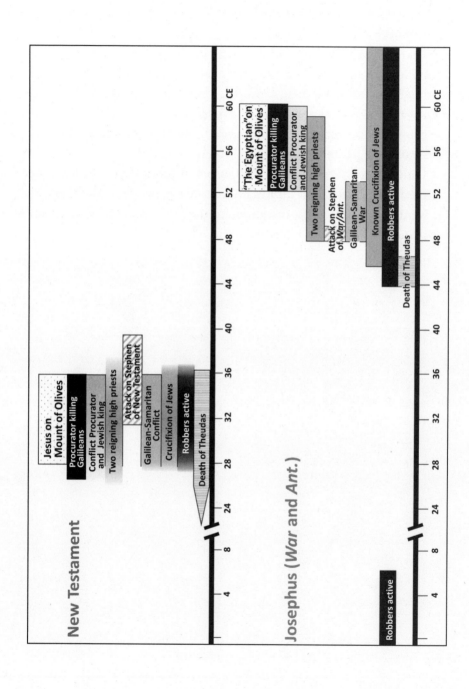

THE NEW TESTAMENT, "THE EGYPTIAN," AND THE SICARII

JUDGING BY JOSEPHUS'S NARRATIVE, "THE EGYPTIAN" WAS DEFEATED IN 55 CE, at the earliest, since Nero had already become Roman emperor.[1] After this defeat, Josephus tells us, "the Egyptian" vanished and "did not appear any more." Despite this, the name of this messianic leader appears again, toward the end of Felix's reign. It is not in the works of Josephus, however, but in the New Testament—in Acts 21:38— that we suddenly read: "Then you are not the Egyptian who recently stirred up a revolt and led the four thousand Sicarii out into the wilderness?" The person the question is directed to is Paul, who has just been discovered in the Jerusalem Temple. No further explanation for this question is given. Nor has "the Egyptian" been mentioned in the New Testament texts prior to this, or later. And it is only here, in Acts, that "the Egyptian" is associated with the Sicarii. Josephus makes no mention of this.

Is Acts wrong about this? Not necessarily. Josephus, after all, writes that "there sprang up another sort of robbers in Jerusalem, which were called Sicarii" at the very time when "the Egyptian" was active, during the procuratorship of Felix.[2] So at least in theory, Acts could here be providing accurate historical information—which its author could not have acquired from Josephus.

The question is, however: why does the author of Acts find it imperative to mention not only "the Egyptian," but also his association with the Sicarii?

Let us briefly take a closer look at this radical rebel faction, the Sicarii. What was their actual role in the fight against Rome? Well, if Josephus is correct when he indicates, as he seems to in *War*, that the Sicarii were the heirs of Judas the Galilean—the instigator of the tax revolt during the census of 6 CE—but that they reappeared again only in the 50s, one might say that they created the frame around the Jewish struggle against Rome. The beginning and the end. Because the Sicarii would come to play a pivotal role also in the final struggle, the Jewish War.

When war broke out, in 66 CE, the triggering event was not a violent one, but was—as so often—of a religious nature. It started when the captain of the Temple, Eleazar, son of High Priest Ananias, admonished those who officiated at the Temple service to abandon the sacrifice for the wellbeing of the Roman emperor. This aggravated not so much the Romans as the leading citizens of Jerusalem, who were terrified of the Roman response. These leading citizens begged of those who ministered about the Temple to abstain from such provocations. But they were not listened to, and the multitude supported the defiance of Eleazar and the priests. The leading citizens then requested aid from Jewish King Agrippa II, who ruled the northeastern region and parts of Galilee. The king sent troops to Jerusalem, and they entered into a fight with what had now turned into a rebel force under Eleazar, the captain of the Temple. Perhaps Eleazar's men had been destined for defeat, if it were not for the fact that they were now joined by a particularly radical faction among the Jewish rebels, namely the Sicarii. The Sicarii are at this very point headed by a very charismatic leader by the name of Menahem, who, according to Josephus, is "the son of Judas, that was called the Galilean."[3]

The Sicarii have just conquered a very important spot in the Judean desert, the hilltop fortress of Masada. As Josephus writes:

> And at this time it was that some of those that principally excited the people to go to war made an assault upon a certain fortress called Masada. They took it by treachery, and slew the Romans that were there, and put others of their own party to keep it.[4]

Menahem and his Sicarii men would from Masada bring back heavy Roman weaponry. The king's troops were now chased away, and the rebels burned the palaces of both High Priest Ananias, and that of King Agrippa II and his sister (and likely mistress) Bernice, as well as the archives of the moneylenders ("that they might persuade the poorer sort to join in their insurrection"). They also seized the Fortress of Antonia, next to the Temple, where the Roman garrison was stationed, and they "took the garrison, and slew them, and set the citadel on fire." With this, the war is ignited.[5]

The two rebel groupings—the one under Eleazar, and the Sicarii under Menahem—would soon, however, enter into competition with each other. Menahem demanded the leadership role, entered the Temple in royal robes, as a Messiah, and had (former?) High Priest Ananias killed. But the Sicarii would soon lose this power struggle against the bigger rebel faction, and Menahem was himself tortured and killed. After this, the Sicarii no longer seemed to play the dominant role in the war against Rome.

But they were tenacious, and they would regroup. As mentioned, the Sicarii had just before the outbreak of the war captured, and ensconced themselves on, a spot which would eventually acquire immense symbolic meaning: the desert rock Masada, next to the Dead Sea. They will have this desolate rock all through the war as their base, and under the leadership of Menahem's relative Eleazar, the son of Jairus (not to be confused with Eleazar, Captain of the Temple), they will eventually constitute the last hold-out against Rome, on Masada, where they are finally defeated in the year 73 CE.

So was "the Egyptian" a Sicarii leader? What speaks against this is that he does not seem to have been of kin to Judas the Galilean—which most Sicarii leaders were. And Josephus's words, "there came out of Egypt about this time," seem to imply that this messianic leader is someone coming from the outside. Furthermore, Josephus makes no mention of "the Egyptian" being affiliated with this group. The only information of such an affiliation comes from Acts.

On the other hand, why would Acts provide this information? And from where did the author get it?

CHRONOLOGICAL ENIGMA TEN: JOHN THE BAPTIST

LET US NOW TURN TO THE OTHER MAJOR MESSIANIC LEADER PRESENTED in the Gospels, the person described as Jesus's teacher and forerunner: John the Baptist, the man who baptizes Jesus by the Jordan River. How does he fit into the emerging picture?

The prominence of John the Baptist is so great in the New Testament that all the Gospels except Matthew start with a description not of Jesus, but of John. And also in Matthew, an account of the missionary activity of John the Baptist fills up most of chapter three. At the same time, however, John seems to be a complication to the Gospel authors; he must be deferred to, and at the same time he must be diminished. Thus, in introducing John, the Synoptic Gospels quote Isaiah: "See, I am sending my messenger ahead of you, who will prepare your way; the voice of one crying out in the wilderness: 'Prepare the way of the Lord, make his paths straight.'"[1] And in the Gospel of John it says: "He himself was not the light, but he came to testify to the light."[2] The man at the top of the Gospel narratives is simply a messenger of someone greater than himself: Jesus. To make this even clearer, all four Gospels have John the Baptist proclaim his own lesser importance than the man from Nazareth, who comes to the river Jordan to be baptized by him: "I am not," says John, "worthy to stoop down and untie the thong of his sandals."[3]

Who, then, was this forerunner, whose place in history was so impossible to ignore?

The one Gospel which gives a description of John's origins is Luke. According to this account, John's mother Elizabeth was a relative of Mary, the mother of Jesus. And the mothers appear to be pregnant simultaneously (Mary is told she will give birth to a son conceived with the Holy Spirit, upon which she travels to see Elizabeth, who is then six months pregnant with John. Mary herself seems to be already pregnant at this point, since Elizabeth, when she meets her, exclaims: "Blessed are you among women, and blessed is the fruit of your womb"[4]).

All the other Gospels introduce John the Baptist when he begins his mission. He appears "in the wilderness, proclaiming a baptism of repentance for the forgiveness of sins."[5] And "the people of Jerusalem and all Judea were going out to him, and all the region along the Jordan, and they were baptized by him in the river Jordan, confessing their sins."[6]

John the Baptist is thus described as a man of the desert, of the wilderness. He wore "clothing of camel's hair with a leather belt around his waist, and his food was locusts and wild honey."[7] He lived simply, and he preached simplicity and compassion: "Whoever has two coats must share with anyone who has none; and whoever has food must do likewise."[8] Nevertheless, his message to those who came down to him by the river Jordan was at times harsh, and decidedly eschatological: "Repent, for the Kingdom of Heaven has come near." And to the Sadducees and Pharisees who came to be baptized, he said: "You brood of vipers! Who warned you to flee from the wrath to come? Bear fruit worthy of repentance."[9]

Scholars have traditionally assumed that John was a member of the Essenes, who lived in quiet opposition, and mostly in isolation, in the wilderness. Josephus describes them as one of the major Jewish factions, and unlike "the fourth philosophic sect," the Zealots, whom he despises, Josephus professes admiration for the Essenes: "Yet is their course of life better than that of other men."[10] Although Jews by confession, the Essenes rejected the leadership establishment at the Temple in Jerusalem. And very atypically for a Jewish faction, they were mostly celibate.

After introducing John the Baptist's missionary activity, all four Gospels proceed to describe how Jesus comes down to the river Jordan, to be baptized. The reason is not stated, except in the apocryphal Gospel according to the Hebrews, where it says that the mother and brothers of Jesus tell him to come with them, as "John Baptist baptizes for the remission of sins." To this, Jesus responds: "What sin have I committed that I should go and be baptized by him? Unless, haply, the very words which I have said are only ignorance."[11] At any rate, this is the first time any of the Gospels introduces us to Jesus as an adult, and Luke states that he is then about thirty years old.[12] After being baptized, Jesus spends forty days in the wilderness (*eremia*), resisting temptation. It is not clearly stated that he begins his own missionary work immediately after this. The Synoptic Gospels—at least Mark and Matthew—indicate that he started preaching only after John the Baptist was arrested (in the Gospel of John it is implied that both of them carry out baptisms for a while in parallel, and possibly in competition).[13]

So what do we know about the arrest of John the Baptist?

The Gospels tell us that he was imprisoned by order of the authorities. But not the authorities of Judea, which is where John the Baptist was active; curiously, it is Herod Antipas, tetrarch of Galilee and Perea, who orders his arrest. Herod Antipas feels insulted by John's criticism of his having taken his brother Philip's wife Herodias as his mistress and later wife.[14] And as Mark and Matthew tell us, the punishment that Herod Antipas bestows upon John does not stop at imprisonment: at a party to celebrate the birthday of the tetrarch, Herodias's daughter performs a dance. Herod Antipas is so delighted that he tells his stepdaughter she may have anything she wishes. After consulting with her mother, the girl comes back and says: "Give me the head of John the Baptist here on a platter." The tetrarch, although reluctantly, orders a soldier to go to the prison and chop off John's head. "The head was brought on a platter and given to the girl, who brought it to her mother."[15]

The scene is macabre enough to have inspired many artistic endeavors through the ages—from paintings to opera. And the parallel with a reluctant Pilate ordering the execution of Jesus is obvious.

From the events described, we can deduce that John the Baptist must have been an important person in his own time—not only because he, judging by the Gospels, threatened the authorities, but also because of his prominent placement in the New Testament. Prominent, and yet problematic—present as if by obligation. In fact, John the Baptist is considered one of the best examples of the so called "criterion of embarrassment" for authenticity. This criterion holds that if, say, a story in the New Testament gives cause for embarrassment on the part of those who are telling it, then this is a sign of likely authenticity—because the narrators would have had no reason to make it up.[16] The Gospel authors are at pains to diminish John in relation to Jesus, and yet, they can not ignore him, presumably because of his fame and importance.

The question then is: do we find John the Baptist also in non-biblical contemporary sources? Is he described by Flavius Josephus?

Perhaps he is. Or perhaps he isn't.

Let us start with the reason the Gospels provide for John's arrest and decapitation: his criticism of Herod Antipas for taking his brother's wife. Do we find this described in Josephus writings?

No, but we find something similar.

In Book 18 of his *Antiquities of the Jews*, Josephus writes about a quarrel between Herod Antipas and the king of the Nabateans, Aretas. The quarrel concerns the love life of Herod Antipas. Antipas was married to the daughter of Aretas. But on a visit to Rome, he had stayed with his brother, and fell in love with the brother's wife, Herodias. With her consent, Herod Antipas decided to marry her, and divorce Aretas' daughter. Aretas became infuriated, and prepared for war. "And when they had joined battle," writes Josephus, "all Herod's army was destroyed."

So according to Josephus's account, it is Aretas, not John the Baptist, who is infuriated at Herod Antipas for marrying Herodias.

So what happens next? What happens, according to Josephus, is that Herod Antipas contacts Emperor Tiberius, who becomes very angry at Aretas, and orders the governor of Syria, Vitellius, to make war on Aretas, "and either to take him alive, and bring him to him in bonds, or to kill him, and send him his head."[17]

Thus, someone *is* really threatened with decapitation on account of this quarrel—but again, it is not John the Baptist. It is Aretas. So far, John the Baptist is conspicuous by his absence.

But then follows this paragraph in Josephus's text:

> Now some of the Jews thought that the destruction of Herod's army came from God, and that very justly, as a punishment of what he did against John, that was called the Baptist: for Herod slew him, who was a good man, and commanded the Jews to exercise virtue, both as to righteousness towards one another, and piety towards God, and so to come to baptism [. . .] Now when others came in crowds about him, for they were very greatly moved by hearing his words, Herod, who feared lest the great influence John had over the people might put it into his power and inclination to raise a rebellion (for they seemed ready to do any thing he should advise), thought it best, by putting him to death, to prevent any mischief he might cause, and not bring himself into difficulties, by sparing a man who might make him repent of it when it would be too late. Accordingly he was sent a prisoner, out of Herod's suspicious temper, to Macherus, the castle I before mentioned, and was there put to death. Now the Jews had an opinion that the destruction of this army was sent as a punishment upon Herod, and a mark of God's displeasure to him.[18]

Is this passage in *Antiquities of the Jews* really written by Flavius Josephus? Or is it a later addition to, or modification of, Josephus's text—like the *Testimonium Flavianum* is thought to be?

Well, in this case—the passage on John the Baptist—a majority of scholars seem to think that the text is authentic.[19] There are several reasons put forth:

- Jesus is not mentioned in this passage on John the Baptist. If it had been a later addition—a Christian interpolation, as it is

called—Jesus would surely have been alluded to in relation to
John the Baptist.

- The text differs from—and yet does not contradict—the Gospels in their presentation of John the Baptist.
- In contrast to the *Testimonium Flavianum*, this paragraph is
mentioned by Church Father Origen, in the third century.[20]

There are, however, awkward elements in Josephus's passage on John
the Baptist, elements which would seem to argue against it being
authentic. The problem with Josephus's description of John the Baptist
is that it sticks out. And it sticks out in more ways than one:

- The appearance of John the Baptist is very sudden, considering his implied importance. He is mentioned in one single
passage, where it is stated that God made Herod Antipas lose
a war as a punishment for what he had done to John. But
prior to this, we have never heard of John.
- More importantly, the passage on John disturbs the flow of
the narrative. At the end of the previous paragraph, we are
told how Emperor Tiberius wrote to Vitellius, ordering him
to make war on Aretas.[21] And the paragraph *following* the one
about John the Baptist begins with the following words: "So
Vitellius prepared to make war with Aretas, having with him
two legions of armed men."[22] Clearly, the text would flow
considerably better if the passage on John the Baptist was not
in the middle.
- A couple of chapters later, when Herod Antipas loses power,
Josephus once again writes that God had punished the
tetrarch. But this time God punished him "for giving ear to
the vain discourses of a woman."[23] John the Baptist is not
mentioned.
- In the passage about John the Baptist, Josephus shows an
atypical reverence toward this messianic leader, considering
the contempt with which he treats other charismatic Jewish
religious leaders—such as "the Egyptian," or Theudas. He
calls them "impostors" and "sorcerers."

- That Josephus would use the very explicitly Christian term "the Baptist"—which became the distinctive epithet for John in Christian sources—and leave it unexplained in a work addressed at Greek and Roman readers is perplexing.
- If we were to rely on the information supplied in this passage, John the Baptist would have been killed later than Jesus is assumed to have been killed.
- In the passage about John the Baptist, it says that Herod Antipas sent John to the castle of Macherus to have him put to death. But in the previous passage, Josephus writes that Macherus is controlled not by Herod Antipas, but by Aretas, the man with whom Herod Antipas is at war![24]
- John the Baptist is not at all mentioned in Josephus's previous work, *War of the Jews*, although when it was written in the 70s, John had been dead for several decades. This, incidentally, is the case with all three references to people connected with Jesus. Also the *Testimonium Flavianum* and the passage about James the brother of Jesus are found only in *Antiquities*. In *War of the Jews* (excepting the very late Slavonic version) these three people are not mentioned at all.

In conclusion, although not a majority opinion, there are enough inconsistencies to throw doubt on the authenticity of the passage on John the Baptist, and a number of scholars have.[25]

But were we to assume that this passage in *Antiquities of the Jews* is a later interpolation, we are left with another problem: could Josephus have omitted mentioning John the Baptist? If the "criterion of embarrassment" for authenticity is met—and it certainly would seem to be—then we should expect Josephus to write about John.

But where? And when?

If we look for a time shift applied to the New Testament narrative also in the case of John the Baptist—in line with the pattern that events similar to those described in the New Testament can be found in Josephus, but with a delay of fifteen to twenty years—we should expect Josephus to describe someone similar to John the Baptist in the mid to late 40s CE.

And indeed, he does.

> Now it came to pass, while Fadus was procurator of Judea, that a certain magician, whose name was Theudas, persuaded a great part of the people to take their effects with them, and follow him to the river Jordan; for he told them he was a prophet, and that he would, by his own command, divide the river, and afford them an easy passage over it; and many were deluded by his words. However, Fadus did not permit them to make any advantage of his wild attempt, but sent a troop of horsemen out against them; who, falling upon them unexpectedly, slew many of them, and took many of them alive. They also took Theudas alive, and cut off his head, and carried it to Jerusalem.
>
> *Antiquities of the Jews* 20.97–98

The forerunner of Jesus was John the Baptist. The last major messianic leader to be named by Josephus before the emergence of "the Egyptian" was Theudas. And the similarities of the forerunners are apparent:

- Like John the Baptist, Theudas is a spiritual leader who brings his followers to the Jordan River.
- Like John the Baptist, Theudas is killed by the authorities, and in the same manner: they sever his head.
- Just as the New Testament describes John the Baptist and Jesus in similar terms, so does Josephus describe Theudas and "the Egyptian" in similar terms. Josephus, however, uses negative terms: he talks about them as aspiring prophets (in the case of "the Egyptian," "false prophet"), and he calls both of them "magician" or "sorcerer" (*goes*). This negative portrayal is something to factor in when evaluating the motive behind a possible time shift in the writing of the Gospels.
- In addition, there is a greater logic to the description of the capture of Theudas than to that of John the Baptist: the ruler who had Theudas arrested, Fadus, was indeed procurator of Judea, the province where John the Baptist was active. This is unlike Herod Antipas, who was only the ruler of Galilee and Perea.

So Theudas shares numerous characteristics and experiences with John the Baptist—although fifteen years later.

But if Theudas is really defeated under Procurator Fadus, 44–46 CE, this is at least six years—more likely nine or ten—before "the Egyptian" is defeated on the Mount of Olives. Were we to assume that Theudas is his forerunner, it seems to be a time gap greater than that described between John the Baptist and Jesus in the Gospels, at least with regard to the time of their defeats.

On the other hand, the length of Jesus's ministry varies considerably in the New Testament texts. In none of the Gospels it is as long as six to ten years, but the mere fact that one year in the Synoptic Gospels is portrayed as perhaps as many as four in the Gospel of John would seem to indicate that the length of his ministry is at least open to interpretation. One of the earliest church fathers, Irenaeus (ca. 130–200), in fact, claims that Jesus was active for many years, and says that he gleaned his information from people who met with the apostles long after Jesus's crucifixion.[26]

And then we have this statement by Origen, another one of the very early church fathers, born already in the second century: "For the Jews do not connect John with Jesus, nor the punishment of John with that of Christ."[27]

One intriguing thing, of course, is the fact that the name Theudas is mentioned not only by Josephus, but also, as we have noted, in Acts.

But so is the name "the Egyptian."

The question is why.

We shall discuss this in the next chapter.

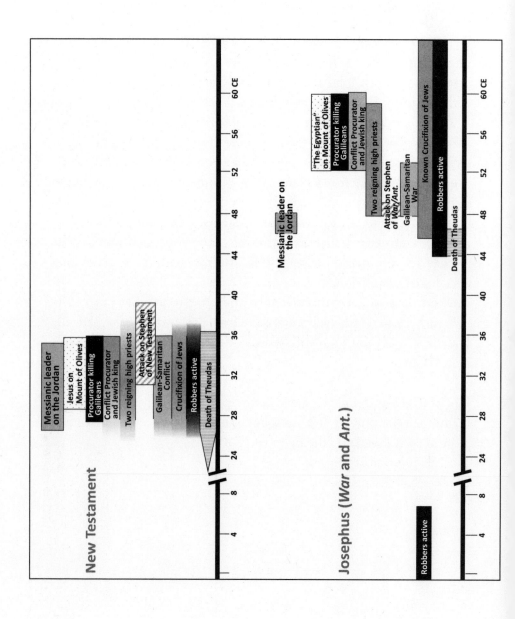

WRITING ON TWO LEVELS

THE AUTHOR OF ACTS, THE FIFTH BOOK OF THE NEW TESTAMENT, CURI-ously manages to mention three of the major messianic rebel leaders of the first century: Judas the Galilean, Theudas, and "the Egyptian." In all three instances, the person is thrown into the New Testament narrative, without much context. And in all three instances the name is mentioned only once. Theudas and Judas the Galilean are brought up in connection with the apostles being interrogated by the Sanhedrin—but we are not told who these two men are.[1] "The Egyptian" is mentioned in connection with Paul's arrest in Jerusalem—but we are not told who he is.[2]

This random dropping of names seems inexplicable, when the names are taken one by one. Taken together, they may form a pattern: all three men are, after all, messianic rebel leaders. And if we look beyond names, to events, the pattern of dropping rebellion-related references becomes even more noticeable. Remember that Luke (considered to be the author also of Acts) defines the time of Jesus's birth by an event—the tax census—that in the chronicles of Josephus is significant for one reason only: it heralds the birth of the organized anti-Roman rebel movement.[3] As Josephus scholar Steve Mason points out:

"Josephus places great emphasis on this early rebellion as a prototype of the later revolt [. . .] the census is not mentioned in passing by Josephus; it is for him a watershed event in recent Jewish history."[4]

That Luke in this instance mentions the tax census without mentioning the rebellion is eye-catching. Whereas in Acts, the author does mention that Judas the Galilean rose up "at the time of the census," in Luke he only links the census to the birth of Jesus.[5] The birth of the anti-Roman resistance movement has been replaced by the birth of Jesus.

Once again, the rebels seem to be present in the New Testament, but mostly as a subtext.

Could it be that the New Testament was written on two levels, one obvious, one concealed?

If so, there was most certainly a contemporaneous precedent for this.

The century before the fall of Jerusalem was a time of intense scriptural interpretation. This is seen not least in the Dead Sea Scrolls, which were first discovered in caves at Qumran, in the Judean Desert, in the late 1940s, and which have traditionally been linked to the Essenes. The scrolls contain some of the oldest copies of sections from the Hebrew bible ever found. And a recurring phenomenon in some of these scrolls—presumably mostly written between the second century BCE and the time of the Jewish War against Rome—is biblical quotations followed by their assumed interpretation, or *pesher* (sometimes compared to later rabbinic biblical interpretation, found in so called *midrash*).[6] The *pesher* is considered to be divinely inspired, and perhaps on par with the biblical passage itself. It, in fact, builds on the assumption that the true, or at least full, meaning of the biblical passage is *lost* without the interpretation. The writers of the Qumran interpretations believed that scripture was written on two levels: one obvious, one concealed—to be interpreted—and that everything in the text had a hidden, foretold, eschatological meaning, relevant to the tumultuous times when the interpretation—rather than the biblical passage itself—was written.[7] The problem was how to find this hidden meaning. Sometimes it was done through allegory; that is, a biblical narrative became metaphorical when interpreted, and thus was transformed into a parable. The biblical verse Habakkuk 2:17, for instance, describes how the Chaldeans will be punished for having destroyed the lands of Lebanon, and the city, and for having killed the animals. The interpretation provided in the *Habakkuk pesher* of the Dead Sea Scrolls is that "Lebanon" is the Council of the Community, "the animals" are "the simple ones of Judah, who observe the Law," "the city" is Jerusalem, and the perpetrator is the so called "Wicked Priest"—an unidentified opponent of the community and its leader, the "Teacher of Righteousness" (an equally unidentified central figure and organizer of the Qumran community).[8]

Essentially, both the original biblical text, and the interpretation, *pesher*, were given by divine revelation—the biblical text, containing an unrevealed mystery, to the biblical prophet, but the full explanation, the interpretation of the text, only to the Teacher of Righteousness, and from him to his disciples. To those who had understood the hidden, full meaning of the scriptural text, a new world was revealed. All others, it was assumed, remained in darkness.

Although there is not much to suggest that Jesus (or, for that matter, John the Baptist, as has been proposed by some[9]) was identical to the Teacher of Righteousness of the Qumran sect, both the eschatological content of many of the Qumran texts, and the concept of overt versus hidden meaning in the prophetic narrative find echoes in the New Testament. A mystical, and eschatological, approach to scripture, and life, may have been a common response to the existential uncertainties of the times. From the Gospels—particularly Matthew 13, Mark 4 and 8, and Luke 8—we see that also Jesus admonishes his disciples to look at the deeper level of his parables, for the hidden story: "Do you still not perceive or understand? Are your hearts hardened? Do you have eyes, and fail to see? Do you have ears, and fail to hear?"[10] We read, for instance, of how Jesus speaks to a crowd, surrounded by his disciples:

> When a great crowd gathered and people from town after town came to him, he said in a parable: "A sower went out to sow his seed; and as he sowed, some fell on the path and was trampled on, and the birds of the air ate it up. Some fell on the rock; and as it grew up, it withered for lack of moisture. Some fell among thorns,

and the thorns grew with it and choked it. Some fell into good soil, and when it grew, it produced a hundredfold." As he said this, he called out, "Let anyone with ears to hear listen!"

Then his disciples asked him what this parable meant. He said, "To you it has been given to know the secrets of the kingdom of God; but to others I speak in parables, so that 'looking they may not perceive, and listening they may not understand.'"[11]

It is perhaps not a far-fetched idea that also the narrative describing the life of Jesus, the master of parables, would utilize this technique of writing on two levels: one obvious, one hidden, to be interpreted. It is noteworthy that when we do see parallels between Josephus's accounts and the New Testament, almost every word in the New Testament text seems to bear significance. But the action is sometimes modified—or even completely reversed. In at least two situations which have been related in this book, a pacifist action in the Gospels closely corresponds to a more violent one in Josephus's accounts: when the Galileans react to the hostility in the Samaritan village ("'Lord, do you want us to command fire to come down from heaven and consume them?' But he turned and rebuked them. Then they went on to another village"[12]); and when Jesus meets his adversaries on the Mount of Olives ("Suddenly, one of those with Jesus put his hand on his sword, drew it, and struck the slave of the high priest, cutting off his ear. Then Jesus said to him, 'Put your sword back into its place; for all who take the sword will perish by the sword'" [13]).

One could, however, see that yet another, perhaps unveiling, level is introduced when the word "robber" is thrown into the Gospel narrative ("Have you come out with swords and clubs to arrest me as though I were a robber?" Jesus says when he is arrested[14]), and a similar, seemingly contradictory, move is seen in Jesus's admonition to the disciples that "the one who has no sword must sell his cloak and buy one," or when he says: "You must not think I have come to bring peace to the earth; I have not come to bring peace, but a sword."[15] If indeed the New Testament narrative is written on different levels, it would appear that whenever the story is disguised on one level, it is opened up on another. Another example of this may be the reversal of the order of

Theudas and Judas the Galilean in Acts 5:36–37. The mentioning of Theudas as a precursor to the apostles could be interpreted as a disclosing subtext—revealing that the apostles were active after the time of Fadus (44–46 CE). And the ensuing mention of Judas as Theudas's successor, rather than predecessor, as a disguise, aimed at hiding the previous disclosure. In light of his evident knowledge of the political events of the period, it is hard to believe that the author of Luke-Acts would not have known that Judas the Galilean—who started the census revolt at the time of Jesus's birth—was active long before Theudas.

Finally, there may be parallels within the New Testament itself that become visible only after a time shift has been assumed: note, for instance, that Acts 21:38 mentions "the Egyptian" leading "four thousand" into the "wilderness," whereas Matthew 15 and Mark 8 mention Jesus leading "four thousand" into the "wilderness" (*eremia, eremos*).

The New Testament accounts by themselves do not provide the reader with enough information to elucidate anything but the obvious story. Occasional oddities, such as the name-dropping of rebel leaders, or Jesus's admonition to his disciples to buy swords, remain unexplained. It is only when we put the accounts of Josephus next to those of the New Testament that certain similarities, and possible underlying patterns of storytelling, can be discerned. The relevance of these similarities is of course open to interpretation. In some cases—for instance when the only similarity is a common name—it is fairly meaningless to attribute any significance to this. It is when two factors or more coincide that the probability of a true association increases, and the likelihood of the similarities being just coincidental significantly decreases.

Thus, when evaluating each parallel between the New Testament and Josephus, it has to be looked at with a statistical eye: How many coinciding elements are there for each suggested parallel? How many diverging elements? How unique are the coinciding elements? To what extent do the different parallels form a pattern? And do the diverging elements for each parallel *also* form a pattern, i.e. do they co-vary?

Let us look at an example: Stephen. In this case, the name is unique in each source. In addition, central to the narrative in both the New Testament and Josephus, is that both men named Stephen are attacked by a crowd, that both attacks happen on a road outside Jerusalem, and that both attacks initiate a period of violence. Those are four strong coinciding elements—especially in light of the unusual name—but they have to be weighed against the diverging elements: the described identities of the victim and of the attackers, and the time when the attack takes place.

Is there, then, a pattern also to the diverging elements? Something which makes the disagreeing factors of a piece?

With regard to the hypothesis explored in this book, there is so far one consistent diverging element when comparing the New Testament accounts and the suggested parallels in the works of Josephus: time. The events presented in the Gospels mainly occur in the late 20s and 30s. The suggested parallel events presented in the works of Josephus occur from 44 CE to the mid-50s, thus in a different era. On the other hand: the time shift is uniform. In other words, when we find parallels to the Gospel accounts in Josephus's works, these are not spread out all over his books, one here, one there. Instead, the vast majority are found in a narrow historical period, in each of his two major works: in Book 20 of *Antiquities*, in Book 2 of *War*. That is, they are consistently found with a specific delay, of about fifteen to twenty years.

Furthermore, although rarely overtly so in the Gospel accounts, the parallels found in Josephus's chronicles almost invariably concern themselves with one issue: rebel activity.

Still, and this has to be remembered: in the presentation of this hypothesis, and throughout this book, we are dealing with varying degrees of likelihood, never with absolute certainties.

And in the next chapter, we shall look at some examples where the parallelism is quite ambiguous—and yet difficult to entirely dismiss.

CHRONOLOGICAL ENIGMA ELEVEN: THE RAISING OF THE DEAD

IN THE GOSPELS, THERE ARE THREE INSTANCES WHERE JESUS IS RAIS-ing someone from the dead. The first one concerns the daughter of Jairus, a tale which we find in Mark, Luke, and—without the mentioning of the name Jairus—also in Matthew.[1] The second case is the raising of Lazarus, found in the Gospel of John.[2] And the third one is the raising of the son of the widow from Nain, found in the Gospel of Luke.[3]

Let us start with the resurrection of the daughter of Jairus: when Jesus is preaching in the Galilee, a man named Jairus, "one of the leaders of the synagogue," approaches him, falls at his feet, and begs him repeatedly, "My little daughter is at the point of death. Come and lay your hands on her, so that she may be made well, and live." Right after this—and in all three Synoptic Gospels—we are told of a woman who had been suffering from hemorrhages for twelve years:

> She had endured much under many physicians, and had spent all that she had; and she was no better, but rather grew worse. She had heard about Jesus, and came up behind him in the crowd and touched his cloak, for she said, "If I but touch his clothes, I will

be made well." Immediately her hemorrhage stopped; and she felt in her body that she was healed of her disease.[4]

In the meantime, the daughter of Jairus—who, incidentally, "was twelve years of age"—is said to have died. But when Jesus comes to their house, he claims that the child is "not dead but sleeping," and goes on to heal, or resuscitate, her. "And immediately the girl got up and began to walk about."

The connection between the twelve-year-old dying girl and the woman who has been suffering for twelve years is thus made in all three Synoptic Gospels: Mark, Matthew, and Luke.

In the Gospel of John, however, we do not at all see the tale of Jairus's daughter. Instead, we find the raising of Lazarus (Eleazar, in Hebrew). In this story, Jesus is informed by two women whom he knows that their brother, Lazarus, is ill. But Jesus delays for two days, and then tells his disciples: "Our friend Lazarus has fallen asleep, but I am going there to awaken him." When Jesus arrives, he is met by one of the despondent sisters, who tells him that Lazarus is already dead and buried. But he answers her: "Your brother will rise again." After removing the stone from the grave, Jesus cries: "Lazarus, come out!" The dead man emerges, wrapped in cloth.

The story of the raising of Lazarus is not found in Mark, Matthew, or Luke—where instead we find the raising of Jairus' daughter.

But beside the actual resurrection, the accounts do bear some additional similarities:

- In both cases, Jesus is summoned by the relatives of the dying person.
- In both cases, Jesus first says that the person is sleeping.
- In both cases, when Jesus arrives, he is met by crying and mourning relatives.
- In both cases, Jesus tells the dead person to get up or come out.
- In both cases, the person immediately gets up and walks.

The fact that the story of the resurrection of Jairus' daughter is missing in the Gospel of John, and is replaced by the similar story of the resurrection of Lazarus, has led some to suggest that the daughter of Jairus could be identical to Lazarus. And that Lazarus, thus, was Lazarus son of Jairus—Eleazar son of Jairus.[5] If it were to be true—and this, of course, is mere speculation—an alternate underlying narrative would immediately spring to mind: Eleazar son of Jairus was a *Sicarius*, and the last of the rebel leaders of the Jewish realm, the man who led the final Jewish defense in the War against Rome, on the hilltop fortress of Masada. He was, according to Josephus, "of kin to Menahem," who in turn was son, or grandson, of Judas the Galilean.[6]

In the Gospels, the man named Jairus is said to be "one of the leaders of the synagogue"; his child, who is twelve years old, is near death, at the same time as a woman has been hemorrhaging for twelve years. If there is any symbolism in this tale, the twelve years of suffering, and the subsequent redemption must be significant.

When "the Egyptian" emerges on the scene, in the 50s, discontent and anti-Roman resistance has been brewing for somewhere between eight and fourteen years—ever since King Agrippa I died. Not long after Agrippa's death, two sons of Judas the Galilean, Simon and Jacob, were crucified, and Theudas was decapitated. After that, the tumults only increased. But no major Jewish spiritual leader has emerged. Not until "the Egyptian." Soon, also the surviving relatives of Judas the Galilean—Menahem and Eleazar son of Jairus—will come out of hibernation. It is easy to see an analogy between the Gospel accounts—of Jesus saving the twelve-year-suffering woman, and resuscitating the twelve-year-old child of Jairus—and the suffering people of Judea and Galilee longing for deliverance. It is possible to take the analogy even further, to identify particular individuals, even if only for symbolic purposes—if Lazarus is the child of Jairus. "Eleazar son of Jairus" would fit right into our narrative, as would the twelve years of suffering, and the longing for deliverance through a messianic leader.

But how strong are these parallels? Are we merely inventing analogies here? Or are the similarities enough to warrant consideration? Again, this must depend on the number, and uniqueness, of the coinciding factors we find. In the case of Lazarus and Eleazar son of Jairus we tread on fairly thin ice, since we actually do not know that Lazarus and the daughter of Jairus are the same person. We only know that one of them is raised from the dead in three Gospels whereas the other one is raised from the dead in the fourth one. And "Jairus" by itself is simply too common a name to make an analogy. Not to speak of "Eleazar."

But then we have the third tale of Jesus raising someone from the dead. We find it in Luke:

> Soon afterwards he [Jesus] went to a town called Nain, and his disciples and a large crowd went with him. As he approached the gate of the town, a man who had died was being carried out. He was his mother's only son, and she was a widow; and with her was a large crowd from the town.
>
> When the Lord saw her, he had compassion for her and said to her, "Do not weep."
>
> Then he came forward and touched the bier, and the bearers stood still. And he said, "Young man, I say to you, rise!"
>
> The dead man sat up and began to speak, and Jesus gave him to his mother.[7]

Curiously, this last resurrection—of the son of the widow from Nain—also provides a name which, in Josephus's chronicles, is linked to a rebel leader.

Simon bar Giora, one of the major leaders of the Jewish War, made the small village of Nain his base.[8] Indeed, this is the only context in which Josephus mentions this village in his chronicles.

Again, we have little more than the name of an obscure village, and the emergence—"revival"—of another rebel leader in the Jewish War against Rome. Is this enough to make an analogy between Luke's text and that of Josephus? Hardly, if the only common element is the village name. With the further association of yet another rebel leader, it could be part of a pattern.

In fact, the New Testament provides us with even more rebel associated names. In one single verse, Acts 13:1, we find three, or possibly even four, such names, lumped together: "Now in the church at Antioch there were prophets and teachers: Barnabas, Simeon who was called Niger, Lucius of Cyrene, Manaen, who had been brought up with Herod the Tetrarch, and Saul."

Niger was the name of one of the main commanders in the beginning and middle of the Jewish revolt.[9] And Cyrene (a name that appears in several places in the New Testament[10]) was a city in North Africa—in present-day Libya—where, after the end of the Jewish War, many of the fleeing Sicarii settled. In the final chapter of the final book of *War of the Jews*, Josephus writes: "And now did the madness of the Sicarii, like a disease, reach as far as the cities of Cyrene."[11] And Manaen? Manaen is the Greek form of the Hebrew name Menahem.[12] Menahem, in the works of Josephus, was the Sicarii leader who at the beginning of the Jewish War captured Masada. Being a Galilean, he could be said to have been "brought up with Herod the Tetrarch," the then ruler of Galilee. Josephus does mention two other Menahem in his works, one of them a king in the eighth century BCE, the second an Essene, born perhaps a century before Jesus.[13]

Finally, we come to the fourth name, Barnabas, later missionary partner of Saul/Paul. When Barnabas is first mentioned in Acts, he is introduced in the following way: "Barnabas (which means 'son of Parakleseos')." The translation given is usually "son of consolation," or "son of comfort." [14] *Parakletos* means paraclete, comforter, helper. In Hebrew, the word for "paraclete, comforter" is *Menahem*. And so Barnabas name could be read as "son of Menahem."

Is there a connection? Or are these coincidences?

Well, there is only one Niger in all of Josephus's chronicles, and only one Niger in the Bible, so that would seem to be significant. Cyrene is of course more common. And Manaen or Menahem is also not unique.[15] But adding to this, all the names are in Josephus's texts connected with Jewish rebel activity, and all the names are in Acts listed in the same sentence, where it is stated that they belong to one and the same grouping—in this case "the church at Antioch."

But even if we were to accept that the conglomeration of four such rebel associated names in one single sentence is hard to simply dismiss, we could not thereby say that this fits with the time shift pattern that we have up until now seen.

Because these last names are not names that in Josephus's chronicles appear in the 40s or 50s. They appear during another period of intense rebellious activity: the Jewish War, 66–73 CE.

Yes, it is certainly a period associated with insurrection.
But it is a different period.

Before we write these last parallels off, however, let us look at two more episodes. Two episodes where people or events described in the New Testament appear to resemble people or events described by Josephus—but during the Jewish War.

The first one concerns one of the resistance fighters we have already become acquainted with: Simon bar Giora, commander of the fortress at the village of Nain.

CHRONOLOGICAL ENIGMA TWELVE:
THE MAD MAN FROM GERASA

SIMON WAS ONE OF THE MOST SIGNIFICANT REBEL LEADERS OF THE Jewish War; he was one of the two, in fact, who finally surrendered Jerusalem to the Romans, in 70 CE. The other one was John of Gischala, known to us as the arch-enemy of Josephus.

Simon was, according to Josephus, known for his superior bodily strength and courage. He was born, not in Nain, but further to the east, in the town of Gerasa—a place we also recognize from the New Testament.[1] His name, bar Giora, in Aramaic means "son of a proselyte." Indeed, Gerasa was a city of mixed population.

Simon first distinguished himself during the Jewish War in the autumn of 66, when, as a young man, he led a successful action against Roman troops under the legate of Syria, Cestius Gallus.[2] He subsequently withdrew from center-stage, and, according to Josephus, "betook himself to ravage the country." [3]

It seems, from Josephus's description, that Simon at a certain point cooperated with the Sicarii. Not long after the beginning of the war, he arrived at Masada, the Sicarii stronghold. "At first," writes Josephus, "they suspected him, and only permitted him to come with the women he brought with him into the lower part of the fortress, while they dwelt in the upper part of it themselves. However, his manner so well agreed with theirs, and he seemed so trusty a man, that he went out with them, and ravaged and destroyed the country with them about Masada. Yet when he persuaded them to undertake greater things, he could not prevail with them so to do; for as they were accustomed to dwell in that citadel, they were afraid of going far from that which was their hiding-place."[4]

So Simon left the Sicarii, and grew in strength, "so that his army was no longer composed of slaves and robbers, but a great many of the populace were obedient to him as to their king." Now needing a base from which to act, Simon "built a wall at a certain village called Nain, and made use of that as a fortress for his own party's security."[5]

From his base in Nain, Simon conquers the Idumeans, "and did not only ravage the cities and villages, but laid waste the whole country . . . so was there nothing left behind Simon's army but a desert."[6] But his violent rampages create fear in a competing rebel grouping, the Zealots in Jerusalem. So in an ambush, they seize his wife and her entourage, hoping that Simon will lay down his arms, and make an appeal to them for the wife.

But this is not how Simon responds. Instead, he rushes to Jerusalem, "and like wild beasts when they are wounded, and cannot overtake those that wounded them, he vented his spleen upon all persons that he met with. Accordingly, he caught all those that were come out of the city gates, either to gather herbs or sticks, who were unarmed and in years; he then tormented them and destroyed them, out of the immense rage he was in, and was almost ready to taste the very flesh of their dead bodies."[7] The wife is now set free, and Simon retreats. But he soon returns to Jerusalem, and is at this point—to their later regret—invited in by citizens hoping to be saved from the equally violent Zealot group led by John of Gischala. "Now it was God who turned their opinions to the worst advice," writes Josephus, "and thence they devised such a remedy to get themselves free, as was worse than the disease itself."[8]

There will soon be three major rebel factions inside the walls of Jerusalem: Simon bar Giora's, John of Gischala's, and a break-away Zealot faction under the leadership of one Eleazar son of Simon, who has seized the inner court of the Temple. And these three factions proceed to butcher each other. During the fighting that ensues, Eleazar's men are at the highest point, John's are below them, and Simon's are even further down. "And the same advantage that Eleazar and his party had over him [John], since he was beneath them, the same advantage had he [John], by his higher situation, over Simon."[9] The rebels kill each other and the populace mercilessly. On top of this, almost all the food supplies of the city are burnt, supplies that would have allowed them to sustain a prolonged siege. And in this bloodbath, the civilians of Jerusalem have absolutely nowhere to go. This is how Josephus describes their plight:

> Loyal citizens, for their part, were in dire despondency and alarm, having no opportunity for planning any change of policy, no hope of coming to terms or of flight, if they had the will; for watch was kept everywhere, and the brigand chiefs, divided on all else, put to death as their common enemies any in favor of peace with the Romans or suspected of an intention to desert, and were unanimous only in slaughtering those deserving of deliverance. The shouts of the combatants rang incessantly by day and night, but yet more harrowing were the mourners' terrified lamentations. Their calamities provided, indeed, perpetual cause for grief, but consternation locked their wailings within their breasts, and while fear suppressed all outward emotion they were tortured with stifled groans. No regard for the living was any longer paid by their relations, no thought was taken for the burial of the dead—negligences both due to personal despair; for those who took no part in sedition lost interest in everything, momentarily expecting certain destruction. The rival parties, meanwhile, were at grips, trampling over the dead bodies that were piled upon each other, the frenzy inhaled from the corpses at their feet increasing their savagery.[10]

It is a frightful expression of a society in the process of disintegration, an accelerating vortex of self-destruction. Josephus likens it to "a wild beast grown mad, which, for want of food from abroad, fell now upon eating its own flesh."[11]

In this carnage, Simon bar Giora has the greatest number of armed men under his command, fifteen thousand—the size of three Romans legions.[12]

While all this has been going on, the Romans have patiently lingered, waiting for their enemies to destroy themselves. But now they decide to attack, something which finally brings the various Jewish rebel factions together. But is too late. After a prolonged siege, the Romans conquer Jerusalem, and the surviving population is either slaughtered or carried away as captives by the furious Roman army. And when there remained no more people to kill, "Caesar gave orders that they should now demolish the entire city and temple."[13]

And so, Jerusalem, and the Jewish nation, is destroyed.

But Simon still lives. He has taken the most faithful of his friends with him, among them some that are stone cutters, and has gone down into some subterranean caverns, from which they start digging a mine, "and this in hopes that they should be able to proceed so far as to rise from under ground, in a safe place, and by that means escape." But, continues Josephus, "the miners could make but small progress, and that with difficulty also; insomuch that their provisions, though they distributed them by measure, began to fail them." So Simon eventually emerges from underground, and "thinking he might be able to astonish and elude the Romans, put on a white frock, and buttoned upon him a purple cloak." But he will not be treated as formerly Josephus. Simon bar Giora is put in shackles, taken out of the country, and forced to partake in Titus's triumphal march in Rome, after which he is killed.[14]

Compare this gruesome narrative from *War of the Jews* with a tale in the New Testament, one that we find in all three Synoptic Gospels. It transpires in a place called Gerasa:

> They came to the other side of the sea, to the country of the Gerasenes. And when he had stepped out of the boat, immediately a man out of the tombs with an unclean spirit met him. He lived among the tombs; and no one could restrain him any more, even with a chain; for he had often been restrained with shackles and chains, but the chains he wrenched apart, and

the shackles he broke in pieces; and no one had the strength to subdue him. Night and day among the tombs and on the mountains he was always howling and bruising himself with stones. When he saw Jesus from a distance, he ran and bowed down before him; and he shouted at the top of his voice, "What have you to do with me, Jesus, Son of the Most High God? I adjure you by God, do not torment me." For he had said to him, "Come out of the man, you unclean spirit!" Then Jesus asked him, "What is your name?" He replied, "My name is Legion; for we are many." He begged him earnestly not to send them out of the country.

Now there on the hillside a great herd of swine was feeding; and the unclean spirits begged him, "Send us into the swine; let us enter them." So he gave them permission. And the unclean spirits came out and entered the swine; and the herd, numbering about two thousand, rushed down the steep bank into the sea, and were drowned in the sea.

The swineherds ran off and told it in the city and in the country. Then people came to see what it was that had happened. They came to Jesus and saw the demoniac sitting there, clothed and in his right mind, the very man who had had the legion. [15]

On the surface, the Gospel tale of the mad man from Gerasa has very little in common with Josephus's narrative of the destruction of Jerusalem. Josephus tells us about a furious, one might say possessed, rebel warrior. The Gospels of Mark and Luke talk of a man possessed by demons. But it is hard to ignore the coinciding elements:

In both cases the main character comes from Gerasa (which, incidentally, lies far from any lake, and about forty-five miles from the Sea of Galilee); in both cases the man is regarded as mad, or acting "in a mad rage"; in both cases he, and his demons, interact with an equally possessed group on the hill above them, and the members, numbering in the thousands, proceed to fall to their death (worth noting is that also Roman soldiers fell to their death in the battle for Jerusalem; as the Temple walls were so impenetrable, the Romans climbed ladders, and were instantly killed by Simon's men, and "some of the ladders they threw down from above when they were full of armed men"); in both cases the man from Gerasa had lived in the tombs, but he is now above ground, clothed, and kept under guard; in both cases he fears being taken out of the country. And finally, also this time, the story in Josephus's chronicles concern a rebel leader (and in both Luke and Mark it immediately precedes the story of the daughter of Jairus).

Oddly, although the story is told also in the Gospel of Matthew, there are two decisive differences from the one in Mark and Luke: according to Matthew, the event does not occur in the country of the *Gerasenes*, but rather in the country of the *Gadarenes*. And it is not *one* man who comes out of the tombs, but *two*.

> When he came to the other side, to the country of the Gadarenes, two demoniacs coming out of the tombs met him. They were so fierce that no one could pass that way. Suddenly they shouted, "What have you to do with us, Son of God? Have you come here to torment us before the time?" Now a large herd of swine was feeding at some distance from them. The demons begged him, "If you cast us out, send us into the herd of swine." And he said to them, "Go!" So they came out and entered the swine; and suddenly, the whole herd rushed down the steep bank into the sea and perished in the water. [16]

It is a fact that not only Simon bar Giora, but also John of Gischala hid in the subterranean caverns at the end of the war ("Yet did God avenge himself upon them both, in a manner agreeable to justice," writes Josephus. "As for John, he wanted food, together with his brethren, in these caverns, and begged that the Romans would now give him their right hand for his security, which he had often proudly rejected before").[17] Before arriving in Jerusalem, John had defended his hometown Gischala against an attack by the neighboring Gadarenes, who, together with fighters from surrounding towns, had entirely demolished the city. "Upon which John was so enraged, that he armed all his men, and joined battle with the people forementioned; and rebuilt Gischala after a manner better than before."[18]

Yes, we have left the 50s CE. Just like Menahem and Eleazar son of Jairus, Simon bar Giora and John of Gischala are rebel leaders who appear much later than Theudas and "the Egyptian." They are commanders in the Jewish War.

But it is hard not to see the similarities with an event described in the New Testament.

And perhaps this is true also of the next example.

CHRONOLOGICAL ENIGMA THIRTEEN: ANANIAS AND PETER

U͏P UNTIL NOW, THE PARALLELS BETWEEN JOSEPHUS'S NARRATIVES AND those of the New Testament have mostly involved the Gospels, and the interval has been fairly consistent, at fifteen to twenty years (28 to 36 CE in the New Testament vs. 44 to mid-50s CE in Josephus's works). But in the last two chapters we have seen some parallels which appear to deviate from this pattern—if indeed parallels they are. In Josephus's chronicles the seemingly related events instead occur during the Jewish War. And we shall now concern ourselves with another such example. Like the mention of Barnabas, Niger, Cyrene, and Manaen, this text is found in the Acts of the Apostles.

As is known by all New Testament scholars, Acts presents a very complicated situation chronologically. At times, episodes in this book seem jumbled, something which we shall come back to in a later chapter. But it is nevertheless taken for granted that events portrayed in this, the fifth book of the New Testament, invariably occur after the crucifixion of Jesus.

We shall now look at an account in chapter five of this book, the Acts of the Apostles. It is a chapter which presents events in Jerusalem, when the apostles strive to continue the missionary work of Jesus, but are met with resistance from the Jewish establishment. And we shall compare this text with the description of some situations that Josephus places in the early and mid 60s. In one of the excerpts, Josephus relates how High Priest Ananias (most likely Ananias son of Nebedeus[1]) hoards up money, and curries favor with Procurator Albinus. In the second one—taking place at the beginning of the Jewish War—he relates how this Ananias is killed, and the aftermath.

Although it may strain credulity, placing Acts 5:1–33 next to *Antiquities* 20.204–210 and *War* 2.441–446 has to provoke some thought. Not least in light of the two names given to Jesus's chief apostle: Simon Bariona, and Simon Peter ("Peter" is Greek for "rock").

The excerpts on the following pages are broken up, but for each source they are consecutive, i.e. the entirety of Acts 5:1–33, *Antiquities* 20.204–210, and *War* 2.441–446 is shown, and in order.[2]

Acts	Antiquities	War
Acts 5:1–4	**Ant. 20.204–207**	
But a man named **Ananias**, with the consent of his wife Sapphira, sold a piece of property. With his wife's knowledge, he kept back some of the proceeds, and brought only a part and laid it at the apostles' feet. "Ananias," Peter asked, "why has Satan filled your heart to lie to the Holy Spirit and to ***keep back part of the proceeds of the land?*** While it remained unsold, did it not remain your own? And after it was sold, were not the proceeds at your disposal? How is it that you have contrived this deed in your heart? You did not lie to us but to God!"	Now as soon as Albinus was come to the city of Jerusalem, he used all his endeavors and care that the country might be kept in peace, and this by destroying many of the Sicarii. But as for the High Priest **Ananias**, he increased in glory every day, and this to a great degree, and had obtained the favor and esteem of the citizens in a signal manner; for he ***was a great hoarder up of money;*** he therefore cultivated the friendship of Albinus, and of the [current/other] high priest, by making them presents. He also had servants who were very wicked, who joined themselves to the boldest sort of the people, and went to the threshing-floors, and took away the tithes that belonged to the priests by violence, and did not refrain from beating such as would not give these tithes to them. So the other high priests acted in the like manner, as did those his servants without anyone being able to prohibit them; so that priests, that of old were wont to be supported with those tithes, died for want of food.	

Acts 5:5–16		War 2.441–442
Now when **Ananias** heard these words, he *fell down and died*. And great fear seized all who heard of it. The young men came and wrapped up his body, then carried him out and buried him. After an interval of about three hours **his wife came in**, not knowing what had happened. Peter said to her, "Tell me whether you and your husband sold the land for such and such a price." And she said, "Yes, that was the price." Then Peter said to her, "How is it that you have agreed together to put the Spirit of the Lord to the test? Look, the feet of those who have buried your husband are at the door, and they will carry you out." Immediately *she fell down at his feet and died*. When the young men came in they found her dead, so they carried her out and buried her beside her husband. *And great fear seized the whole church and all who heard of these things.* Now many signs and wonders were done among the people through the apostles. And they were all together in Solomon's Portico. *None of the rest dared to join them, but the people held them in high esteem.* Yet more than ever believers were added to the Lord, great numbers of both men and women, so that they even carried out the sick into the streets, and laid them on cots and mats, in order that Peter's shadow might fall on some of them as he came by. A great number of people would also gather from the towns around Jerusalem, bringing the sick and those tormented by unclean spirits, and they were all cured.		On the following day the high priest **Ananias** was caught near the canal in the palace grounds, where he was hiding, and, **with his brother** Ezechias, *was killed* by the brigands [robbers]; while the rebels invested and kept strict watch on the towers, to prevent any soldier from escaping. But the reduction of the strongholds and the murder of the high-priest Ananias *inflated and brutalized Menahem to such an extent that he believed himself without a rival in the conduct of affairs and became an insufferable tyrant.*

Acts 5:17–23	Ant. 20.208–210	
Then **the high priest** took action; he and all who were with him (that is, the sect of the Sadducees), being filled with jealousy, ***arrested the apostles and put them in the public prison***. But during the night an angel of **the Lord opened the prison doors, brought them out**, and said, "Go, stand in the temple and tell the people the whole message about this life." When they heard this, they entered the temple at daybreak and went on with their teaching. **When the high priest and those with him arrived**, they called together the council and the whole body of the elders of Israel, and sent to the prison to have them brought. But when the temple police went there, **they did not find them in the prison; so they returned and reported, "We found the prison securely locked and the guards standing at the doors, but when we opened them, we found no one inside."**	But now the Sicarii went into the city by night, just before the festival, which was now at hand, and took the scribe belonging to the captain of the temple, whose name was Eleazar, who was the son of Ananias, **the high priest**, and bound him, and carried him away with them; after which they sent to **Ananias**, and said that they would send the scribe to him, if he would persuade Albinus to release ***ten of those prisoners which he had caught of their party***; so Ananias was plainly forced to persuade Albinus, and gained his request of him. This was the beginning of greater calamities; for **the robbers perpetually contrived to catch some of Ananias's servants; and when they had taken them alive, they would not let them go, till they thereby recovered some of their own** Sicarii. And as they were again become no small number, they grew bold, and were a great affliction to the whole country.	

Acts 5:24–33		War 2.443–447
Now when **the captain of the temple and the chief priests heard these words**, they were perplexed about them, wondering what might be going on. Then someone arrived and announced, **"Look, the men whom you put in prison are standing in the temple and teaching the people!" Then the captain went with the temple police and brought them**, but without violence, **for they were afraid of being stoned by the people**. When they had brought them, they had them stand before the council. The high priest questioned them, saying, "We gave you strict orders not to teach in this name, yet here you have filled Jerusalem with your teaching and you are determined to bring this man's blood on us." But Peter and the apostles answered, "We must obey God rather than any human authority. The God of our ancestors raised up Jesus, whom you had killed by hanging him on a tree. God exalted him at his right hand as Leader and Savior that he might give repentance to Israel and forgiveness of sins. And we are witnesses to these things, and so is the Holy Spirit whom God has given to those who obey him." **When they heard this, they were enraged and wanted to kill them.**		**The partisans of Eleazar [the captain of the temple]** now rose against him [Menahem]; they remarked to each other that, after revolting from the Romans for love of liberty, they ought not to sacrifice this liberty to a Jewish hangman and to put up with a master who, even were he to abstain from violence, was anyhow far below themselves; and that if they must have a leader, anyone would be better than Menahem. **So they laid their plans to attack him in the Temple, whither he had gone up in state to pay his devotions, arrayed in royal robes and attended by his suite of armed fanatics. When Eleazar [the captain] and his companions rushed upon him**, and the rest of **the people to gratify their rage took up stones and began pelting the arrogant doctor**, imagining that his downfall would crush the whole revolt, Menahem and his followers offered a momentary resistance; then, **seeing themselves assailed by the whole multitude, they fled whithersoever they could; all who were caught were massacred, and a hunt was made for any in hiding.** A few succeeded in escaping by stealth to Masada, among others Eleazar, son of Jairus and a relative of Menahem, and subsequently despot of Masada. [3]

Could these parallels be coincidental? Two men named Ananias, who both lay claim to proceeds that rightfully belong to others, are both later killed with their next-of-kin (in one case the wife, in the other the brother). In both cases, Ananias's accusers have been imprisoned, and in both cases they have been released from prison, against the wishes of the authorities, and in the presence of the prison guards. Then later, in both cases, the leaders of these ex-prisoners go straight into the Temple and start preaching and worshipping. Something which, in both cases, leads the captain of the Temple to confront them, and with his people to try to kill them.

Yes, the similarities could be coincidental. But if they are not, this would mean that Simon Peter—Simon Bariona—is no other than Menahem, the next messianic rebel leader to be named by Josephus after "the Egyptian." Menahem, a *Bariona*, who leads his followers to a rock on which they build their community: Masada (cf. Matthew 16:18: "And I tell you, you are Peter, and on this rock I will build my church").

The preceding verses of *War* describe Menahem and his men arriving from Masada, entering Jerusalem, and in the process setting a tower on fire, "and when the foundations were burnt below, the tower fell down suddenly."[4] A falling tower is mentioned not in Acts, but in Luke: "Unless you repent, you will all perish as they did. Or those eighteen who were killed when the tower of Siloam fell on them."[5] If one approached Jerusalem from the direction of Masada, one arrived at Siloam, which lay just by the city walls.[6]

As mentioned, the Hebrew name Menahem means "comforter" or "paraclete" in English. *Parakletos* in Greek. This is the same term that Jesus, in the Gospel of John, repeatedly uses for the one who will come after him: "And I will ask the Father, and he shall give you another Paraclete, that he may abide with you for ever" (John14:16); "But when the Paraclete cometh, whom I will send you from the Father, the Spirit of truth, who proceedeth from the Father, he shall give testimony of me" (John 15:26); "But I tell you the truth: it is expedient to you that I go: for if I go not, the Paraclete will not come to you; but if I go, I will send him to you" (John 16:7).[7]

AN ALTERNATE ROLE
FOR THE NEW TESTAMENT?

ON THE FACE OF IT, THE NEW TESTAMENT IS A COLLECTION OF WORKS which concern themselves with the emerging religion of Christianity, with its central figure, Jesus of Nazareth, and with the apostles who initially spread the faith, locally and around the world.

That is the outward, and also the deeper, essence and mission of the New Testament canon.

At the same time, the activities described in this religious anthology transpire in an era of great upheaval, occurring in the very setting where Jesus and the apostles are active. At first glance, very little of this comes across in the text. But the more one engages in comparisons of the New Testament with parallel historical sources, the more these tumultuous events shine through in the subtexts of the narratives. And not only in the subtexts. Of the militant messianic rebel leaders named by Josephus—from the census in 6 CE, to the fall of Masada in 73 CE—the Gospels and Acts manage to name almost all: Judas the Galilean, Theudas, "the Egyptian," and possibly Menahem (Manaen). In addition, Niger, Dorcas, and the Captain of the Temple are all singular names or epithets found in the New Testament, that also happen to be names and epithets held by leaders during the Jewish

War. Furthermore, Luke and Acts manage to refer to a number of events identical, or distinctly similar, to events highly significant in the emergence of the Jewish rebellion: the Census under Quirinius (6 CE), the sudden death of Herod dressed in royal robes (44 CE), a pivotal attack on a man named Stephen on a road outside Jerusalem (48 CE), a conflict between Galileans and Samaritans, beginning in a Samaritan village (48 CE), a man emerging from the village of Nain (c. 68 CE).

And although there is certainly a significant number of rebel leaders, and rebellion-related events, that the New Testament fails to mention, surprisingly often they seem to be there in the undertext of parables.

If the mad men in Gerasa/Gadara really are Simon bar Giora and John of Gischala, and if the similarities of Simon Peter and Menahem are no mere overinterpretations, and if Judas Iscariot really means Judas the Sikarios—a name appropriately given to Judas the Galilean—and if Simon the Zealot really is a Zealot, and if Lazarus really is the son of Jairus, and if, as has been suggested, the disciple name Thaddeus is the same name as Theudas,[1] then perhaps we have reason to start suspecting that the disciples are not really disciples. But a procession of rebel leaders, spread out over the first seven decades of the first century.

And that perhaps the New Testament, in addition to being a religious canon, is a text documenting a history that the authors feared otherwise would be lost—just like *War of the Jews* was to Flavius Josephus.

Yes, we are in the realm of speculation here. Not much can be unequivocally proven. Some of it seems relatively incontestable—Luke and Acts beyond any doubt name several messianic rebel leaders—other names remain guesses. In some cases it seems that one and the same person may have been given several different names. And perhaps one and the same name at different places in the text could denote different persons. Let's not forget that Josephus in *Antiquities* writes that Felix was informed of the plans of "the Egyptian" ahead of time. So maybe there was a betrayer—someone like the Judas Iscariot of the Gospels—also in this story?

Reading the New Testament with Flavius Josephus as chaperon means entering a labyrinth. A labyrinth where the path at times seems clear, and at other times is so intricate that one marvels at the complexity and sophistication of the narrative. It is a web best perceived from a distance. And yet, it is one which never comes into perfect focus.

Take the parable of the rich man and Lazarus, found not in the Gospel of John—where the other Lazarus tale is—but in Luke, chapter 16. The tale begins with a description of "a rich man who was dressed in purple and fine linen and who feasted sumptuously each day," and of Lazarus, a poor man who lies at the rich man's gate covered with sores. Who could the rich man be? According to the Bible, the high priest wore a garment "of gold, of blue, purple and crimson yarns, and of fine twisted linen."[2] As the parable in Luke proceeds, both Lazarus and the rich man die. The rich man goes to Hades, where he is being tormented, whereas Lazarus is carried away by the angels to be with Abraham, the Patriarch. When the rich man begs Abraham to have mercy, "and send Lazarus to dip the tip of his finger in water and cool my tongue," Abraham responds: "Child, remember that during your lifetime you received your good things, and Lazarus in like manner evil things; but now he is comforted here, and you are in agony." In the Greek original, the word for "he is comforted" is *parakaleitai*. A word we know by now.

Is this parable merely a moral tale about doing good in your lifetime? Or is it also a story about two struggling relatives, Eleazar and Menahem—rebels against Rome as well as against the Jewish religious establishment?

The New Testament is a brilliant, multilayered work of faith, art, and history. And a mystery book.

Again and again we see the pattern. Again and again, we are nevertheless left speculating.

And while we are speculating, let's end this chapter with two highly speculative thoughts:

When Jesus goes to Capernaum, by the Sea of Galilee, he starts gathering the disciples around him. Several of them are fishermen, laboring with their nets by or in the water. Two are called James son of Zebedee, and his brother John. Jesus finds them sitting in a boat on the lake with their father Zebedee, mending their nets.[3] He calls them, and immediately they leave the boat and the father, and follow him (later, we also hear of their mother, named Salome).[4]

Who are these people, the family of Zebedee? Of course, we do not know. But the name Zebedee (Zebadiah) has a meaning in Hebrew. It means "Gift of God." This is the meaning also of the name Matitiahu (Matthias, in Greek).

Josephus was born Yosef ben Matitiahu, Joseph son of Matthias.

The idea may seem absurd. Josephus was a sworn enemy of "the fourth sect of Jewish philosophy."

But Joseph son of Matthias, a member of an aristocratic family, later abandoned the more moderate position taken by the aristocracy, and became one of the leading Jewish commanders during the war against Rome. His brother and parents were in Jerusalem during the siege. And when Josephus expressed his hatred against the "fourth sect," he was already a distinguished Roman, an ally of his former enemies.

On the other hand: Josephus was born in 37 or 38 CE. And could hardly have been causing tumults in a Samaritan village in 48 CE.

And then there is this, in Acts:

> "So one of the men who have accompanied us during all the time that the Lord Jesus went in and out among us, beginning from the baptism of John until the day when he was taken up from us—one of these must become a witness with us to his resurrection." So they proposed two, Joseph called Barsabbas, who was also known as Justus, and Matthias.[5]

The two main witnesses of the era, outside of the New Testament, were Justus of Tiberias, and Joseph son of Matthias.[6] Both of them leaders during the Jewish War. Both of them subsequent chroniclers.

Barsabbas is a name of unknown etymology, but has been interpreted as "son of fighting" ("bar"=son; "[t]saba"=to fight, to swell).[7]

Justus real name was Justus son of Pistus. *Pistus* is Latin, derived from the word which means "to beat, to pound, to crush" (compare "piston").

POSSIBLE ARGUMENTS
AGAINST A TIME SHIFT

BY NOW, A NUMBER OF EXAMPLES OF SEEMINGLY DELAYED PARALLELS between events described in the New Testament and events described in the chronicles of Josephus have been presented in this book. Most of the matches seem to pertain to events Josephus places in the mid-40s to mid-50s—during the build-up phase to the Jewish War. A few instead look like events Josephus places during the war itself, 66–70 CE.

Are there then no facts which would seem to argue against this pattern of delay? No circumstances which would speak against a deliberate—or accidental—time shift having been implemented on the New Testament texts?

Indeed there are. And the most evident ones will be listed, and discussed, in this chapter.

1 TACITUS

One obvious argument against a time shift is that Cornelius Tacitus—often considered the foremost historian of the Roman Empire—in his *Annals* writes the following passage (the context is the great fire in Rome, 64 CE, a fire that Emperor Nero himself was suspected of having started):

> Consequently, to get rid of the report, Nero fastened the guilt [for the fire] and inflicted the most exquisite tortures on a class hated for their abominations, called Christians by the populace. Christus, from whom the name had its origin, suffered the extreme penalty during the reign of Tiberius at the hands of one of our procurators, Pontius Pilate, and a most mischievous superstition, thus checked for the moment, again broke out not only in Judea, the first source of the evil, but even in Rome, where all things hideous and shameful from every part of the world find their center and become popular.[1]

From this passage, it would seem that there is an important Roman source placing the crucifixion of Jesus in the time of Pilate. At first glance, this would appear to be firm evidence. Furthermore, this passage by Tacitus is hardly a confessional text, not even a sympathetic one, which ought to increase the probability of it being authentic.

But there are problems with the passage. Because Tacitus makes some mysterious mistakes. The first one is not unequivocal: he calls Pontius Pilate a "procurator," the title the Roman governors in *Iudaea* would later be given. But at least according to the only known ancient inscription naming Pilate, he was titled *praefectus Iudaeae*—prefect of *Iudaea*.[2] Some scholars have, however, argued that equestrian governors of Roman provinces could have been both prefects and procurators, or that Tacitus just used a title which was more common at the time when he wrote *Annals*. As John Dominic Crossan puts it: "Tacitus simply retrojected the title of *procurator*, current from the time of the emperor Claudius between 41 and 54, back onto Pilate, who was actually *prefect* at that earlier period."[3] Josephus, who wrote in Greek, refers to Pilate with the generic Greek term *hegemon*, "leader" or "governor"—as do the Gospels. But Josephus, as well as Philo, sometimes also use *epitropos*, which means "guardian," or "steward," or "administrator," but can be translated as "procurator."[4]

Thus, Tacitus makes a mistake with regard to Pilate's title, but it is not necessarily a significant one.

The next anomaly in Tacitus' passage is, however, more conspicuous. He gives Jesus the name *Christus*. If Tacitus had used official Roman records, he ought to have called him by a proper name, i.e. "Jesus ben Joseph," or something similar. *Christus* is a theological term, and it means "the anointed," as does "messiah." Many therefore believe that Tacitus received his information from the Christian community in Rome, rather than from official Roman records. Importantly, he wrote this passage around 116 CE, thus well after Luke, and the assumed implementation of the time shift (see below).

Finally, although not a majority opinion, the authenticity of the passage has been called into question, not least because early Christian writers do not refer to it.[5]

2 THE CENSUS

If we go to the Gospels, one circumstance possibly arguing against a time shift is the description of the census under Quirinius. The information in Luke fits well with the description of this census (ca. 6 CE) as related by Josephus—and it seems to be the only social or political event in the Gospels which does fit Josephus's description, chronologically as well as content-wise. Although the information of the ensuing revolt is absent in Luke, everything else matches, and it simply has to be the same event.

One could argue that if Jesus was active in the late 40s and 50s, as the time shift hypothesis suggests, he would not have been born as early as 6 CE (although the only argument against it is Luke 3:23—stating that he began his work when he was about thirty. John 8:57 actually suggests that he may have been older: "Then the Jews said to him, 'You are not yet fifty years old, and have you seen Abraham?'" John 2:19–21 strengthens this: "Jesus answered them, 'Destroy this temple, and in three days I will raise it up.' The Jews then said, 'This temple has been under construction for forty-six years, and will you raise it up in three days?' But he was speaking of the temple of his body").[6]

Jesus's age aside, the problem with Luke's chronological parameter for the time of his birth is that there is something odd with it: the time-point differs by at least ten years from that suggested in Matthew, and the choice of the census as a chronological parameter is filled with unstated significance. The question is, simply put, if the time-point Luke provides for Jesus's birth is a symbolic one, rather than a factual one: the census marks the birth of the anti-Roman resistance movement.

In a similar vein, one could, as mentioned, argue that the attack on Stephen the Roman servant, as well as the conflict after Galileans enter a Samaritan village, as well as the death of Herod Agrippa I, seated in royal robes in the theater at Caesarea, constitute milestones in the re-emergence of the anti-Roman resistance movement. All four events—or events markedly similar to those—are mentioned by the author of Luke-Acts, but not by the other Gospel authors.[7] In each case, Luke mentions these rebellion-related events in an entirely different context than Josephus does, and thus they fill a different purpose for Luke. One could hypothesize that they function as a subtext—a context of Zealotry never mentioned overtly, always hidden under an unrelated story.

One might here even find an explanation for the puzzling "Lysanias ruler of Abilene" reference, used in Luke 3:1 to define the time when John the Baptist began his ministry ("In the fifteenth year of the reign of Emperor Tiberius, when Pontius Pilate was governor of Judea, and Herod was ruler of Galilee, and his brother Philip ruler of the region of Ituraea and Trachonitis, and Lysanias ruler of Abilene, during the high priesthood of Annas and Caiaphas, the word of God came to John son of Zechariah in the wilderness"). Whereas the other dignitaries mentioned all were active in the late 20s and 30s, the only Lysanias known to have exercised authority in this area was Lysanias tetrarch of Chalcis, executed by Mark Antony about 36 BCE, more than sixty years earlier.[8] However, Josephus, in *Antiquities* 19.275, does mention that Emperor Claudius in 41 CE bestows upon Agrippa I "Abila of Lysanias." In other words, the town of Abila, in the district of Abilene, retained its byname after its former ruler. If this, again, is an example of the Lukan subtext, one interpretation could be that John the Baptist actually started his ministry during the time when Agrippa I ruled over Abila of Lysanias, i.e. 41–44 CE.

As mentioned, it is a fairly common opinion that Luke had read *Antiquities of the Jews* by Josephus. Irrespective of whether he had, Luke is the historian among the Gospel writers, and he has been "investigating everything carefully from the very first" (Luke 1:3). One could speculate that if a time shift was implemented, then Luke might have been active in accomplishing this, as well as more deliberate when making veiled references to Zealot activity. Looking at his writing through the prism of a time shift, one can discern a definite pattern. This is less the case with Mark and Matthew (which were presumably written earlier). Perhaps changes in these two Gospels were made retroactively, and through more simple means—something which could have produced the seemingly incomprehensible statement in Matthew that John the Baptist started preaching at the same time as Jesus returned from Egypt, as a child.[9] If this assumption is correct, Luke would have been written with a time shift in mind, whereas Matthew and Mark would have had to have been changed retroactively.

As will be argued below, the same could possibly be hypothesized with regard to Acts, in relation to the Letters of Paul.

3 ACTS

The Acts of the Apostles is considered to be one of the most problematic of the New Testament texts. And also in relation to the time shift hypothesis it constitutes a particular case.

There are some features of Acts which, on the surface, would appear to argue against a time shift: as a rule, we expect Acts to describe events occurring *after* the events in the Gospels. Acts, after all, begins with Jesus being taken up to heaven, and he never appears in the flesh after that. The problem for the time shift hypothesis—and the assumption that the Gospels predominantly describe events occurring during the procuratorships of Cumanus and Felix (48–60 CE)—is that Acts describes a couple of events that seem to occur earlier than that. One example concerns Acts 12:21–23, beginning with the words: "On an

appointed day Herod put on his royal robes, took his seat on the plat-
form, and delivered a public address to them," and proceeding to tell
the story of how Herod dies, "eaten by worms." The description closely
resembles that in *Antiquities* of the death of Agrippa I, estimated to
have occurred in 44 CE.[10] Thus, if Acts in this case details an event
preceding the defeat of "the Egyptian" (which happened in the 50s), it
would seem to argue against him being identical to Jesus.

Similarly, if Stephen of Acts is identical to the Stephen portrayed
by Josephus, then the stoning of Stephen occurred ca. 48 CE, also
prior to the defeat of "the Egyptian."

So could there be instances when events portrayed in Acts *precede*
those described in the Gospels? Interestingly, when it comes to the
chronology in Acts, there are other indications that it may be jumbled,
both when compared to Josephus, and, significantly, when compared
to the Letters of Paul.

If we begin by comparing Acts with Josephus, we do find a number
of seeming parallels. But whereas the parallels between the Gospels and
Josephus mostly appear with a fifteen to twenty year delay in Josephus,
the situation with Acts appears much more jumbled: while Acts 5:1–33
(on Ananias and Peter) possibly bears some similarities to events referred
by Josephus to the early to mid 60s, chapters 6 and 7 (concerning the
attack on Stephen) bear certain similarities to an event in the late 40s. Acts
8:9–24 (concerning Simon the magician) possibly resembles an event in
the 50s,[11] and Acts 12:21–23 (on the death of Herod, "eaten by worms")
appears to refer to something in the mid-40s. One explanation could of
course be that these parallels are weaker, and perhaps not relevant.

What is important to take into account, however, is that this cha-
otic structure is not unexpected when it comes to Acts. It is often stated
that the chronology of Acts is not always linear, especially when compared to the Letters of Paul. At least, the two sources are very difficult
to reconcile.[12]

The New Testament contains thirteen letters traditionally attributed to Paul the Apostle (fourteen, counting the anonymous Epistle to
the Hebrews). Most modern scholars consider a number of these to be
pseudepigraphic, i.e. written by someone other than Paul. But seven of
them are usually considered "undisputed." These letters, or epistles, con-

stitute some of the earliest documents within Christianity, most of them are generally dated to the 50s CE (thus well before the Gospels and Acts), and they feel decidedly authentic in their personal tone and here-and-now approach. These Letters appear to be written continuously, and chiefly concern themselves with issues pertaining to Paul's missionary journeys.

Now what do these two sources on Paul—Acts and the Letters—tell us about his activities? As described in Acts, Paul after undergoing his conversion on the road to Damascus (a conversion clearly subsequent to the crucifixion of Jesus), begins his missionary activity—with journeys around the Mediterranean, interspersed with brief visits to the Jerusalem community (visits which are mostly done in secret). Finally, after twenty to twenty-five years of missionary activity, Paul appears more openly in Jerusalem, in the Temple, and is arrested and imprisoned. This, Acts tells us, takes place two years before the end of procurator Felix's reign, thus around 57 or 58 CE.[13] But when Felix leaves office two years later, and is replaced as procurator by Festus, Paul is allowed to leave prison, to travel to Rome (incidentally, not only Felix and Festus, but also High Priest Ananias son of Nebedeus, and later King Agrippa II, are said to be involved in these procedings). After a lengthy journey, Paul arrives in Rome, probably around the year 61, judging by the chronological parameters provided.

Now if the time-span described is accurate, and the period between Paul's conversion and arrest is twenty to twenty-five years, this would be a strong argument against the time shift hypothesis. Because if Jesus was crucified or defeated under Felix (52 to 59/60 CE)—and after Nero became emperor in 54 CE—and Paul underwent his conversion after that, the addition of another twenty to twenty-five years before Paul's arrest would put us well beyond the Jewish War. This would of course be impossible. There was no Temple—there hardly was a Jerusalem—after 70 CE. And none of the events described in connection with Paul's arrest could have taken place.

The only thing is: there is something odd with the time-span described. Because although Paul's Letters seem to tell the same story as that in Acts—and the story seems to fill up a similar amount of time—the sequences of events described in the two sources are almost impossible to align.

PAULINE CHRONOLOGY
(from conversion to imprisonment in Jerusalem)

YEARS AFTER CONVERSION	ACTS	LETTERS OF PAUL
0	Conversion, outside Damascus. (Acts 9:1–22; 22:6–16; 26:12–18) Has to flee Damascus, is lowered from the wall in a basket. Leaves for first visit to Jerusalem. Then goes to Tarsus in Cilicia. (Acts 9:23–30; 22:17–21)	Conversion, probably outside Damascus. (Galatians 1:15–16) Goes to Arabia. (Galatians 1:17) Returns to Damascus. (Galatians 1:17)
3	Goes to Syrian Antioch for a year (unclear when). (Acts 11:25–26) Collects money for famine relief. (Acts 11:27–29) Second visit to Jerusalem, to deliver funds. (Acts 11:29–30;12:25) First Missionary Journey: Syrian Antioch, Seleucia, Cyprus, Perga in Pamphylia, Pisidian Antioch, Iconium, Lystra, Derbe, Lystra, Iconium, Pisidian Antioch, Pamphylia, Perga, Attalia, Syrian Antioch. (Acts 13:4–14:26)	Has to flee Damascus, is lowered from the wall in a basket. Leaves for first visit to Jerusalem. Then goes to "the regions of Syria and Cilicia." (Galatians 1:18–24; 2 Corinthians 11:32–33)
17	Third visit to Jerusalem, for Jerusalem Council. (Acts 15:2–29)	Second visit to Jerusalem, for Jerusalem Council. Paul is asked to "remember the poor." (Galatians 2:1–10)

	Second missionary journey. No mention of collecting money. (Acts 15:40–18:21)	Missionary journey. Paul collects money for the poor of Judea. (Galatians 2:9–10; 1 Corinthians 16:1–4; 2 Corinthians 8–9; Romans 15:25–26)
	Fourth visit to Jerusalem, to "greet the Church." (Acts 18:22)	
	Third missionary journey. No mention of collecting money.[14] (Acts 18:23–20:38)	
ca. 22	Fifth visit to Jerusalem, arrest and imprisonment. (Acts 21:17–27:1)	Third visit to Jerusalem, to deliver funds for the poor. (Romans 15:25–29; see also 2 Corinthians 8–9; 1 Corinthians 16:1–3)
ca. 24	Release from prison. Then journey to Rome. (Acts 27:1–28:14)	

> But when God, who had set me apart before I was born and called me through his grace, was pleased to reveal his Son to me, so that I might proclaim him among the Gentiles, I did not confer with any human being, nor did I go up to Jerusalem to those who were already apostles before me, but I went away at once into Arabia, and afterwards I returned to Damascus. Then after three years I did go up to Jerusalem to visit Cephas [Peter] and stayed with him fifteen days.

This is how Paul, in his letter to the Galatians, describes what he did just after his conversion on the road to Damascus: he "at once" went to Arabia, and spent three years there and in Damascus again before returning for the first time to Jerusalem.[15] Acts describes the same period, of course, but in much more detail. But here we read of no visit to Arabia. Instead, after the conversion, Jesus stayed in Damascus, and "immediately he began to proclaim Jesus in the synagogues."[16] Nor does Acts tell us of any three years spent there before Paul returns for the first time to Jerusalem.

Thus, the visit to Arabia is absent in Acts, as are the three years before returning to Jerusalem for the first time.

But it is after Paul *leaves* Jerusalem that it gets really confusing: in the Letter to the Galatians, Paul just writes that he then "went into the regions of Syria and Cilicia." And the narrative continues: "Then after fourteen years I went up again to Jerusalem with Barnabas, taking Titus along with me."[17] Thus it seems Saul/Paul remained, seemingly quietly, in "Syria and Cilicia" for as much as fourteen years. The subsequent, second, visit to Jerusalem involved—or so it appears—the so called Jerusalem Council, when the missionary work was divided up, so that the apostles in Jerusalem continued preaching to the Jews, whereas Saul/Paul was entrusted with the Gentiles:

> . . . and when James and Cephas [Peter] and John, who were acknowledged pillars, recognized the grace that had been given to me, they gave to Barnabas and me the right hand of fellowship, agreeing that we should go to the Gentiles and they to the circumcised.[18]

It is very, very difficult to harmonize this chronology in the Letter to the Galatians with Acts. And I will now briefly go into some of the problems facing those who nevertheless try to harmonize them (the reader who does not want to go into details should jump to the next section, "A Hypothesis on Pauline Chronology"):

Acts tells us that after leaving Jerusalem so abruptly after his first visit, Paul is sent by the apostles to his hometown Tarsus in Cilicia (which may well correspond to "the regions of Syria and Cilicia" mentioned in Galatians). At some point, it is unclear when, Barnabas is sent by the apostles in Jerusalem to meet Saul/Paul in Tarsus, and they travel together to Syrian Antioch, where they spend a year, preaching. This thus still fits with the statement in Galatians that Paul "went into the regions of Syria and Cilicia." But then it gets confusing again. Because Acts tells us that while in Antioch, Saul/Paul and Barnabas are informed of a "severe famine over all the world," and are assigned the task to "send relief to the believers living in Judea." This they do, and "after completing their mission Barnabas and Saul returned to

Jerusalem . . ."[19] But which return visit to Jerusalem is this? It is obviously not the journey entailing the Jerusalem Council, because that visit is described in Acts in great detail later.[20] This visit seems entirely devoted to the delivery of collected funds for the people in Judea. Consequently, most scholars agree that Paul's second Jerusalem visit in Galatians corresponds to his *third* one in Acts, involving the Jerusalem Council. So why would Paul omit mentioning a visit to Jerusalem in his Letter to the Galatians?

But that extra Jerusalem visit in Acts is not the only befuddling event: because according to Acts, Paul by no means remains stationary in Syria and Cilicia for fourteen years before going back for the Jerusalem Council, as Galatians tells us. On the contrary, according to Acts, Paul and Barnabas during this time travel on a missionary journey to Salamis and Paphos on Cyprus, then on to the Asian mainland, and Perga in Pamphylia, then further into present-day Turkey to Pisidian Antioch, then down to Iconium, Lystra, and Derbe. After this, they follow pretty much the same route back, finally sailing from Attalia back to Antioch in Syria. Only after this do they return to Jerusalem for the Jerusalem Council.

To solve this impossible equation, some scholars have, despite the evidence to the contrary, chosen to equate the second visit described in the Letter to the Galatians with the second visit in Acts, i.e. the visit for famine relief and delivery of funds. This, however, produces other problems: during the second visit of Galatians, the apostles ask Paul "to remember the poor."[21] But if he had just brought them money, why would he receive this admonition? Furthermore, the collecting of money for the poor in Jerusalem is prominent not only in Acts, but also in a number of the Letters. In fact, Paul wrote Second Corinthians mainly to seek assistance for the poor of Judea, and he mentions the collection in several letters.[22] But these letters were written *after* the Jerusalem Council, during Paul's later journeys. When Acts recounts those same later journeys, however, it does not speak of collecting money. And whereas the Letters describe the final Jerusalem visit—presumably the one leading to Paul's arrest—as one of delivering contributions ("At present, however, I am going to Jerusalem in a ministry to the saints; for Macedonia and Achaia have been pleased to share their resources with the poor among the saints at Jerusalem[23]), Acts only mentions this purpose in passing, and much later.[24]

So it seems that in Acts, the collecting of money mainly precedes the Jerusalem Council, whereas in the Letters it follows it.

Another problem which is produced when equating the second Jerusalem visit in Galatians with the famine-relief visit of Acts 11:30, is that Paul is told by the Holy Spirit that he should be "set apart" for his special work only in Acts 13:2, i.e. after the famine-relief visit. So why then would Paul, according to Galatians, tell the apostles already during this visit that "I had been entrusted with the gospel to the uncircumcised, just as Peter had been to the circumcised"?[25]

A Hypothesis on Pauline Chronology

The differences between Acts and the Letters are so extensive, and the sources so incompatible, that many scholars choose to rely on only one of them. Which leaves scholarship on Pauline chronology in a state of continual flux. As one scholar, Frank Matera, puts it:

> Anyone who carefully compares Galatians and Acts sees that the two accounts present a frustrating mixture of episodes, some of which confirm each other, others of which are in tension with each other. Most will agree that the two narratives do not lend themselves to either simple or complex harmonizations.[26]

Although this is not his own opinion, Rainer Riesner presents the conclusion of many: "For historical purposes, the Acts of the Apostles is all but worthless, and a chronological reconstruction should be based exclusively on the genuine letters of Paul."[27]

When, as in this case, two sets of data on the same events don't match, the choices are usually to either discard one of the sets, or to still try to harmonize what can't be harmonized—essentially to try to fit a square peg into a round hole—or to throw one's hands up in the air.

But the question is, *why* are there such significant chronological discrepancies? Acts and the Letters manage to describe a similar time-span between Paul's conversion and arrest in Jerusalem—twenty to twenty-five years—and yet they fill the time with very different activity: Acts describes five (or perhaps even six[28]) Jerusalem journeys between conversion and arrest, while the Letters only account for three. Acts also describes one missionary journey which is not visible in the Letters. And yet, the Letters provide a similar time span as Acts—twenty to twenty-five years—by presenting seventeen unaccounted-for, and seemingly stationary, years in the Letter to the Galatians (three after the conversion, fourteen after the first Jerusalem visit).

What could all this be about?

I suggest that the extensive discrepancies between Acts and the Letters could be due to the implementation of the time shift, more specifically to a dissimilar implementation of the time shift in the two sources. Just as the internal inconsistencies seen in the Gospels could be explained by an elaborate time shift in Luke, and a retroactive, and not fully implemented, time shift in Mark and Matthew, so could the incompatibilities between Letters and Acts be explained by the same phenomenon: a more elaborate time shift in Acts (presumably written by the same author as Luke), and a more rudimentary, retroactive, one in the earlier source, Paul's Letters.

I suggest that the time shift in the particular case of Paul accomplishes a very specific, and new, task: to adjust the narrative back to real time, perhaps in time for Paul's arrival in Rome—an event which presumably was known in Rome at the time (and thus had to be chronologically correct). And I suggest that the requisite artificial prolongation of Paul's pre-imprisonment activity is handled differently by the two sources, Acts and Letters, leading to two very different stories.

The proposition is thus that the actual period between conversion and imprisonment is considerably shorter than presented; that both events could even fit within Felix's (and Nero's) reign (54–ca. 60 CE) and that the time given for Paul's arrival in Rome is the factual one, i.e. we are brought back to real time.

The two years of imprisonment could of course also be part of an artificial prolongation, in which case Paul would have arrived in Jerusalem at the very end of Felix's procuratorship.

It is worth noting that those historical people presented by Acts in connection with Paul's arrest and imprisonment—Procurator Felix and his Jewish wife Drusilla, King Agrippa II and his ever-present sister Bernice, High Priest Ananias son of Nebedeus,[29] Procurator Festus, the recently disappearing "Egyptian", etc.—all are portrayed in ways which meld well with the descriptions by Josephus of those same people. Which makes sense, if we are at this stage back to real time.

So why would an artificial lengthening of the period between conversion and arrest produce a jumbled chronology when comparing the Letters with Acts? Only because they utilize different techniques to accomplish this expansion of time: in the Letters, the artificial lengthening of this period from perhaps less than five to more than twenty years would have been accomplished simply by inserting seventeen empty years (Letter to the Galatians), and occasional names of authority figures. The seventeen inactive years presented in Galatians are not only out of character when it comes to Paul, they are absent in Acts. In Acts, on the other hand, these seventeen inactive years seem to be replaced by activities not reported in the Letters, or reported at a later date. One possibility is that some later missionary journeys were moved to earlier dates in Acts. This would have accomplished more activity between conversion and arrest. But it would also jumble the chronology in Acts, leading to the general problem of reconciling Acts and the Letters.

It is remarkable that in Acts 26:19–20, an imprisoned Paul says to King Agrippa II: "King Agrippa, I was not disobedient to the heavenly vision, but declared first to those in Damascus, then in Jerusalem and throughout the countryside of Judea, and also to the Gentiles, that they should repent and turn to God and do deeds consistent with repentance."

Paul, according to the same source, has just spent over two decades completing three long missionary journeys all over the Mediterranean! He has, since his conversion, spent at most a few weeks in freedom in Judea and Jerusalem.

Yes, maybe he decided to keep those long missionary journeys a secret to the king.

Or maybe some of them hadn't happened yet.

It is not unlikely that Paul was known in Rome, and a re-adjustment of the narrative back to real time by the time of his arrival in Rome would have had to be accomplished in order to make the story hold together. Thus, the time between Paul's conversion and his arrival in Rome would have had to be stretched out. And events occurring between the mid-50s and the early 60s would have been presented as occurring between the mid-30s and the early 60s.

Although it is the most complicated aspect of the time shift hypothesis, this proposition would not only allow us to fit Paul into the modified chronology, it would also provide an eventual adjustment back to real time, as well as, and perhaps most importantly, an explanation for the puzzling, extensive, and seemingly inexplicable chronological incompatibilities between the Acts of the Apostles and the Letters of Paul.

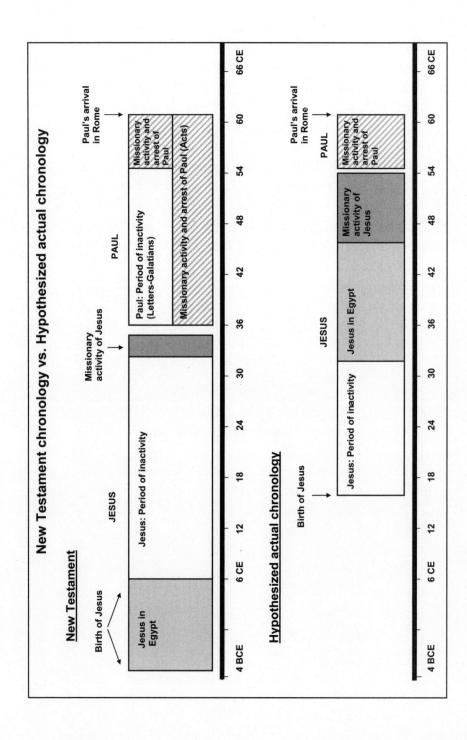

New Testament chronology vs. Hypothesized actual chronology

NATURE OF THE PARALLELS

THE PARALLELS PRESENTED IN THIS BOOK HAVE ALL INVOLVED COM-
monly reported events or individuals in the New Testament and in the
works of Josephus. The book has not, however, tried to make an eval-
uation of the relationship between the two sources. Although much
of the evidence may be in favor of Luke having read Josephus, their
knowledge of events could also be independent of each other. In the
comparisons made in this book, Josephus mainly functions as a historical reference, being the main source of knowledge of Judea and Galilee
in the decades leading up to the Jewish War.[1]

What is fundamental when assessing the relevance of the parallels between the New Testament and the chronicles of Josephus, is the
fact that the New Testament narrative so poorly matches the *concurrent*
events described in *War of the Jews* and *Antiquities of the Jews*. In fact,
of all the historical events presented in the Gospels, only one seems to
fit the description by Josephus, chronologically as well as content-wise:
the census under Quirinius. In Acts, we find a few more, but none of
them are earlier than 44 CE: The famine under Claudius is one.[2] The
death of Agrippa I could be regarded as a second (although the king is
only called "Herod"). And the portrayals of the dignitaries mentioned

in connection with Paul's arrest and trial—Procurator Felix and his wife Drusilla, King Agrippa II and his sister Bernice, High Priest Ananias—do not differ from the descriptions found in Josephus's chronicles. It is as if the people that this book suggests should have been present during the trial of Jesus—if indeed a trial took place—instead are present during the trial of Paul.

It could be argued that the circumstances surrounding the arrest and beheading of John the Baptist—as they are described in the Gospels—are somewhat historical, since Josephus confirms that Herod Antipas married his brother's wife, and that this stirred up controversy.[3] But in fact, not much else in the Gospel story matches Josephus's description. In his narrative, it is the father of the first wife, Aretas, who is angered on account of the new marriage. And it is Aretas who is threatened with decapitation.

As a rule, when dignitaries are introduced in the Gospels, their names match with those of dignitaries who, according to other sources, were active during Pilate. Their actions, however, do not.

This stands in sharp contrast to what would materialize if we were to move the accounts from the Gospels fifteen to twenty years forward in time, and change the names of people in authority accordingly. The number of matches would increase dramatically, and although the matches are separate, not interdependent, they form a pattern with regard to the subject matter. In addition, a person with significant similarities to Jesus would appear in both *War of the Jews* and in *Antiquities of the Jews*. This person, however, was not, as far as is known, tried or crucified.

Barring this last fact, it seems that no new obvious historical inconsistencies are produced with the time shift (and consequent changing of names). It should be noted, however, that in both *War* and *Antiquities*, the description of the murder of High Priest Jonathan precedes the description of how "the Egyptian" arrives at the Mount of Olives, and thus, if this is the correct order of events, there is only one high priest in office by the time this messianic leader is defeated.[4] On the other hand, the two events lie closely together, and possibly the order is not fixed, as Josephus simply writes: "Moreover, there came out of Egypt about this time to Jerusalem one that said he was a prophet . . ."

So are there no statements from early church fathers on this? No pronouncements that would seem to hint at a different original chronology?

Perhaps there are. Without a doubt, at least a couple of assertions made by early Christian theologians have seemed paradoxical when seen through the prism of the conventional chronology. And they may well corroborate the notion of an altered timeline.

To begin with, we have already mentioned the statement by Church Father Irenaeus (ca. 130–200 CE), that Jesus lived and worked into his fifties. Irenaeus, who was bishop in Lyons, with his work *Adversus haereses* (*Against Heresies*) became known as one of the strongest opponents of "heretical ideas." Nevertheless, in this very work, Irenaeus writes as follows:

> On completing His thirtieth year He [Jesus] suffered, being in fact still a young man, and who had by no means attained to advanced age. Now, that the first stage of early life embraces thirty years, and that this extends onwards to the fortieth year, every one will admit; but from the fortieth and fiftieth year a man begins to decline towards old age, which our Lord possessed while He still fulfilled the office of a Teacher, even as the Gospel and all the elders testify; those who were conversant in Asia with John, the disciple of the Lord, [affirming] that John conveyed to them that information. And he remained among them up to the times of Trajan [Roman emperor, 98–117 CE, author's note]. Some of them, moreover, saw not only John, but the other apostles also, and heard the very same account from them . . .[5]

One can possibly interpret the text as meaning that he who "remained among them up to the times of Trajan" was John, rather than Jesus. But Irenaeus nevertheless clearly states that Jesus reached "old age" (which begins "from the fortieth and fiftieth year"), and that he bases this on testimony from the disciples.

As mentioned, even the Gospel of John suggests that Jesus may have lived at least into his late forties (John 2:19–21; John 8:57).

In another work of his, *Demonstration of the Apostolic Preaching*, Church Father Irenaeus writes: "For Herod the king of the Jews and

Pontius Pilate, the governor of Claudius Caesar, came together and condemned Him to be crucified."[6] Irenaeus ought to know that Pilate was not governor under Claudius Caesar, who ruled much later, from 41 to 54 CE. A similar chronological contradiction is found in "The Letter from Pilate to Claudius," embedded in the apocryphal *Acts of Peter and Paul.*

There are other examples of early church fathers providing what seems to be divergent chronological information: curiously, third century bishop Victorinus of Pettau, according to a surviving ninth century fragment in the monastery in Bobbio, northern Italy, wrote that Jesus was born in the consulate of Sulpicius Camerinus, that is in 9 CE, that he was baptised in the consulate of Valerius Asiaticus, that is in 46 CE, and that he died in the third consulate of Nero, with Valerius Messala, that is in 58 CE. Victorinus, according to this fragment, claimed to have found this information "among the parchments of Alexander," Bishop of Jerusalem and founder of the Theological Library there, who died ca. 250 CE. Alexander, in turn, had relied on "apostolic documents."[7]

A parallel fifteenth century fragment, with similar content, was found in Padua.[8]

Whether this information holds any truth is impossible to say (and the contents of the fragments have been dismissed as "blunders," likely built on erroneous information from earlier church fathers).[9] Nevertheless, it is interesting that a bishop of the Church, Victorinus, would come up with this kind of deviating information, information which, in itself, ought to live up to the "criterion of embarrassment." And he was not alone: Church Father Epiphanius, who lived about a century later, states as his own opinion that Jesus was born in 2 BCE, but he also refers to a dissenting Christian group in Asia Minor, which he calls *Alogi* (ca. 170 CE). They, he says, claim that Jesus was conceived "in the consulships of Sulpicius Cammarinus and Betteus Pompeianus."[10]

And then we have George Synkellos, a Byzantine chronicler, and private secretary of the Patriarch of Constantinople, who in 808 CE started writing a massive chronology of universal history—a work "widely praised," as his modern translators write, "for its scope, accuracy and wealth of source material," and also called "the greatest achievement of Byzantine historical scholarship."[11] Similarly to Epiphanius, Synkellos places Jesus's birth in "the forty-third year of the reign of Augustus Caesar" (which likely translates as 1 BCE[12]), but then he continues, "in the consulate of Sulpicius, and Marinus and Gaius Pompeius, as it is reported in accurate and ancient manuscripts."[13] A few pages later, he has this to say about the crucifixion of Jesus: "And although blameless, he was crucified on the 27th of the month of Phamenoth, on the day of preparation, that is the sixth day of the week, 23 March, at the sixth hour of the day, in the consulate of Nero for the third time, and of Valerius Messala."[14]

Quintus Sulpicius Camerinus and Gaius Poppaeus Sabinus were consuls in 9 CE (commentators assume "Gaius Poppeaus" has been corrupted into "Gaius Pompeius" by later copyists).[15] Nero's third consulship, with Valerius Messala, was in 58 CE.

Are all these sources relying on the same erroneous information?

It is of course possible. But remember that Victorinus claimed that his informant, Bishop Alexander of Jerusalem, had based his chronology on "apostolic documents" available to him. Notably, Alexander's predecessor, Narcissus, had presided over the Great council in Jerusalem ca. 198 CE. One of the burning questions at this council was to settle the alleged "disagreement between the Gospels" with regard to certain dating issues, and, as Church Father Eusebius later writes, the information "had come to them in succession from the apostles."[16]

CONCLUSIONS

IN THIS BOOK, A NUMBER OF SEEMING PARALLELS BETWEEN THE NEW
Testament and the works of Josephus have been described. But the
parallel episodes are not located in the same era by the two sources, and
importantly, Josephus locates none of them in the twenties or thirties
CE—the time when the Gospels claim that Jesus was active. Instead,
in Josephus's chronicles, the vast majority occur in the late 40s and 50s,
that is, fifteen to twenty years later than the seemingly analogous events
described in the Gospels. Although the reliability of Flavius Josephus
as a historian has been questioned, the length and consistency of these
delays makes it highly unlikely that they can be ascribed to a consistent
error on his part.

Some tales, however—particularly from the Acts of the Apostles,
but also occasional stories in the Gospels—deviate from this pattern, in
that they seem to involve events Josephus places at other times, chiefly
during the Jewish War, 66 to 70 CE.

Seemingly without exception, however, the events, as described by
Josephus, happen in times of Jewish insurrection, before 7 and after 44
CE. And they tend to concern themselves with rebel activity.

Whether the parallels are true parallels, and refer to identical events or people, is another matter. Some parallels are stronger than others, in that they involve several—and to some extent unique or highly unusual—coinciding elements. Others are weaker, with fewer coinciding elements. In some cases, however, the chronological shift seems undeniable. Theudas, and the "robbers," undoubtedly are historical people, and their activity is evidently placed in the wrong period in the New Testament. Even so, the question remains if this is due to an error on the part of the Gospel writers, or if the time shift is deliberate.

The fact that Josephus describes two messianic claimants in the 40s and 50s, Theudas and "the Egyptian," with significant similarities to John the Baptist and Jesus, and that he does so using decidedly negative terms, could be an argument for the time shift being deliberate. Those who put together the Gospels may have wanted to avoid an unfavorable comparison with established historical sources, even at a high cost. Placing Jesus in an era where no other sources would have described him would have eliminated alternate narratives, but it would also have eliminated, or at least greatly diminished, Jesus as a historical person.

It must be remembered that when these historical accounts were written, the nation which they portrayed had been destroyed, and its people either killed or dispersed. The Gospel writers wrote in exile, for an audience largely removed from the area and events described. The availability of testimonies was limited after the Jewish War, but it was not non-existent. Just like the Gospel writers, Josephus, while in exile, endeavored to rescue to posterity a history he feared would otherwise be lost. He was successful at it. Eusebius called Josephus "the most famous Jew of his time," a statue of him was erected in Rome, and his books were deposited in the Public Library of Rome.[1] In addition, although his works have now been lost, there was at least one other contemporary Jewish historian, Justus of Tiberias, who wrote about the events preceding the Jewish War. If Luke, as is often suggested, had read the works of Josephus, he would have known how this historian depicted the period—and how Josephus now, from his current perspective, portrayed its messianic movements. If he did not know of Josephus, or Justus, then certainly at some later point, these competing historical accounts would have become known. This, one may postulate, could be a reason for Luke, or a later editor, to try to minimize the chances for competing narratives. Shifting the story of Jesus to a different time would have been one way to accomplish this.

In particular, those who put together and edited the Gospels may have wanted to remove Jesus from the political setting in which he, according to this hypothesis, was active: the beginning uprising of "robbers," of Zealot rebels, often with a messianic leader at the helm. It was a violent insurrection targeted primarily against the Romans, but also against the established Jewish leadership, the Pharisees, and the Sadducees.

Whatever its roots, by the time Christianity spread around the Mediterranean, it was a religion that advocated non-violence, and applied ethics to the demands and decisions of human existence. Likely, this attitude to life was present also during the formative years. But the pressure on the people living in Judea and Galilee was immense. Considered the most difficult of all Roman provinces to rule, with a population fiercely protecting its customs and traditions, and having never accepted its loss of independence, the foreign rulers reacted by intensifying oppression. Perhaps the persistent strain put upon the masses living under on-again-off-again foreign occupation in Judea and Galilee, and the recurring disappointments when periods of hope invariably ended in despair, ultimately led to violent rebellion. Something which elicited an annihilating response. As Josephus laments, "God . . . brought the Romans upon us, and threw a fire upon the city to purge it; and brought upon us, our wives, and children, slavery, as desirous to make us wiser by our calamities."[2]

From the ashes of this furnace, the seedlings of not one, but two faiths emerged, managed to take root, and ultimately blossomed.

The scattered sprinkling of references to "robbers" and uprisings still found in the Gospels may be the remnants of parts of a founding story that could not be told, at least not overtly.

THANK YOU

THIS BOOK HAS NOT COME ABOUT IN A VACUUM. IN THE LAST FEW YEARS I have had the opportunity to discuss the hypothesis presented in the book with many people, not least a great number of biblical scholars. From all these talks and written exchanges I have gained much insight. This is a controversial hypothesis, and one not easily processed. It has on occasion met with resistance, but at other times with curiosity and valuable reflection from some of the sharpest minds in the field. I thank you for this.

I would also like to express my gratitude for the thoughts and ideas offered by the late Neil Gillard, with whom I engaged in a very valuable exchange over the Internet during the writing of this book.

And last, but not least, Peter Riva, my literary agent, who has been such a terrific supporter, advisor, and workmate for a very long time. I thank you!

SOURCES FOR ANCIENT TEXTS

Most ancient texts mentioned or quoted in this book can be found online, in the original languages, as well as in various translations.

Below are listed some available, and free, online resources for commonly used English translations of these ancient texts (all accessed 25 August, 2015):

New Testament:
http://unbound.biola.edu/ (English)
http://www.greekbible.com/ (Greek, with translation to English)
http://www.greeknewtestament.com/ (Greek and English)
http://biblehub.com/interlinear/matthew/1.htm (Greek, English and
    Strong's Concordance)

**Josephus, *Antiquities of the Jews, War of the Jews, Life of Flavius
    Josephus (Vita)*, trans. William Whiston:**
http://pace-ancient.mcmaster.ca/york/york/texts.htm (English and
    Greek, also Brill Project translation)
http://www.isdet.com/_PDF/Complete_Works_%20of_Josephus.pdf

http://www.perseus.tufts.edu/hopper/searchresults?q=Josephus
(English and Greek)

http://www.ccel.org/j/josephus/works/JOSEPHUS.HTM

Josephus, *Antiquities of the Jews, War of the Jews, Life of Flavius Josephus (Vita)*, trans. Loeb Classical Library (mostly H. St. J. Thackeray):

https://ryanfb.github.io/loebolus/ (except *Antiquities*, Books 15–20)

Philo, *On the Embassy to Gaius*, trans. Charles Duke Yonge:

http://www.earlychristianwritings.com/yonge/book40.html

Tacitus, *The Histories*, trans. Alfred John Church and William Jackson Brodribb:

http://classics.mit.edu/Tacitus/histories.html

http://www.sacred-texts.com/cla/tac/

http://www.earlychristianwritings.com/text/histories.html

Tacitus, *The Annals*, trans. Alfred John Church and William Jackson Brodribb:

http://classics.mit.edu/Tacitus/annals.html

http://www.sacred-texts.com/cla/tac/

http://www.earlychristianwritings.com/text/annals.html

Suetonius, *The Life of Tiberius*:

http://ancienthistory.about.com/library/bl/bl_text_suettiberius.htm
(trans. A. Thomson)

http://legacy.fordham.edu/halsall/ancient/suet-tiberius-rolfe.asp,
(trans. J.C. Rolfe)

Pliny the Younger to Trajan (10.96–97):

http://www.earlychristianwritings.com/text/pliny.html

http://faculty.georgetown.edu/jod/texts/pliny.html

Origen, *Contra Celsum (Against Celsus)*, trans. Frederick Crombie:

http://www.newadvent.org/fathers/0416.htm

http://www.earlychristianwritings.com/origen.html

Origen, *Commentary on the Gospel of Matthew*, trans. John Patrick:
http://www.newadvent.org/fathers/1016.htm
http://www.earlychristianwritings.com/origen.html

Eusebius of Caesarea, *Church History*, trans. Arthur Cushman McGiffert:
http://www.newadvent.org/fathers/2501.htm
http://www.ccel.org/ccel/schaff/npnf201.toc.html

Eusebius of Caesarea, *The Proof of the Gospel*, trans. William John Ferrar:
http://www.tertullian.org/fathers/eusebius_de_03_book1.htm (http://www.tertullian.org/fathers/)

Eusebius of Caesarea, *Theophania*, trans. Samuel Lee:
http://www.tertullian.org/fathers/eusebius_theophania_02book1.htm (http://www.tertullian.org/fathers/)

Eusebius of Caesarea, *The Preparation of the Gospel*, trans. E.H Gifford:
http://www.tertullian.org/fathers/eusebius_pe_01_book1.htm (http://www.tertullian.org/fathers/)

Irenaeus, *Against Heresies*, trans. Alexander Roberts and William Rambaut:
http://www.newadvent.org/fathers/0103.htm
http://www.earlychristianwritings.com/irenaeus.html

Irenaeus, *The Demonstration of the Apostolic Preaching*:
http://www.tertullian.org/fathers/irenaeus_02_proof.htm
http://www.earlychristianwritings.com/text/demonstrationapostolic.html

Jerome, *De Viris Illustribus (On Illustrious Men)*, trans. Ernest Cushing Richardson:
http://www.newadvent.org/fathers/2708.htm

Jerome, *Against the Pelagians*, trans. W.H. Freemantle, G. Lewis and W.G. Martley:
http://www.newadvent.org/fathers/3011.htm

Photius, *Bibliotheca*, trans. J.H. Freese:
http://archive.org/stream/libraryofphotius00phot/
   libraryofphotius00phot_djvu.txt
http://www.earlychristianwritings.com/fathers/photius_03bibliotheca.
   html

Lactantius, *The Divine Institutes*, trans. William Fletcher:
http://www.newadvent.org/fathers/0701.htm

Talmud (Babylonian Gemara):
http://www.come-and-hear.com/talmud/index.html
http://halakhah.com/indexrst.html
http://ancientworldonline.blogspot.se/2012/01/online-soncino-
   babylonian-talmud.html
http://juchre.org/talmud/

Maimonides, *Mishneh Torah*, trans. Eliyahu Touger:
http://www.chabad.org/library/article_cdo/aid/682956/jewish/
   Mishneh-Torah.htm

Arnobius, *Adversus Gentes*, trans. Hamilton Bryce and Hugh Campbell:
https://archive.org/details/thesevenbooksofa00arnouoft

Tertullian, *Adversus Iudaeos (An Answer to the Jews)*, trans. S. Thelwall:
http://www.tertullian.org/anf/anf03/anf03–19.htm#P2021_691723
http://www.newadvent.org/fathers/0308.htm
http://www.earlychristianwritings.com/text/tertullian08.html

Augustine, *On Christian Doctrine*, trans. James Shaw:
http://www.newadvent.org/fathers/1202.htm

NOTES

PROLOGUE

1 Lena Einhorn, *Vad hände på vägen till Damaskus? På spaning efter den verklige Jesus från Nasaret* (Stockholm: Prisma, 2006); *The Jesus Mystery: Astonishing Clues to the True Identities of Jesus and Paul* (Guilford, CT: Lyons Press, 2007).

2 Lena Einhorn, "A Shift in Time: Parallels between events depicted in the New Testament and later events depicted in the writings of Josephus" (lecture, SBL International Meeting, Tartu, Estonia, July 26, 2010); Lena Einhorn, "Josephus and Messianic Leaders in the First Century" (lecture, SBL International Meeting, London, July 6, 2011); Lena Einhorn, "A Shift From the 50's to the 30's? A Comparison of New Testament Accounts with Accounts of Later Events in the Writings of Josephus" (lecture, SBL International Meeting, London, July 7, 2011); Lena Einhorn, "Josephus and the New Testament: A Different Look at the Sources" (lecture, SBL International Meeting, Amsterdam, July 26, 2012); Lena Einhorn, "Jesus and the 'Egyptian Prophet'" (lecture, SBL Annual Meeting, Chicago, November 17, 2012).

ON TRYING TO FIND JESUS IN THE HISTORICAL SOURCES

1 Hermann Samuel Reimarus, *Apologie oder Schutzschrift für die vernünftigen Verehrer Gottes* (An Apology for the Reasonable Believers in God), compilation by G.E Lessing (Brunswick: 1774–78), fragments entitled "Brief Critical Remarks on the Object of Jesus and His Disciples as Seen in the New

Testament," trans. Charles Voysey (London: Williams & Norgate, 1879), https://archive.org/details/cu31924031784279 (accessed 15 Aug. 2015)

2 Luke 2:1–6, New Revised Standard Version.

3 Josephus, *Antiquities of the Jews* 18.1–2.

4 Josephus, *Antiquities* 18.9,23–25, trans. William Whiston.

5 Josephus, *Antiquities* 18.4.

6 Josephus, *Antiquities* 17.355; 18.1–10; *War of the Jews* 2.118; 7.253.

7 Solomon Zeitlin, "Who were the Galileans?" *Jewish Quarterly Review* 64 (1974): 193; Joseph R. Armenti, "On the Use of the Term 'Galileans' in the Writings of Josephus Flavius: A Brief Note" *Jewish Quarterly Review* 72 (1981):45–49; Richard A. Horsley, *Galilee: History, Politics, People* (Valley Forge, PA: Trinity, 1995), 258–259; Richard A. Horsley, "Early Christian movements: Jesus movements and the renewal of Israel" *HTS Theological Studies* 62 (2006):1213–1214; Lincoln Blumell, "Social Banditry? Galilean Banditry from Herod until the Outbreak of the First Jewish Revolt" *Scripta Classica Israelica* 27 (2008): 35–53; Josephus, *War* 3.41–42.

8 Josephus, *Antiquities* 18.4,23; *War* 2.118.

9 Matthew 2:1.

10 Luke 1:5,24,36,40–44.

11 "Prefect" is a military term, whereas "procurator" is a civilian term that denotes fiscal responsibilities.

12 Cornelius Tacitus, *Histories* 5.9, trans. Alfred John Church and William Jackson Brodribb.

13 Josephus, *Antiquities* 19.344–350.

14 With the possible exception of the small region of Chalcis, in Syria, which had been given to Herod II in 41 CE. He died in 48, after which the territory was given to Agrippa II.

15 Josephus, *Antiquities* 20.1–5.

16 Josephus, *Antiquities* 20.102.

17 Josephus, *Antiquities* 20.97–98.

18 Josephus, *Vita (The Life of Flavius Josephus)* 2.

19 Josephus, *Vita* 10; *Antiquities* 18.4–10, 23–25.

20 Josephus, *Vita* 12.

21 Josephus, *Antiquities* 18.23.

22 Josephus, *War* 3.342.

23 Josephus, *War* 3.387–391.

24 Josephus, *War* 3.400–402.

25 Josephus, *War* 4.622–629.

26 Eusebius, *Church History* 3.9.2; Jerome, *De Viris Illustribus* 13, trans. Ernest Cushing Richardson.

27 *Codex Parisinus Graecus*, kept at the Bibliothèque nationale de France, in Paris; *Codex Ambrosianus*, kept at the Ambrosian Library, in Milan; *Codex Palatinus (Vaticanus) Graecus*, kept at the Vatican Library, in Rome. For a list of the manuscripts, see Heinz Schreckenberg, *Die Flavius-Josephus-Tradition in Antike und Mittelalter* (Leiden: Brill, 1972). Summarized by Roger Pearse online, http://www.tertullian.org/rpearse/manuscripts/josephus_all.htm; see

also http://www.tertullian.org/rpearse/manuscripts/josephus_antiquities. htm; http://www.tertullian.org/rpearse/manuscripts/josephus_jewish_war. htm (accessed Aug. 19, 2015). Today, there are three main translations to English: William Whiston (1737), Loeb Classical Library (1927–1965), and the ongoing Brill Josephus Project, edited by Steve Mason (2000–present). English translations of the works of Josephus are available online, as are the Greek original texts (see under "Sources for Ancient Texts").

28 Josephus, *Antiquities* 18.63–64.

29 Josephus, *Antiquities* 20.200.

30 See, for example, Shlomo Pines, *An Arabic Version of the Testimonium Flavianum and its Implications* (Jerusalem: Israel Acad. Sciences and Humanities, 1971); Paul Winter, "Excursus II—Josephus on Jesus and James," in Emil Schürer, *The History of the Jewish People in the Age of Jesus Christ*, Vol. 1, rev. and ed. by G. Vermes, F. Millar and M. Black (Edinburgh: T.& T. Clark, 1973), 428–441; Louis H. Feldman, "The *Testimonium Flavianum*: The State of the Question," in *Christological Perspectives*, eds. R. F. Berkey and S. A. Edwards (New York: Pilgrim, 1982), 179–199; J. Neville Birdsall, "The Continuing Enigma of Josephus's Testimony About Jesus," *Bulletin of the John Rylands University Library of Manchester* 67 (1985): 609–622; Zvi Baras, "The Testimonium Flavianum and the Martyrdom of James," in *Josephus, Judaism and Christianity,*. eds. L. H. Feldman, G. Hata (Leiden: Brill, 1987), 338–348; Louis H. Feldman, "A Selective Critical Bibliography of *Josephus*," in *Josephus, the Bible, and History*, eds. L. H. Feldman, G. Hata (Detroit: Wayne State U. Press, 1989), 330–448; John P. Meier, "Jesus in Josephus: A Modest Proposal," *Catholic Biblical Quarterly* 52 (1990): 76–103; Steve Mason, *Josephus and the New Testament* (Peabody, MA: Hendrickson, 2003), 225–236; James Carleton Paget, "Some Observations on Josephus and Christianity," *Journal of Theological Studies* 52 (2001): 539–624; Andrew James Carriker, *The Library of Eusebius of Caesarea* (Leiden: Brill, 2003), 160–161; Alice Whealey, *Josephus on Jesus: the Testimonium Flavianum Controversy from Late Antiquity to Modern Times (Studies in Biblical Literature*, vol. 36; Peter Lang, New York, 2003); Alice Whealey, "Josephus, Eusebius of Caesarea, and the *Testimonium Flavianum*," in *Josephus und das neue Testament*, eds. Christfried Böttrich, Jens Herzer and Torsten Reiprich. (Tübingen: Mohr Siebeck, 2007), 73–116; Louis H. Feldman, "On the Authenticity of the *Testimonium Flavianum* attributed to Josephus," in *New Perspectives on Jewish Christian Relations*, ed. Elisheva Carlebach and Jacob J. Schacter (Leiden: Brill, 2012), 14–30; Paul J. Hopper, "A Narrative Anomaly in Josephus: Jewish Antiquities xviii:63", in *Linguistics and Literary Studies / Linguistik und Literaturwissenschaft: Interfaces, Encounters, Transfers / Begegnungen, Interferenzen und Kooperationen*, eds. Monika Fludernik and Daniel Jacob (Berlin: de Gruyter, 2014), 147–169.

31 One of the earliest to do so was Tanneguy Le Fèvre, *Flavii Josephi de Jesu Dom. testimonium suppositum esse/Tanaquilli Fabri diatriba* (Saumur, 1655).

32 See, for example, John P. Meier, *A Marginal Jew: Rethinking the Historical Jesus, Vol. 1: The Roots of the Problem and the Person*, (New York: Doubleday, 1991), 68.

33 Charles Guignebert, *Jesus*, trans. S.H. Hooke (New York: Knopf, 1935), 17.

34 Origen, *Contra Celsum* 1.47; *Commentary on the Gospel of Matthew* 10.17.

35 Louis H. Feldman, "On the Authenticity of the Testimonium Flavianum Attributed to Josephus," in *New Perspectives on Jewish Christian Relations*, ed. Elisheva Carlebach and Jacob J. Schacter (Leiden: Brill, 2012), 15.

36 Origen, *Commentary on the Gospel of Matthew*, trans. John Patrick 10.17; *Contra Celsum* 1.47 trans. Frederick Crombie.

37 Eusebius of Caesarea, *Proof of the Gospel* 3.5.105–106; *Church History* 1.11.7–8; *Theophania* 5.44, for a chronology of Eusebius' works, see Andrew James Carriker, *The Library of Eusebius of Caesarea* (Leiden: Brill, 2003), 37–41.

38 Louis H. Feldman, "Introduction," in *Josephus, Judaism, and Christianity* eds. L.H. Feldman, G. Hata (Detroit: Wayne State U. Press, 1987), 57. See also Louis H. Feldman, "A Selective Critical Bibliography of Josephus," in *Josephus, the Bible, and History*, eds. L. H. Feldman, G. Hata (Detroit: Wayne State U. Press, 1989), 431; Louis H. Feldman, "The *Testimonium Flavianum*: The State of the Question," in *Christological Perspectives: Essays in Honor of Harvey K. McArthur*, eds. R.F. Berkey, S.A. Edwards (New York: Pilgrim, 1982), 179–199, 288–293; Louis H. Feldman, "Josephus (c. 37–100 CE)", in *The Cambridge History of Judaism*, Vol. 3, *The Early Roman Period*, eds. W. Horbury, W.D. Davies and J. Sturdy (Cambridge: Cambridge University Press, 1999), 911–912; Louis H. Feldman, "On the Authenticity of the *Testimonium Flavianum* Attributed to Josephus," in *New Perspectives on Jewish Christian Relations*, ed. Elisheva Carlebach and Jacob J. Schacter (Leiden: Brill, 2012), 14–30. Here, Feldman lists eight Christian writers who lived before Eusebius and who mention Josephus, without making a reference to the *Testimonium:* Theophilus of Antioch, Minucius Felix, Julius Africanus, Hippolytus, Origen, Methodius, Pseudo-Eustathius, and Pseudo-Justin. He furthermore lists seven church fathers who lived in the century after Eusebius, and who refer to the works of Josephus, without citing the *Testimonium:* Ambrose, Basil, John Chrysostom, Josippos, Panodorus, Rufinus, Severus, and Sulpicius. He then adds fifth century Christian writers Orosius, Philostorgius, Theodore of Mopsuestia, and Augustine.

39 Alice Whealey, *Josephus on Jesus: The Testimonium Flavianum Controversy from Late Antiquity to Modern Times (Studies in Biblical Literature*, vol. 36; New York: Peter Lang, 2003), 7–11; see also Michael E. Hardwick, *Josephus as an Historical Source in Patristic Literature through Eusebius* (Atlanta: Scholars Press, 1989), 31,49–50,112; Heinz Schreckenberg and Kurt Schubert, *Jewish Historiography and Iconography in Early and Medieval Christianity* (Minneapolis: Fortress Press, 1991), 51–85 ("Josephus in Early Christian Texts").

40 Solomon Zeitlin, "The Christ Passage in Josephus", *Jewish Quarterly Review* 18 (1927–8): 231–255, http://www.drabruzzi.com/ZEITLIN-1928-The%20Christ%20Passage%20in%20Josephus.pdf (accessed 20 Aug., 2015); Ken Olson, "Eusebius and the Testimonium Flavianum," *Catholic Biblical Quarterly* 61 (1999): 305–22; as a number of authors have pointed out, Eusebius titles the thirty-first chapter of Book 12 of his *Præparatio*

Evangelica: "That it will be necessary sometimes to use falsehood as a remedy for the benefit of those who require such a mode of treatment.", trans. E.H. Gifford, http://www.tertullian.org/fathers/eusebius_pe_12_book12.htm (accessed 15 Aug. 2015).

41 John P. Meier, *A Marginal Jew: Rethinking the Historical Jesus,* Vol. 1: *The Roots of the Problem and the Person* (New York: Doubleday, 1991), 68.

42 Josephus, *Vita* 88.

43 Eusebius, *Church History* 3.10.8; Jerome, *De Viris Illustribus* 14.

44 Photius, *Bibliotheca,* Cod. 33, trans. J.H. Freese.

45 Cornelius Tacitus, *Annals* 15.44. Pliny the Younger to Trajan, 10.96–97.

46 John E. Remsburg, *The Christ: A Critical Review and Analysis of the Evidence of His Existence* (New York: Truth Seeker Company, 1909), 24–26, http://www.gutenberg.org/ebooks/46986 (accessed 19 Aug., 2015).

47 E. P. Sanders, *The Historical Figure of Jesus* (London: Penguin, 1993), 49.

48 Constantin-François Volney, *Les ruines, ou Méditation sur les révolutions des empires* (Paris: Desenne, 1791), http://gallica.bnf.fr/ark:/12148/bpt6k6515487j/f5.image (accessed 20 Aug., 2015); C.F. Dupuis, *Origine de tous les cultes, ou religion universelle* (Paris: Chasseriau, 1794), http://gallica.bnf.fr/ark:/12148/bpt6k61488s/f8.image (accessed 20 Aug., 2015); Will Durant, *Caesar and Christ* (New York: Simon and Schuster, 1944); George Albert Wells, *Did Jesus exist?* (Amherst, NY: Prometheus Books, 1975); Alvar Ellegård, *Myten om Jesus: den tidigaste kristendomen i nytt ljus* (Stockholm: Bonniers, 1992); Alvar Ellegård, *Jesus—One Hundred Years Before Christ: A Study in Creative Mythology,* (Woodstock, NY: Overlook, 1999); Earl Doherty, *The Jesus Puzzle: Did Christianity Begin with a Mythical Christ?* (Ottawa, Canada: Canadian Humanist, 1999); Robert M. Price, *The Incredible Shrinking Son of Man: How Reliable is the Gospel Tradition?* (Amherst, NY: Prometheus, 2003).

THE TIMING OF EVENTS DEPICTED IN THE GOSPELS

1 See, for example, Burnett Hillman Streeter, *The Four Gospels: A Study of Origins* (New York: Macmillan, 1924), http://biblicalstudies.org.uk/book_4gospels_streeter.html (accessed 20 Aug., 2015); Vincent Taylor, *The Gospels, A Short Introduction* (London: Epworth Press, 1930); John A.T. Robinson, *Redating the New Testament* (London: Westminster Press, 1976); Raymond E. Brown, *An Introduction to the New Testament* (New York: Doubleday, 1997); Markus Vinzent, *Marcion and the Dating of the Synoptic Gospels* (Leuven, Belgium: Peeters, 2014).

2 Luke 1:1–4.

3 Acts 1:1.

4 Max Krenkel, *Josephus und Lukas* (Leipzig: Haessel, 1894); F. Crawford Burkitt, *The Gospel History and its Transmission* (Edinburgh: T & T Clark, 1911), 105–110, https://archive.org/details/gospelhistoryits00burk (accessed 20 Aug. 2015); Clark Robinson Smith, "Fresh Light on the Synoptic Problem: Josephus a Lukan Source," *American Journal of Theology* 17 (1913): 614–

621, https://archive.org/details/jstor-3154865 (accessed 20 Aug., 2015); Steve Mason, *Josephus and the New Testament*, 2nd edition (Peabody, MA: Hendrickson, 2003), 251–295; Richard I. Pervo, *Dating Acts: Between the Evangelists and the Apologists* (Santa Rosa, CA: Polebridge, 2006), 149–200. For a critical view, see, for example, F.F. Bruce, *The Acts of the Apostles: Greek Text with Introduction and Commentary* (Grand Rapids: Eerdmans, 1990), 43–44; Gregory E. Sterling, *Historiography and Self-Definition. Josephos, Luke-Acts and Apologetic Historiography* (Leiden: Brill, 1992), 365–69; Ben Witherington III, *The Acts of the Apostles: A Socio-Rhetorical Commentary* (Grand Rapids: Eerdmans, 1998), 235–239; Hans-Josef Klauck, *Magic and Paganism in Early Christianity: The World of the Acts of the Apostles* (Edinburgh: T & T Clark, 2000), 41–43. For a review, see Heinz Schreckenberg, "Flavius Josephus und die lukanischen Schriften," in *Wort in der Zeit: Neutestamentliche Studien*, eds. W. Haubeck, M. Bachmann (Leiden: Brill Archive, 1980), 179–209.

5 Steve Mason, *Josephus and the New Testament* (Peabody, MA: Hendrickson, 2003), 291–292.

6 Rudolf Bultmann, *The Gospel of John: A Commentary*, trans. G.R. Beasley-Murray (Oxford: Blackwell, 1971); Craig L. Blomberg, *The Historical Reliability of the Gospels* (Downers Grove, IL: InterVarsity Press, 1987), 153–189; Craig L. Blomberg, *The Historical Reliability of John's Gospel: Issues & Commentary* (Downers Grove, IL: InterVarsity Press, 2001), 283–294; Richard Bauckham, *The Testimony of the Beloved Disciple: Narrative, History, and Theology in the Gospel of John* (Grand Rapids, MI: Baker Academic, 2007), 9–14.

7 Luke 2:41–51.

8 Luke 3:1–2.

9 Some suggest October in 27 CE to October in 28 CE, based on the Syro-Macedonian calendar. Kenneth F. Doig, *New Testament Chronology* (Lewiston, NY: Edwin Mellen Press, 1992), http://www.nowoezone.com/NTCIII.htm (accessed 17 Aug. 2015).

10 Luke 3:23.

11 Matthew 3:1; 14:3.

12 Josephus, *Antiquities* 17.188–227; *War* 2.1–22; *Antiquities* 18.238–256, 19.351; *War* 2.181–3; see, for example, *International Standard Bible Encyclopedia*, "Chronology of the New Testament", http://biblehub.com/topical/c/chronology_of_the_new_testament.htm (accessed 17 Aug. 2015); Kenneth F. Doig, *New Testament Chronology* (Lewiston, NY: Edwin Mellen Press, 1992), http://www.nowoezone.com/NTC04.html (accessed 17 Aug. 2015).

13 "Pilate": Mark 15:1; Matthew 27:2; Luke 23:1; John 18:29; "Caiaphas": Matthew 26:57; John 18:13; "Annas": John 18:13; "Herod": Luke 23:7. Earlier, Matthew 14:1 and Luke 9:7 speak of "Herod, the tetrarch."

14 In *Antiquities* 18.89 Josephus writes: "Vitellius [. . .] ordered Pilate to go to Rome, to answer before the emperor to the accusations of the Jews. So Pilate, when he had tarried ten years in Judea, made haste to Rome, and this

in obedience to the orders of Vitellius, which he durst not contradict; but before he could get to Rome Tiberius was dead." Tiberius died on March 16, in the year 37 CE. Besides Josephus's statement that Pilate "tarried ten years in Judea," the conclusion that Pilate could not have arrived in Judea later than 27 CE is supported by Suetonius statement, that from 27 on Tiberius "so far abandoned all care of the government, that he never filled up the decuriae of the knights, never changed any military tribunes or prefects, or governors of provinces" (Suetonius, *The Life of Tiberius* 41, trans. Alexander Thomson). That Pilate could not have arrived earlier than 25 CE is supported by Josephus's statement that "Tiberius [. . .] was now the third emperor, and he sent Valerius Gratus to be prefect (eparchos) of Judea," and that Gratus "went back to Rome, after he had tarried in Judea eleven years, when Pontius Pilate came as his successor." (*Antiquities* 18.33,35) Tiberius, as mentioned, became emperor in 14 CE.

15 Josephus, *Antiquities* 17.188–227; *War* 2.1–22; *Antiquities* 18.238–256, 19.351; *War* 2.181–183.

16 As Joseph Caiaphas was appointed by Gratus, and deposed by Vitellius while Tiberius was still alive (*Antiquities* 18.95–96), we may feel certain that he was deposed no later than March of 37 CE, and instated prior to 27 CE. In fact, upon arriving in Judea, Gratus is said to have appointed four high priests in less than three years—the last of whom was Caiaphas—which makes 18 CE a reasonable time for Caiaphas instatement (*Antiquities* 18.33–35).

CHRONOLOGICAL ENIGMA ONE: ON THEUDAS, AND OTHER MESSIANIC LEADERS

1 Acts 5:36–37; Acts 21:38.
2 Acts 21:38.
3 Acts 5:12–18.
4 Acts 5:19–21.
5 Acts 5:33–38.
6 2 Cor. 11:32.
7 See, for instance, Rainer Riesner, *Paul's Early Period: Chronology, Mission Strategy, Theology*, trans. D. Stott (Grand Rapids: Eerdmans, 1998), 75–77.
8 Josephus, *Antiquities*, 20.97–98.
9 Josephus, *Antiquities* 19.363; 20.1–2; Josephus, *War* 2.220.
10 Karl Theodor Keim, *Geschichte Jesu von Nazara*, Vol. III, (Zürich: Orell, Füssli, 1872), 134, http://reader.digitale-sammlungen.de/de/fs1/object/display/bsb10271732_00150.html (accessed 20 Aug. 2015); Max Krenkel, *Josephus und Lukas* (Leipzig: Haessel, 1894), 162–174; Geoffrey Arthur Williamson, *The World of Josephus* (London: Secker & Warburg, 1964), 129; F. F. Bruce, *The New Testament Documents: Are They Reliable?* (Cambridge: Eerdmans, 1981 (1943)), 106; F. F. Bruce, *The Acts of the Apostles: Greek Text with Introduction and Commentary* (Grand Rapids: Eerdmans, 1990), 32, 176; Ben Witherington III, *The Acts of the Apostles: A Socio-Rhetorical Commentary*

(Grand Rapids: Eerdmans, 1998), 238–239; Steve Mason, *Josephus and the New Testament* (Peabody, MA: Hendrickson, 2003), 277–282; Paul Barnett, *The Birth of Christianity: The First Twenty Years* (Grand Rapids, MI: Eerdmans, 2005), 199–200.

11 See, for example, Steve Mason, *Josephus and the New Testament* (Peabody, MA: Hendrickson, 2003), 279–280.

12 Josephus, *War* 2.118,433; Josephus, *Antiquities* 18.1–10,23.

13 G.A. Williamson, *The World of Josephus* (London: Secker & Warburg, 1964), 129; Jack P. Lewis, *Historical Backgrounds of Bible History* (Grand Rapids: Baker Book House, 1971), 170; Colin J. Hemer, *The Book of Acts in the Setting of Hellenistic History* (Tübingen: Mohr, 1989), 162–163; F. F. Bruce, *The Acts of the Apostles: Greek Text with Introduction and Commentary* (Grand Rapids: Eerdmans, 1990), 32, 176; Paul Barnett, *The Birth of Christianity: The First Twenty Years* (Grand Rapids, MI: Eerdmans, 2005), 199–200

14 Josephus, *Antiquities* 20.100–102; Karl Theodor Keim, *Geschichte Jesu von Nazara*, Vol. III, (Zürich: Orell, Füssli, 1872), 134; Max Krenkel, *Josephus und Lukas* (Leipzig: Haessel, 1894), 162–174; Steve Mason, *Josephus and the New Testament* (Peabody, MA: Hendrickson, 2003), 279–280.

CHRONOLOGICAL ENIGMA TWO: OF ROBBERS AND REBELS

1 Matthew 27:38; 27:44; Mark 15:27; John 18:40. In NRSV, the term "bandit" is used, but the original Greek word, *lestes*, is the same.

2 Matthew 26:55; Mark 14:48; Luke 22:52.

3 Mark 15:7.

4 Josephus, *War* 2.651. In *War* 7.253–274 Josephus distinguishes between different factions of rebels.

5 Josephus, *Antiquities* 18.4–10, 23–25.

6 Babylonian Talmud: B'rakhot 10a; Ta'anith 23b and 24a; Gittin 56a; Yalkut Genesis 115; Harris Hirschberg, "Simon Bariona and the Ebionites," *Journal of Biblical Literature* 61 (1942): 172.

7 For further discussion, see Kaufmann Kohler, "Zealots," *Jewish Encyclopedia* (New York: Funk and Wagnalls,1906), http://www.jewishencyclopedia.com/articles/15185-zealots (accessed 15 Aug. 2015); Shimon Appelbaum, "The Zealots: The Case for Revaluation," *Journal of Roman Studies* 61(1971): 155–170; Martin Hengel, *The Zealots: Investigations into the Jewish Freedom Movement in the Period from Herod I until A.D. 70*, trans. David Smith (Edinburgh: T & T Clark, 1989); Richard A. Horsley, "Josephus and the Bandits," *Journal for the Study of Judaism* 10(1979): 37–63; Gerhard Kittel, Gerhard Friedrich, and Geoffrey W. Bromiley, eds., *Theological Dictionary of the New Testament: Abridged in one Volume* (Grand Rapids: Eerdmans, 1985), 532–533; Jonathan J. Price, *Jerusalem under Siege: The Collapse of the Jewish State, 66–70 CE* (Leiden: Brill, 1992), 17–24; Mark A. Brighton, *The Sicarii in Josephus's Judean War: Rhetorical Analysis and Historical Observations* (Atlanta, GA: Society of Biblical Literature, 2009), 7.

8   Josephus, *Antiquities* 20.166.
9   Acts 21:38.
10 Josephus, *War* 2.254–256.
11 Josephus, *War* 7.253–254.
12 Josephus, *Antiquities* 18.23; see also *Antiquities* 18.9.
13 Josephus, *Antiquities* 15.284–291.
14 Josephus, *War* 1.204; *Antiquities* 14.159.
15 1 Maccabees 2:27.
16 Numbers 25:1–14.
17 Numbers 25:11.
18 Acts 21:38.
19 Matthew 26:55; 27:38; 27:44; Mark 14:48; 15:27; Luke 10:30; 22:52; John 10:1,8; 18:40.
20 Luke 23:19.
21 Tacitus, *Histories* 5.9.
22 Josephus, *War* 2.253.
23 Josephus, *Antiquities* 20.121.
24 Josephus, *Antiquities* 18.55–59,60–62; Philo, *On the Embassy to Gaius* 299–305, trans. Charles Duke Yonge.
25 Josephus, *Antiquities* 18.257–309; *War* 2.184–203.
26 Menahem Stern, "The Political and Social History of Judea Under Roman Rule," in *A History of the Jewish People,* ed. H.H. Ben-Sasson (London: Weidenfeld & Nicolson, 1976), 258.
27 See, for example, Friedrich Schulthess, *Das Problem der Sprache Jesu* (Zürich: Schulthess, 1917), 41,54–55; Harris Hirschberg, "Simon Bariona and the Ebionites," *Journal of Biblical Literature* 61 (1942): 182–184; Oscar Cullmann, *The State in the New Testament* (New York: Scribner, 1956), 15–16; Robert Eisenman, *James, the Brother of Jesus: The Key to Unlocking the Secrets of Early Christianity and the Dead Sea Scrolls* (New York: Viking Penguin,1997), 179. For other interpretations of the name, see, for example, Richard Bauckham, *Jesus and the Eyewitnesses: The Gospels as Eyewitness Testimony* (Cambridge: Eerdmans, 2006), 106; Joan E. Taylor, "The Name 'Iskarioth' (Iscariot)," *Journal of Biblical Literature* 129 (2010): 367–383; *Encyclopaedia Britannica*: "Judas Iscariot."
28 bGittin 56a; for an analysis of the name "Bariona," see, for example, Harris Hirschberg, "Simon Bariona and the Ebionites," *Journal of Biblical Literature* 61 (1942): 171–191, http://www.christmylife.info/PerversionsHeresies1/Perversions1/SIMON%20BARIONA%20AND%20THE%20EBIONITES.pdf (accessed 20 Aug., 2015); Markus Bockmuehl, "Simon Peter's name in Jewish Sources," *Journal of Jewish Studies* 55 (2004): 58–80, http://www.jjs-online.net/doc.php?id=055_01_058_1 (accessed 20 Aug., 2015).
29 John 18:10.
30 Cf. Old Testament: Psalm 2:1; Psalm 46:6; Isaiah 17:12; see Strong's Concordance 993: *Boanerges*; 7285, 7283: *regesh, ragash*, http://biblehub.com/hebrew/ (accessed 15 Aug. 2015).

31 See, for example, Joseph Klausner, *Jesus of Nazareth: His Life Times and Teaching* (New York: MacMillan, 1925), 206.

CHRONOLOGICAL ENIGMA FOUR: THE CONFLICT BETWEEN JEWS AND SAMARITANS

1 Josephus, *War* 2.223.
2 Josephus, *War* 2.223–227. A direct translation is "thrice ten thousand"; see also *Antiquities* 20.105–112.
3 Josephus, *Antiquities* 20.118–136; Josephus, *War* 2.232–246.
4 Josephus, *Antiquities* 18.85–89.
5 Josephus, *Antiquities* 20.118.
6 Josephus, *War* 2.232–235.
7 Josephus, *Antiquities* 20.124.
8 Alan D. Crown, "Redating the schism between the Judaeans and the Samaritans," *Jewish Quarterly Review* 82 (1991): 17–50; Ingrid Hjelm, "What do Samaritans and Jews have in Common? Recent Trends in Samaritan Studies," *Currents in Biblical Research* 3 (2004): 9–59.
9 John 4:3–9.
10 Matthew 10:5; Luke 9:51–56; Luke 10:25–37; Luke 17:11–19; John 8:48.
11 Acts 1:8; Acts 8:5, 14, 25; Acts 9:31; Acts 15:3.
12 See, for example, Paul Barnett, *The Birth of Christianity: The First Twenty Years* (Grand Rapids: Eerdmans, 2005), 100; Albert L.A. Hogeterp, *Paul and God's Temple: A Historical Interpretation of Cultic Imagery in the Corinthian Correspondence* (Leuven: Peeters, 2006), 157, n.168; Jürgen Zangenberg, "Between Jerusalem and the Galilee: Samaria in the Time of Jesus," in *Jesus and Archaeology*, ed. James H. Charlesworth (Grand Rapids: Eerdmans, 2006), 394; Reinhard Pummer, *The Samaritans in Flavius Josephus* (Tübingen: Mohr Siebeck, 2009), 28–29; G.J. Goldberg, "New Testament Parallels to the Works of Josephus," http://www.josephus.org/ntparallels. htm#Samaritans (accessed 13 Aug. 2015).

CHRONOLOGICAL ENIGMA FIVE: STEPHEN

1 Josephus, *Antiquities* 20.113–117; *War* 2.228–231.
2 Acts 6:11.
3 Acts 6:14.
4 Mishnah: Ta'anit, iv, 6, https://en.wikisource.org/wiki/Translation: Mishnah/ Seder_Moed/Tractate_Taanit/Chapter_4/6 (accessed 21 Aug., 2015); Kaufmann Kohler, Marcus Jastrow, and Louis Ginzberg, "Apostomus," *Jewish Encyclopedia* (New York: Funk and Wagnalls, 1906), http://www. jewishencyclopedia.com/articles/1660-apostomus (accessed 21 Aug. 2015); Joseph Derenbourg, *Essai sur l'histoire et la géographie de la Palestine, d'après les Thalmuds et les autres sources rabbiniques* (Paris: L'impremerie Impériale, 1867), 58, https://books.google.se/books/about/Essai_sur_l_histoire_et_

la_g%C3%A9ographie_d.html?id=vUvLiRQTQ0cC&redir_esc=y (accessed 21 Aug., 2015); Joseph Schwarz, Israel Schwarz, *Das Heilige Land: nach seiner ehemaligen und jetzigen geographischen Beschaffenheit* (Frankfurt am Main: Kaufmann, 1852), 279–280, https://archive.org/details/dasheiligelandn00unkngoog (accessed 21 Aug., 2015).

5 Hermann Samuel Reimarus, *Apologie oder Schutzschrift für die vernünftigen Verehrer Gottes* (An Apology for the reasonable believers in God) compilation by G.E Lessing, (Brunswick: 1774–78), fragments entitled "Brief critical remarks on the object of Jesus and his disciples as seen in the New Testament," trans. Charles Voysey (London: Williams & Norgate, 1879), 27.

6 Robert Eisler, *Iesous Basileus ou Basileusas* (Heidelberg: Carl Winter, 1929–30); Joel Carmichael, *The Death of Jesus* (New York: Macmillan, 1962); S.G.F. Brandon, *Jesus and the Zealots: A Study of the Political Factor in Primitive Christianity* (Manchester U. Press, 1967); Hyam Maccoby, *Revolution in Judaea: Jesus and the Jewish Resistance* (London: Ocean Books, 1973); Fernando Bermejo-Rubio, "Jesus and the Anti-Roman Resistance. A Reassessment of the Arguments", *Journal for the Study of the Historical Jesus* 12 (2014): 1–105; Fernando Bermejo-Rubio, "Why is the Hypothesis that Jesus was an Anti-Roman Rebel alive and well? Theological Apologetics versus Historical Plausibility" (2013) http://www.bibleinterp.com/articles/2013/ber378008.shtml (accessed 16 Aug. 2015).

7 Lactantius, *Divine Institutes* 5.3, trans. William Fletcher. The anti-Christian he refers to is likely late third century Roman governor Sossianus Hierocles.

8 Origen, *Contra Celsum* 3.7.

9 Matthew 10:34.

10 Mark 13:7–8.

11 Mark 3:18, Matthew 10:4; Kaufmann Kohler, "Zealots," *Jewish Encyclopedia* (New York: Funk and Wagnalls,1906), http://www.jewishencyclopedia.com/articles/15185-zealots (accessed 15 Aug. 2015).

12 John 11:47–50.

13 Luke 22:36–37.

14 Cf. Matthew 4:18–19.

15 See also Amos 4:2, and Habakkuk 1:15.

16 Jeremiah 16:1–16.

17 Martin Hengel, *Was Jesus a Revolutionary?*, trans. William Klassen (Philadelphia: Fortress, 1971), 9.

18 Acts of the Apostles, 22:3.

19 Letter to the Galatians, 1:14.

20 Luke 6:15; Acts 1:13; Acts 21:20; Acts 22:3; Galatians 1:14; 1 Corinthians 14:12; 1 Peter 3:13; Titus 2:14.

21 Mark R. Fairchild, "Paul's Pre-Christian Zealot Associations: a Re-examination of Gal. 1.14 and Acts 22.3," *New Testament Studies* 45(1999): 514–532; Justin Taylor, "Why Did Paul Persecute the Church?" in *Tolerance and Intolerance in Early Judaism and Christianity*, eds. Graham N. Stanton and Guy G. Stroumsa (Cambridge: Cambridge U. Press, 1998), 99–120.

CHRONOLOGICAL ENIGMA SIX: THE TWO HIGH PRIESTS

1 Josephus, *Antiquities* 20.224–251.
2 Numbers 18:7; 25:11–13; 35:25,28. But already in king Solomon's time, a high priest seems to have been dismissed for political reasons (1 Kings 2:27).
3 1 Macc.14:28,41.
4 See, for example, Emil G. Hirsch, "High Priest," in *Jewish Encyclopaedia* (New York: Funk and Wagnalls, 1906), http://www.jewishencyclopedia.com/articles/7689-high-priest (accessed 22 Aug. 2015).
5 John 11:49; 18:13.
6 Luke 3:2; John 18:13,24; Acts 4:6.
7 Josephus, *Antiquities* 20.198.
8 Josephus, *Antiquities* 18.26.
9 Josephus, *Antiquities* 18.33–34.
10 Maimonides, *Mishneh Torah*, "Kli ha-Mikdash" 4.15, trans. Eliyahu Touger.
11 Acts 4:6; 23:2–5; 24:1.
12 Josephus, *Antiquities* 19:313–316.
13 Josephus, *War* 2:240,243; Josephus, *Antiquities* 20.162.
14 Josephus, *Antiquities* 20.103; 20.131.
15 Josephus, *War* 2.243.
16 Josephus, *War* 2.239–240.
17 See, for example, Emil G. Hirsch, "High Priest," in *Jewish Encyclopaedia* (New York: Funk and Wagnalls, 1906), http://www.jewishencyclopedia.com/articles/7689-high-priest (accessed 22 Aug. 2015).
18 Josephus, *Antiquities* 20.162 and *War* 2.256.
19 Acts 23:2–5,24–26; 24:1–3,22–27.
20 Josephus, *Antiquities* 20.204–207.

CHRONOLOGICAL ENIGMA SEVEN: PILATE VS. FELIX

1 Philo, *On the Embassy to Gaius* 299–305.
2 Josephus, *Antiquities* 18.55–59. See also *War* 2.169–174.
3 Philo, *On the Embassy to Gaius* 299–305.
4 Josephus, *Antiquities* 18.60–62; *War* 2.175–177.
5 Josephus, *Antiquities* 18.62.
6 Josephus, *War* 2.177.
7 Tacitus, *Histories* 5.9.
8 According to Tacitus (*Annals* 12.54), Felix had governed Samaria also during the war, whereas Cumanus ruled Galilee.
9 Josephus, *War* 2.247,252.
10 Tacitus, *Annals* 12.54; Josephus, *Antiquities* 20.162–164; Josephus, *War* 2.247.
11 Josephus, *Antiquities*, 20.142–143; cf. Acts 24:24.
12 Josephus, *Antiquities*, 20.137–140.
13 Tacitus, *Histories* 5.9.
14 Tacitus, *Annals* 12.54.

15 Josephus, *Antiquities* 20.160–161.
16 Josephus, *War* 2.253.
17 Luke 13:1–3.
18 Josephus, *War* 2.175–177.
19 Josephus, *War* 2.247.
20 Josephus, *Antiquities* 20.119–124,160; *War* 2.253; Richard A. Horsley, *Galilee: History, Politics, People* (Valley Forge, PA: Trinity, 1995), 258–259; Solomon Zeitlin, "Who were the Galileans?" *Jewish Quarterly Review* 64 (1974): 193.
21 Philo, *On the Embassy to Gaius* 299–305.
22 Josephus, *Antiquities* 20.137–144.
23 Josephus, *Antiquities* 20.158–159: "For in the first year of the reign of Nero[54–55 CE], upon the death of Azizus, king of Emesa, Soemus, his brother, succeeded in his kingdom, and Aristobulus, the son of Herod, king of Chalcis, was intrusted by Nero with the government of the Lesser Armenia. Caesar also bestowed on Agrippa a certain part of Galilee, Tiberias, and Taricheae, and ordered them to submit to his jurisdiction." See also *War* 2.252.

CHRONOLOGICAL ENIGMA EIGHT: THE RETURN FROM EGYPT

1 Matthew 2:22.
2 Luke 2:2.
3 Josephus, *Antiquities* 17.355; 18.1.
4 Luke 1:5,36,42.
5 Matthew 2:21–3:2.
6 Matthew 2:19–21.
7 Luke 1:36,42.
8 bSanhedrin 43a, http://www.come-and-hear.com/sanhedrin/sanhedrin_43.html (accessed 24 Aug., 2015).
9 For views for and against, see: Bernhard Pick, *The Talmud: What it is and what it knows of Jesus and his Followers,* (New York: Alden, 1887), http://docslide.us/documents/1887-the-talmud-what-it-is-and-what-it-knows-about-jesus-and-his-followers.html (accessed 24 Aug., 2015); G.H. Dalman, *Was sagt der Thalmud über Jesum?* (Berlin: Reuther, 1891), https://docs.google.com/document/d/1Wvs3WPtbzhSvIo4REm5SQXBKUI-K79TdvydPwILlRL8/edit?pli=1 (accessed 28 Aug., 2015); H. Laible, *Jesus Christus im Thalmud* (Berlin: Reuther, 1891), https://archive.org/details/jesuschristusim00dalmgoog (accessed 24 Aug., 2015); R. Travers Herford, *Christianity in Talmud and Midrash* (London: Williams & Norgate, 1903), https://archive.org/details/christianityinta00herfuoft (accessed 24 Aug., 2014); A. Meyer, "Jesus, Jesu Jünger und das Evangelium im Talmud und verwandten jüdischen Schriften," in *Handbuch zu den neutestamentlichen Apokryphen,* ed. Edgar Hennecke (Tübingen: Mohr, 1904), 47–71, https://archive.org/stream/handbuchzudenne01henngoog#page/n68/mode/2up

(accessed 24 Aug., 2015); H.L. Strack, *Jesus, die Häretiker und die Christen nach den ältesten jüdischen Angaben* (Leipzig: Hinrichs, 1910); Bernhard Pick, *Jesus in the Talmud: His Personality, his Disciples and his Sayings* (Chicago: Open Court Publishing, 1913), https://archive.org/details/jesusintalmudhis00pick (accessed 24 Aug., 2015); Joseph Klausner, *Jesus of Nazareth: His Life, Times, and Teaching*, trans. Herbert Danby (New York: Macmillan, 1925), 18–54; R. Travers Herford, "Jesus in Rabbinical Literature," *Universal Jewish Encyclopedia* 6 (1942): 87–88; Morris Goldstein, *Jesus in the Jewish Tradition.* (New York: Macmillan, 1950), 57–81; J. Z. Lauterbach, "Jesus in the Talmud," in *Rabbinic Essays*, ed. J. Z. Lauterbach (Cincinnati: Hebrew Union College, 1951), 473–570); E. Bammel, "Christian Origins in Jewish Tradition," *New Testament Studies* 13(1967): 317–335; D.R. Catchpole, *The Trial of Jesus: A Study in the Gospels and Jewish Historiography from 1770 to the Present Day* (Leiden: Brill, 1971), 1–71; Johann Maier, *Jesus von Nazareth in der Talmudischen Überlieferung* (Darmstadt: Wissenschaftliche Buchgesellsch., 1978); Jacob Neusner, *Judaism in the Matrix of Christianity* (Philadelphia: Fortress Press, 1986); John P. Meier, *A Marginal Jew: Rethinking the Historical Jesus*, Vol. 1: *The Roots of the Problem and the Person* (New York: Doubleday, 1991), 94–98; Craig A. Evans, "Jesus in Non-Christian Sources," in *Dictionary of Jesus and the Gospels*, eds. Joel B. Green, Scot McKnight and I.H. Marshall (Diners Grove, Ill.: InterVarsity, 1992), 364–368; Robert E. Van Voorst, *Jesus outside the New Testament: And Introduction to the Ancient Evidence* (Grand Rapids, MI: Eerdmans, 2000), 104–120; Peter Schäfer, *Jesus in the Talmud* (Princeton: Princeton University Press, 2007).

10 bSanhedrin 67a, http://www.come-and-hear.com/sanhedrin/sanhedrin_67. html (accessed 24 Aug., 2015).

11 bShabbat 104b, http://www.come-and-hear.com/shabbath/shabbath_104. html#104b_19 (accessed 24 Aug., 2015).

12 jShabbat 13d; G.R.S. Mead, *Did Jesus Live 100 B.C.?* chapter 10 (London: Theosophical Publishing Society, 1903); R. Travers Herford, *Christianity in Talmud and Midrash* (London: Williams & Norgate, 1903), 54–55.

13 Book of Revelation 19:12,16; William Hendriksen, *More than Conquerors: An Interpretation of the Book of Revelation* (Grand Rapids, MI: Baker 1967 (1940)).

14 bSanhedrin 107b, http://www.come-and-hear.com/sanhedrin/sanhedrin_ 107.html (accessed 24 Aug., 2015); bSotah 47a.

15 In 1903, G.R.S. Mead published an account where he, partially based on this Talmud story, suggests that Jesus lived in 100 BCE: G.R.S. Mead, *Did Jesus Live 100 B.C.?* (London: Theosophical Publishing Society, 1903), https://archive.org/details/didjesuslive100b00meaduoft (accessed 24 Aug., 2015).

16 Luke 15:11–32.

17 Origen, *Contra Celsum* 1.32, trans. Frederick Crombie.

18 Epiphanius of Salamis, *Against Heresies (Panarion)* 78.7.5. (*The Panarion of Epiphanius of Salamis*, trans. Frank Williams (Leiden: Brill, 1994)).

19 John of Damascus, *Exposition of the Orthodox Faith* 4.14, trans. E.W. Watson and L. Pullan, http://www.newadvent.org/fathers/3304.htm (accessed 15 Aug. 2015).

20 For dating, see Samuel Krauss, *Das Leben Jesu nach jüdischen Quellen* (Berlin: S. Calvary, 1902), 245–248, https://archive.org/details/daslebenjesunac00kraugoog (accessed 24 Aug., 2015); Hugh J. Schonfield, *According to the Hebrews* (London: Duckworth, 1937) 214–227; William A. Horbury, *A Critical Examination of the Toledoth Jeshu* (dissertation, Cambridge University, 1970), 443–445; Frank R. Zindler, *The Jesus the Jews Never Knew: Sepher Toldoth Yeshu and the Quest of the Historical Jesus in Jewish Sources* (Cranford, NJ: Am. Atheist Press, 2003), 267–278, 323–328; Michael Meerson and Peter Schäfer, *Toledoth Yeshu: The Life Story of Jesus: Two Volumes and Database*, Vol. 1, *Introduction and Translation* (Tübingen: Mohr Siebeck, 2014), 22.

21 Origen, *Contra Celsum*, 1.28.

22 Origen, *Contra Celsum*, 1.29.

23 Arnobius, *Adversus Gentes* 1.43, trans. Hamilton Bryce and Hugh Campbell (Edinburgh: T& T Clark, 1871), 34.

24 Luke 3:23.

25 Josephus, *Antiquities* 18.240–252; Josephus, *War* 2.181–183; Josephus, *Antiquities* 19.345–350.

CHRONOLOGICAL ENIGMA NINE: JESUS VS. "THE EGYPTIAN"

1 Josephus, *Antiquities* 20.167–168; Josephus, *War* 2.258–260; Josephus nevertheless describes a Samaritan messianic leader in the times of Pilate (*Antiquities* 18.85–89).

2 See also Luke 21:5–9; Matthew 24:1–6.

THE EVENTS ON THE MOUNT OF OLIVES

1 Mark 15:7.

2 Luke 23:19.

3 Matthew 26:55.

4 Matthew 26:47; Mark 14:43; Luke 22:52.

5 Luke 22:36–37.

6 Mark 14:47; Matthew 26:51–54; Luke 22:49–51; John 18:10–11.

7 Matthew 27:16; Mark 15:7; Luke 23:18; John 18:40.

8 Hjalmar Söderberg, *Jesus Barabbas* (Stockholm: Bonniers, 1928), http://litteraturbanken.se/#!/forfattare/SoderbergH/titlar/JesusBarabbas/sida/3/etext (accessed 24 Aug., 2015); Hjalmar Söderberg, *Den förvandlade Messias: Jesus Barabbas II* (Stockholm: Bonniers, 1932), http://litteraturbanken.se/#!/forfattare/SoderbergH/titlar/DenForvandladeMess/sida/3/etext (accessed 24 Aug., 2015); Horace Abram Rigg, Jr., "Barabbas," *Journal of Biblical Literature* 64(1945): 417–456, https://www.yumpu.com/en/document/

view/6627630/horace-abram-rigg-jr-source-journal-of-biblical-yoyopl/41 (accessed 24 Aug., 2015); Hyam Z. Maccoby, "Jesus and Barabbas," *New Testament Studies* 16 (1970): 55–60; Hyam Maccoby, *Revolution in Judaea: Jesus and the Jewish resistance* (London: Ocean Books, 1973), 159; Stevan L. Davies, "Who is called Bar Abbas?" *New Testament Studies* 27(1981): 260–262.

9 Horace Abram Rigg, Jr., "Barabbas." *Journal of Biblical Literature* 64(1945): 421; Matthew 27:15; Mark 15:6; John 18:39.

10 Horace Abram Rigg, Jr., "Barabbas," *Journal of Biblical Literature* 64(1945): 455–456.

11 R. Travers Herford, *Christianity in Talmud and Midrash* (London: Williams & Norgate, 1903), 345, n.1, https://archive.org/stream/christianityinta00h erfuoft#page/344/mode/2up/search/345 (accessed 24 Aug., 2015); Robert Eisler later brings up Herford's interpretation, in *The Messiah Jesus and John the Baptist,* (trans. Alexander Haggerty Krappe (London: Methuen, 1931), 577,582–583,592). Eisler also briefly touches upon the similarities between "the Egyptian" and the depiction of Jesus's arrest in the *Testimonium* of the Slavonic version of *War of the Jews*, but does not conclude that the events are the same (pp. 458–459), http://www.christianjewishlibrary.org/PDF/ LCJU_MessiahJesus.pdf (accessed 24 Aug., 2015).

12 See also Lena Einhorn, *Vad hände på vägen till Damaskus? På spaning efter den verklige Jesus från Nasaret* (Stockholm: Prisma, 2006), 178–181; *The Jesus Mystery: Astonishing Clues to the True Identities of Jesus and Paul* (Guilford, CT: Lyons Press, 2007), 190–194.

13 Possibly an early version of *Sepher Toldoth Yeshu*. The earliest unequivocal reference to a text reminiscent of *Toldoth Yeshu* comes from Amulo's predecessor as Archbishop of Lyons. Agobard, ca. 826, in *De Judaicis Superstitionibus*.

14 Amulo, *Epistola, seu Liber contra Judaeos, ad Carolum Regem*, 39. Although "Hamizri" undoubtedly means "the Egyptian," the word "Ussum" is interpreted by other authors to be a faulty rendering of Hebrew words meaning "his name" or "sorcerer." For references and discussions, see, for example, Samuel Krauss, *Das Leben Jesu nach jüdischen Quellen* (Berlin: S. Calvary, 1902), 13, https://archive.org/details/daslebenjesunac00kraugoog (accessed 24 Aug., 2015); Hugh J. Schonfield, *According to the Hebrews* (London: Duckworth, 1937), 128–129; Bat-Sheva Albert, *"Adversus Iudaeos* in the Carolingian Empire," in *Contra Iudaeos: Ancient and Medieval Polemics Between Christians and Jews,* eds. Ora Limor and Guy G. Stroumsa (Tübingen: Mohr, 1996), 139; Frank R. Zindler, *The Jesus the Jews Never Knew: Sepher Toldoth Yeshu and the Quest of the Historical Jesus in Jewish Sources* (Cranford, NJ: Am. Atheist Press, 2003), 277–278; G.R.S. Mead, *Did Jesus Live 100 B.C.?* (New York: Cosimo, 2005), 292–293; Michael Meerson and Peter Schäfer, *Toledoth Yeshu: The Life Story of Jesus: Two Volumes and Database,* Vol. 1, *Introduction and Translation* (Tübingen: Mohr Siebeck, 2014), 67,307.

15 Johann Jacob Huldreich, *Sepher Toldoth Yeshua haNotzri—Historia Jeschuae Nazareni* (1705), 20,24,26. Digital version at Bayerische Staatsbibliothek,

http://reader.digitale-sammlungen.de/resolve/display/bsb10239719.html; also https://books.google.se/books?id=TSNSAAAAcAAJ (accessed 15 Aug. 2015); see also Michael Meerson and Peter Schäfer, *Toledoth Yeshu: The Life Story of Jesus: Two Volumes and Database*, Vol. 1, *Introduction and Translation* (Tübingen: Mohr Siebeck, 2014).

16 *The Jewish Life of Christ. Being the Sepher Toldoth Jeshu*, trans. G.W. Foote and J.M. Wheeler (London: Progressive Pub. Co., 1885), chapter 3, verses 24–29, http://www.ftarchives.net/foote/toldoth/tjtitle.htm (accessed 15 Aug. 2015).

17 N.A. Meščerskij, *Istorija Iudejskoj Vojny Iosifa Flavija v drevnerusskom perevode* (Moscow, 1958), trans. H. Leeming, in H. Leeming, K. Leeming, L. Osinkina, *Josephus' Jewish War and its Slavonic Version: A Synoptic Comparison* (Leiden: Brill, 2003), 261–262.

18 Origen, *Contra Celsum* 2.9.

19 An arrest, followed by an escape, followed by a second arrest and subsequent execution is found also in several versions of *Sepher Toldoth Yeshu*.

20 A short, temporary release is described also in the apocryphal *Narrative of Joseph of Arimataea* 2:1–4.

THE NEW TESTAMENT, "THE EGYPTIAN," AND THE SICARII

1 Josephus, *Antiquities* 20.158–159. The description of "the Egyptian" starts at 20.169.

2 Josephus, *War* 2.254–257.

3 Josephus, *War* 2.433.

4 Josephus, *War* 2.408.

5 Josephus, *War* 2. 425–430.

CHRONOLOGICAL ENIGMA TEN: JOHN THE BAPTIST

1 Mark 1:2–3; see also Matthew 3:3, Luke 3:4.

2 John 1:8.

3 Mark 1:7; Luke 3:16; Matthew 3:11; John 1:27.

4 Luke 1:5–42.

5 Mark 1:4.

6 Matthew 3:5–6.

7 Matthew 3:4; Mark 1:6.

8 Luke 3:11.

9 Matthew 3:2,7–8.

10 Josephus, *Antiquities*, 18.18–22.

11 Jerome, *Against the Pelagians* 3.2, trans. W.H. Freemantle, G. Lewis and W.G. Martley.

12 Luke 3:23.

13 Luke 4:14; Luke 3:19–20; Mark 1:14; Matthew 4:12; John 3:22–30; 4:1–3.

14 Matthew 14:3–4; Mark 6:17–19; Luke 3:19–20.

15 Matthew 14:1–12; Mark 6:17–29.

16 John P. Meier, *A Marginal Jew: Rethinking the Historical Jesus* (New York: Doubleday, 1991), 168–171; see also, for example, E. P. Sanders, *The Historical Figure of Jesus* (London: Penguin, 1993), 94; Stanley E. Porter, *The Criteria for Authenticity in Historical-Jesus Research: Previous Discussions and New Proposals* (Sheffield: Sheffield Academic Press, 200), 108–110.

17 Josephus, *Antiquities* 18.109–115.

18 Josephus, *Antiquities* 18.116–119.

19 See, for example, John P. Meier, "John the Baptist in Josephus: Philology and Exegesis," *Journal of Biblical Literature* 111 (1992): 225–237; Robert L. Webb, *John the Baptizer and Prophet: A Socio-historic Study* (Eugene, OR: Wipf and Stock, 2006), 39–41.

20 Origen, *Contra Celsum* 1.47.

21 Josephus, *Antiquities* 18.115.

22 Josephus, *Antiquities* 18.120.

23 Josephus, *Antiquities* 18.255.

24 Josephus, *Antiquities* 18.112.

25 Heinrich Graetz, *Geschichte der Juden: von den ältesten Zeiten bis auf die Gegenwart* (Leipzig: Leiner, 1888), 277–278, n.3, https://archive.org/details/geschichtederjud03grae (accessed 25 Aug., 2015); S. Krauss, *Das Leben Jesu nach jüdischen Quellen* (Berlin: Calvary, 1902), 257, https://archive.org/details/daslebenjesunac00kraugoog (accessed 24 Aug., 2015); E. Schürer, *Geschichte des Jüdischen Volkes im Zeitalter Jesu Christi*, Vol. I (Leipzig: Hinrichs, 1890), 364, n.24, http://sammlungen.ub.uni-frankfurt.de/freimann/content/pageview/13709 (accessed 25 Aug., 2015); L. Herrmann, *Chrestos. Témoignages païens et juifs sur le christianisme du premier siècle* (Brussels: Latomus, 1970), 99–104; Frank R. Zindler, *The Jesus the Jews never knew* (Cranford, NJ: Am. Atheist Press, 2003), 95–99; Clare K. Rothschild, "'Echo of a Whisper': The Uncertain Authenticity of Josephus' Witness to John the Baptist," in *Ablution, Initiation and Baptism: Late Antiquity, Early Judaism, and Early Christianity,* eds. David Hellholm, Tor Vegge, Øyvind Norderval and Christer Hellholm (Berlin: de Gruyter, 2011), 255–290; Rivka Nir, "Josephus' Account of John the Baptist: A Christian Interpolation?" *Journal for the Study of the Historical Jesus* 10 (2012): 32–62, http://www.academia.edu/9556504/Josephus_Account_of_John_the_Baptist_A_Christian (accessed 25 Aug., 2015).

26 Irenaeus, *Against Heresies* 2.22.5.

27 Origen, *Contra Celsum* 1.48.

WRITING ON TWO LEVELS

1 Acts 5:36–37.

2 Acts 21:38.

3 Josephus, *Antiquities* 18.1–10.

4 Steve Mason, *Josephus and the New Testament* (Peabody, MA: Hendrickson, 2003), 274.

5 Acts 5:37.

6 For a review, see, for example, Rivka Kern-Ulmer, "Midrash and the Hebrew Bible," *Religion Compass* 2/5 (2008): 754–768; Timothy H. Lim, *Pesharim* (Sheffield: Sheffield Academic Press, 2002), 48–51.

7 W.H. Brownlee, "Biblical Interpretation among the Sectaries of the Dead Sea Scrolls," *Biblical Archaeologist* 14 (1951): 60–62; Timothy H. Lim, *Pesharim* (Sheffield: Sheffield Academic Press, 2002), 44–45.

8 1QpHab 11:17–12:10. See, for example, Timothy H. Lim, *Holy Scripture in the Qumran Commentaries and Pauline Letters* (Oxford: Clarendon, 1997), 49, 97.

9 See, for example, Barbara Thiering, *Jesus and the Riddle of the Dead Sea Scrolls* (San Francisco: Harper, 1992).

10 Mark 8:17–18.

11 Luke 8:4–10.

12 Luke 9:51–56.

13 Matthew 26:51–52.

14 Matthew 26:55; see also Matthew 21:13.

15 Luke 22:36; Matthew 10:32–39.

CHRONOLOGICAL ENIGMA ELEVEN: THE RAISING OF THE DEAD

1 Mark 5:21–43; Luke 8:40–56; Matthew 9:18–26.

2 John 11:1–44.

3 Luke 7:11–16.

4 Mark 5:26–29.

5 See, for example, Peter Cresswell, *Jesus, the Terrorist* (Hants, U.K.: O Books, 2010), 307–308.

6 Josephus, *War* 2.433,447.

7 Luke 7:11–15.

8 Josephus, *War* 4.509–513.

9 Josephus, *War* 2.520,566; *War* 3.11,20,25–28; *War* 4.359–363.

10 Mark 15:21, Matthew 27:32, Luke 23:26, Acts 2:10; 6:9; 11:20; 13:1.

11 Josephus, *War* 7.437.

12 International Standard Bible Encyclopedia: "Manaen", http://www.internationalstandardbible.com/M/manaen.html (accessed 15 Aug. 2015).

13 Josephus, *Antiquities* 15.373.

14 Acts 4:36.

15 See also 2 Kings 15.

CHRONOLOGICAL ENIGMA TWELVE: THE MAD MAN FROM GERASA

1 Josephus, *War* 4.503–504; Luke 8:26; Mark 5:1.

2 Josephus, *War* 2.521.

3 Josephus, *War* 2.652.

4 Josephus, *War* 4.505–507.

5 Josephus, *War* 4.509–511.
6 Josephus, *War* 4.534–536.
7 Josephus, *War* 4.540–541.
8 Josephus, War 4.573.
9 Josephus, *War* 5.12.
10 Josephus, *War* 5.29–34, trans. H. St. J. Thackeray.
11 Josephus, *War* 5.4.
12 Josephus, *War* 5.248–249.
13 Josephus, *War* 7.1.
14 Josephus, *War* 6.433–434; 7.25–36.
15 Mark 5:1–15. See also Luke 8:26–35.
16 Matthew 8:28–32.
17 Josephus, *War* 6.433.
18 Josephus, *Vita* 45.

CHRONOLOGICAL ENIGMA THIRTEEN: ANANIAS AND PETER

1 Alexander Büchler: "Ananias, son of Nebedeus," *Jewish Encyclopedia* (New York: Funk and Wagnalls,1906), http://www.jewishencyclopedia.com/articles/1469-ananias-son-of-nebedeus (accessed 21 Aug., 2015).
2 To facilitate readability, the Loeb Classical Library translation by Thackeray is used for *War* 2
4 Josephus, *War* 2.433–440.
5 Luke 13:3–4.
6 Josephus, *War* 5.145,253,410.
7 Douay Rheims version. See also John 14:26.

AN ALTERNATE ROLE FOR THE NEW TESTAMENT?

1 See, for example Adam Clarke, *The New Testament: Commentary and Critical Notes* (New York: Waugh and Mason, 1833) 682.
2 Exodus 28:6.
3 Matthew 4:21–22; Mark 1:19–20; Luke 5:10–11.
4 Mark 15:40; Matthew 27:56.
5 Acts 1:21–23.
6 Josephus, *Vita* 7.
7 Abarim Publications: Barsabbas, http://www.abarim-publications.com/Meaning/Barsabbas.html#.VdOn6vntlBc (accessed 19 Aug. 2015).

POSSIBLE ARGUMENTS AGAINST A TIME SHIFT

1 Tacitus, *Annals* 15.44 trans. Alfred John Church and William Jackson Brodribb.
2 The inscription was found in 1961, in Caesarea. It is currently kept at the Israel Museum.

3 Jerry Vardaman, "A New Inscription Which Mentions Pilate as 'Prefect,'" *Journal of Biblical Literature*, 81 (1962): 70–71; S.G.F Brandon, "Pontius Pilate in history and legend," *History Today* 18 (1968): 523–530; John Dominic Crossan, *The Birth of Christianity: Discovering what happened in the Years immediately after the execution of Jesus* (Edinburgh: T&T Clark, 1999), 9; Robert E. Van Voorst, *Jesus Outside the New Testament: An Introduction to the Ancient Evidence* (Grand Rapids, Michigan: Eerdmans, 2000), 42–53; Richard Carrier, "On the Dual Office of Procurator and Prefect" (2012), http://www.richardcarrier.info/TheProvincialProcurator.pdf (accessed 13 Aug. 2015).

4 Josephus, *Antiquities* 18.55; *War* 2.169; Matthew 27:2; Luke 3:1. See also Matthew 10:18; 27:11,14,15,21,27; 28:14; Mark 13:19; Luke 20:20; 21:12; Philo, *On the Embassy to Gaius* 299. Incidentally, Josephus uses the term *epitropos* for governors preceding Pilate (Coponius; *War* 2.117) as well as for some succeeding him (Fadus, Tiberius Alexander, Felix; *War* 2.220; 2.247). But he also uses the term *eparchos* ("prefect") for both predecessors (Gratus; *Antiquities* 18.33) and successors (Festus; *Antiquities* 20.193). And in the case of Fadus he uses both terms (*Antiquities* 19.363; 20.14; *War* 2.220); see, for example, Warren Carter, *Matthew and Empire: Initial Explorations* (Harrisburg: Trinity Press, 2001), 215, n.2.

5 Robert Taylor, *The Diegesis: Being a Discovery of the Origin, Evidences, and Early History of Christianity* (London: Carlile, 1829), 394–397, https://archive.org/details/diegesisbeingdis01tayl (accesed 24 Aug., 2015); Arthur Drews, *The Christ Myth* (London: T. Fisher Unwin 1910), 231–235, http://www.gutenberg.org/files/45540/45540-h/45540-h.htm (accessed 27 Aug. 2015); Jean Rougé, "L'incendie de Rome en 64 et l'incendie de Nicomédie en 303," in *Mélanges d'histoire ancienne, offerts à William Seston* (Paris: Boccard, 1974), 433–441; Richard Carrier, "The Prospect of a Christian Interpolation in Tacitus, Annals 15.44," *Vigiliae Christianae*, 3 (2014): 264–283. Some authors have even questioned the authenticity of *Annals* itself: John Wilson Ross, *Tacitus and Bracciolini: The Annals forged in the XVth Century* (London: Diprose & Bateman, 1878), http://www.gutenberg. org/cache/epub/9098/pg9098-images.html (accessed 27 Aug., 2015); Polydore Hochart, *De l'authenticité des Annales et des Histoires de Tacite* (Paris: Thorin,1890), https://archive.org/details/delauthenticitd00hochgoog (accessed 27 Aug., 2015). For a view defending the authenticity of the passage, including the use of the name Christus, see, for instance, Robert E. Van Voorst, *Jesus outside the New Testament: An Introduction to the Ancient Evidence* (Grand Rapids: Eerdmans, 2000), 39–53.

6 See commentary on this by Augustine, *On Christian Doctrine* 2.28, trans. James Shaw; see also Benjamin Wisner Bacon, *The Fourth Gospel in Research and Debate.* (New York: Moffat, Yard, 1910), 396–397, https://archive.org/ details/fourthgospelinre00baco (accessed 15 Aug. 2015).

7 Luke 2:1–3; Acts 12:21–23; Acts 7:54–60; Luke 9:51–56.

8 Josephus, *Antiquities* 15.92; an inscription found at Suk Wadi Barada, near Damascus, could possibly be interpreted to support the existence of a younger Lysanias, but there is no historical narrative supporting it; see Emil Schürer, *Geschichte des jüdischen Volkes im Zeitalter Jesu Christi*, Vol I. (Leipzig: Hinrichs, 1890), 602–603, http://sammlungen.ub.uni-frankfurt.de/freimann/content/pageview/13709 (accessed 25 Aug., 2015); F.F. Bruce, *The Acts of the Apostles: The Greek Text with Introduction and Commentary* (Grand Rapids: Eerdmans, 1990), 44, n.15.

9 Matthew 2:21–3:2.

10 Josephus, *Antiquities* 19.344–350.

11 Josephus, *Antiquities* 20.141–144.

12 For a survey of scholarship on Pauline chronology, see Rainer Riesner, "Pauline Chronology," in *The Blackwell Companion to Paul*, ed. Stephen Westerholm (Chichester, UK: Wiley-Blackwell, 2011), 9–27; see also Rainer Riesner, *Paul's Early Period: Chronology, Mission Strategy, Theology*, trans. D. Stott (Grand Rapids: Eerdmans, 1998), 3–28.

13 Acts 24:27.

14 Unless Acts 20:33–35 is interpreted that way: "I coveted no one's silver or gold or clothing. You know for yourselves that I worked with my own hands to support myself and my companions. In all this I have given you an example that by such work we must support the weak, remembering the words of the Lord Jesus, for he himself said, 'It is more blessed to give than to receive.'"

15 Galatians 1:15–18.

16 Acts 9:20.

17 Galatians 2:1.

18 Galatians 2:9.

19 Acts 11:28–30; 12:25.

20 Acts 15:1–30.

21 Galatians 2:10.

22 Acts 11:27–30; Galatians 2:9–10; 1 Corinthians 16:1–4; 2 Corinthians 8:1–4; 9:1–2; Romans 15:25–26.

23 Romans 15:25–26; see also 2 Corinthians 8–9; 1 Corinthians 16:1–3.

24 Acts 24:17.

25 Galatians 2:7.

26 Frank J. Matera, *Galatians*, Sacra Pagina Series (Collegeville, Minnesota: Liturgical Press, 1992, 2007), 110

27 Rainer Riesner, "Pauline Chronology," in *The Blackwell Companion to Paul*, ed. Stephen Westerholm (Chichester, UK: Wiley-Blackwell, 2011), 9.

28 Depending on how one reads Acts 12:25.

29 Ananias was succeeded by Ismael son of Phabi before the end of Felix's time in power, although it is not clear when. Possibly, Ananias may also have continued as co-reigning high priest (*Antiquities* 20.204–210; *War* 2.441–442).

NATURE OF THE PARALLELS

1 For discussions on Josephus, and on his reliability as a historian, see, for example, Shaye J.D. Cohen, *Josephus in Galilee and Rome: His Vita and Development as a Historian* (Leiden: Brill,1979); Tessa Rajak, *Josephus: The Historian and His Society* (London: Duckworth, 1983); Louis H. Feldman, *Josephus and Modern Scholarship, 1937–80.* (Berlin: de Gruyter,1984); Per Bilde, *Flavius Josephus between Jerusalem and Rome: His Life, his Works and their Importance* (Sheffield: Sheffield Academic Press, 1988); Steve Mason, *Josephus, Judea, and Christian Origins: Methods and Categories* (Peabody, MA: Hendrickson, 2009).

2 Acts 11:27–28; Josephus, *Antiquities* 20.49–53.

3 Josephus, *Antiquities* 18.109–129.

4 Josephus, *Antiquities* 20.162–172; *War* 2.256, 2.261–263. Interestingly, although Luke 3:2 clearly states that Annas and Caiaphas had a joint high priesthood, John is the only Gospel that makes Annas present at the trial. Acts 4:6, however, mentions a high priest by the name of Annas at what seems to be a later stage.

5 Irenaeus, *Against Heresies* 2.22.5.

6 Irenaeus, *The Demonstration of the Apostolic Preaching* 74.

7 Victorinus, Saint, and Centre Traditio Litterarum Occidentalium, *Fragmentum Chronologicum Victorino Ascriptum, Secundum Notitiam in Codice Bobiensi Saec. IX Editum: (cod. Bibl. Ambros. H 150 F, Fol. 137v. - 138r)* (Turnhout: Brepols Publishers, 2010); for commentary, see, for example, Benjamin Wisner Bacon, *The Fourth Gospel in Research and Debate.* (New York: Moffat, Yard, 1910), 398–402, https://archive.org/details/fourthgospelinre00baco (accessed 15 Aug. 2015); George Ogg, *The Chronology of the Public Ministry of Jesus* (Cambridge: Cambridge University Press, 1940), 94; Charles E. Hill, review of *Victorin de Poetovio: Sur L'Apocalypse et autre écrits*, by Martine Dulaey, *Journal of Theological Studies* 49 (1998), 835–836; Frank R. Zindler, *The Jesus the Jews never knew* (Cranford, NJ: Am. Atheist Press, 2003), 127–129.

8 Padoue, Bibl. Univ. *1473*, Fol. 164; D. Germain Morin, "Notes sur Victorin de Pettau," *Journal of Theological Studies* 7 (1906): 456–459.

9 Tertullian, *Adversus Iudaeos* 8. For a detailed critical analysis of both fragments, see John Chapman, "On an Apostolic Tradition that Christ was Baptized in 46 and Crucified under Nero," *Journal of Theological Studies* 8 (1906–7): 590–606, http://biblicalstudies.org.uk/pdf/jts/008_590.pdf (accessed 28 Aug. 2015).

10 Epiphanius of Salamis, *Against Heresies (Panarion)* 51.22.24; 51.29.2.

11 William Adler and Paul Tuffin, "Introduction", in *The Chronography of George Synkellos: A Byzantine Chronology of Universal History from the Creation* (Oxford: Oxford University Press, 2002) xxix; Cyril Mango and Roger Scott, in *The Chronicle of Theophanes Confessor: Byzantine and Near Eastern HistoryAD 284–813* (Oxford: Clarendon Press, 1997) 17.

12 The reign of Augustus was often counted from 44 or 43 BCE.

13 He then says he received his information from "traditions that have come down from Hippolytus . . . [and] Annianos."

14 *The Chronography of George Synkellos: A Byzantine Chronology of Universal History from the Creation*, trans. W. Adler, P. Tuffin (Oxford: Oxford University Press, 2002), 455(381), 463(389); see also, for the Greek spellings, John Chapman, "On an Apostolic Tradition that Christ was Baptized in 46 and Crucified under Nero," *Journal of Theological Studies* 8 (1906–7): 595–597 http://biblicalstudies.org.uk/pdf/jts/008_590.pdf (accessed 28 Aug., 2015).

15 Adler and Tuffin, 455; Chapman, 596.

16 Eusebius, *Church History* 5.25.1.

CONCLUSIONS

1 Eusebius, *Church History* 3.9.2; Jerome, *De Viris Illustribus* 13.

2 Josephus, *Antiquities* 20.166.

INDEX